Contents

Social scientists meet the media

Social scientists often dismiss the media as untrustworthy and irresponsible and the media frequently regard social scientists as incapable of giving a straight answer. Many of the contributors to this volume complain of having been misrepresented, misquoted and edited out of all recognition. That this clash of cultures should occur is not surprising given the different priorities and perspectives of the social sciences and the media. *Social Scientists Meet the Media* examines these issues from the viewpoint of the media and social scientists who have had extensive media contact. The academics who have contributed to this book have conducted research on a diverse range of topics including: education, stress, football hooliganism, intelligence, risk factors for illness, drug use, performance appraisal in universities, politics, sex, religion, pornography, female sexuality, terrorism, youth culture and media studies. There are also chapters from three well-known media practitioners, from radio, the television and newspapers. Based on the contributions, the editors offer practical suggestions for social scientists to help them work more effectively with the media and thereby reach a wider audience.

Cheryl Haslam is Lecturer in Health Psychology at the Department of Epidemiology and Public Health, Leicester University. **Alan Bryman** is Professor of Social Research, the Department of Social Sciences, Loughborough University.

Contributors: Robert Burgess, Cary L. Cooper, Eric Dunning, Hans Eysenck, Helen Haste, Dennis Howitt, Graham Murdock, Jane Ussher, Paul Wilkinson, Peter Evans, Martin Freeth and Oliver Gillie.

Social scientists meet the media

Edited by Cheryl Haslam
and Alan Bryman

London and New York

First published 1994
by Routledge
11 New Fetter Lane, London EC4P 4EE

Simultaneously published in the USA and Canada
by Routledge
29 West 35th Street, New York, NY 10001

Typeset in Baskerville by LaserScript, Mitcham, Surrey
Printed and bound in Great Britain by
TJ Press (Padstow) Ltd, Padstow, Cornwall

British Library Cataloguing in Publication Data
A catalogue record for this book is available from the British Library.

Libary of Congress Cataloging in Publication Data
Social scientists meet the media/edited by Cheryl Haslam and
    Alan Bryman.
        p. cm.
    Includes bibliographical references and index.
    ISBN 0–415–08190–4: $5.00. – ISBN 0–415–08191–2 (pbk.): $17.95
    1. Mass media – Social aspects. 2. Communication in the social
sciences. 3. Social sciences – Research. I. Haslam, Cheryl II. Bryman,
Alan.
HM258.S586 1994
302.23 – dc20
                                                        93-24572
                                                        CIP

ISBN 0–415–08190–4 (hbk)   0–415–08191–2 (pbk)

Notes on contributors

Alan Bryman is Professor of Social Research in the Department of Social Sciences, Loughborough University of Technology. He is author of *Leadership and Organizations* (Routledge and Kegan Paul, 1986), *Quantity and Quality in Social Research* (Unwin Hyman, 1988), *Research Methods and Organization Studies* (Unwin Hyman, 1989) and *Charisma and Leadership in Organizations* (Sage, 1992), co-author of *Clergy, Ministers and Priests* (Routledge and Kegan Paul, 1977) and *Quantitative Data Analysis for Social Scientists* (Routledge, 1990), editor of *Doing Research in Organizations* (Routledge, 1988) and co-editor of *Rethinking the Life Cycle* (Macmillan, 1987), *Women and the Life Cycle* (Macmillan, 1988) and *Becoming and Being Old* (Sage, 1988). His chief research interests lie in the fields of leadership theory, research methodology and organization studies.

Robert Burgess is Director of CEDAR (Centre for Educational Development, Appraisal and Research) and Professor of Sociology at the University of Warwick. His main teaching and research interests are in social research methodology, especially qualitative methods and the sociology of education, and the study of schools, classrooms and curricula. He has written ethnographic studies of secondary schools and is currently working on case studies of schools and higher education. His main publications include *Experiencing Comprehensive Education* (Methuen, 1983), *In the Field: An Introduction to Field Research* (Allen and Unwin, 1984), *Education, Schools and Schooling* (Macmillan, 1985), *Sociology, Education and Schools* (Batsford, 1986), *Schools at Work* (Open University Press, 1988 with Rosemary Deem), and *Implementing In-Service Education and Training,* (Falmer Press, 1993 with John Connor, Sheila Galloway, Marlene Morrison and Malcolm Newton), together with 14 edited volumes on qualitative methods and education. He has held the position of President of the British Sociological Association and is currently President of the Association for the Teaching of the Social Sciences. He was a member of the Economic and Social Research Council (ESRC) Training Board and is currently on the ESRC Research Resources Board.

Cary L. Cooper is currently Professor of Organizational Psychology and Deputy Chairman of the Manchester School of Management at the University of Manchester Institute of Science and Technology. He is the author of over 60 books (on stress, women at work and industrial and organizational psychology), has written over 250 articles for academic journals, and is a frequent contributor to national newspapers, TV and radio. He was founding President of the British Academy of Management, is currently Editor-in-Chief of the *Journal of Organizational Behavior*, and Fellow of the British Psychological Society and Royal Society of Arts.

Eric Dunning is Professor of Sociology at the University of Leicester and Research Director of its Centre for Research into Sport and Society. Since 1959, his research interests have lain primarily in the sociology of sport. His publications include *Quest for Excitement* (Blackwell, 1985, with Norbert Elias), *The Roots of Football Hooliganism* (1988) and *Football on Trial* (1990), both published by Routledge and written jointly with Patrick Murphy and John Williams. Eric was formerly an active soccer player and cricketer but his direct sporting interests are currently restricted to watching Leicester City and his 17-year-old son, Michael, who is already a better footballer in all departments of the game except for heading.

Peter Evans graduated from Oxford University in 1964, since when he has worked in all branches of the media as a writer, editor, presenter and producer. He has presented *Science Now* on BBC Radio 4 for many years and authored 12 popular books on psychological, scientific or medical topics. He frequently acts as tutor on media training courses for scientists and others wishing to be more effective when they meet the media.

Hans J. Eysenck is Professor Emeritus of Psychology at the University of London. Professor Eysenck was born in Berlin in

1926, and left Germany in 1934 as a political refugee. He obtained his Ph.D. in psychology from the University of London in 1940, and spent the remainder of his professional career at the Maudsley Hospital, and as Professor at the associated Institute of Psychiatry, which is part of the University of London. He retired eight years ago, but is still actively engaged in research. His main research interests have been in individual differences in personality and intelligence, social attitudes, behaviour therapy, and behaviour genetics. He has published about 1,000 articles and over 70 books.

Martin Freeth is an Executive Producer for BBC Television, Science and Features Department. Martin has worked for the BBC since 1971. Before joining the BBC he was a film editor in the freelance sector, having graduated with distinction (gaining an M.Art Degree) from the Film and Television School of the Royal College of Art in London. He has produced *The Trouble with Medicine, The Mind Machine* and several *Antenna* programmes such as *Immunising Against Poverty?*, which won a 1992 BMA award. Previous work has included popular studio and invited-audience shows, in particular *Tomorrow's World, The Burke Special* and *Young Scientist of the Year*. He has made 19 *Horizon* documentaries, one of which, *Finding a Voice* was shown in the US as a NOVA, and there won a Blue Ribbon and other awards. He directed and produced a 70-minute *Horizon* drama documentary, *The Intelligence Man*, written by Stephen Davis, and starring John Shrapnel as the allegedly fraudulent psychologist Cyril Burt. Martin was the principal subject of the book *Framing Science: the Making of a BBC Documentary*, by the sociologist Roger Silverstone, who followed him during the research, shooting and editing of the *Horizon* film *A New Green Revolution?* filmed in Mexico, Bangladesh and the Phillipines.

Oliver Gillie, Reporter and Writer for the *Independent*, trained in genetics at the University of Edinburgh in the 1950s. Following his doctorate degree he spent three years working in research and published a number of academic papers. He had written only a small number of freelance articles, mainly for the *Guardian*, when he decided to give up research and start a career in writing. He began to work for science and medical publications and became the editor of *General Practitioner*. He later became the medical correspondent of *The Sunday Times* where he worked for 15 years.

He moved to the *Independent* when it was launched in October
1986, initially as the medical editor, but he now writes on a wide
range of topics.

Cheryl Haslam is a Lecturer in Health Psychology at the Department of Epidemiology and Public Health, Leicester University.
She graduated in Psychology at the University of London in 1982,
and then undertook postgraduate research at Nottingham
University which led to the award of her Ph.D. in 1986. She has
held research posts at the Medical Research Council Institute of
Hearing Research in Nottingham, Department of Social Sciences
at Loughborough University, Department of Psychiatry at St George's
Hospital Medical School and The Sports Council. She has
published articles in a number of journals including: *British Journal
of Psychology, Psychopharmacology, British Journal of Addiction, Work
and Stress, Construction Management and Economics, Public Money and
Management, Higher Education Management* and *Higher Education.*
Her research interests include: lifestyle factors in relation to health,
health promotion and addictive behaviour.

Helen Haste is Reader in Psychology in the School of Social
Sciences at the University of Bath. In 1991 she was President of the
Psychology Section of the British Association for the Advancement
of Science. She has also been Honorary Secretary of the Association for Learned Societies in the Social Sciences (ALSISS) which
is in part concerned with improving relations between social
scientists and the wider world. Her research fields are, broadly, the
development of values, and social and psychological issues
concerned with gender. This has increasingly included issues in
gender and science, and the relationship between metaphors of
gender and metaphors associated with the history of concepts of
science and rationality. Her recent work on metaphor has brought
her into such fields as dinosaurs, and the development of scientific
thinking. She is the author of numerous scientific papers, editor of
several books and author of *The Sexual Metaphor* (Wheatsheaf,
1993).

Dennis Howitt is Senior Lecturer in Social Psychology at Loughborough University. As well as a long-standing interest in mass
communication research (*Mass Media Violence and Society,* Elek,
1975; *Mass Media and Social Problems,* Pergamon, 1982; *A Measure of*

Uncertainty, Libby/Broadcasting Standards Council, 1989; *Pornography: Impacts and Influences*, Home Office, 1990), his research interests have stretched much more widely to include many areas of psychology and social issues including racism, loneliness, child abuse and drugs. His most recent books are *Concerning Psychology: Psychology Applied to Social Issues* (Open University Press, 1991), *Child Abuse Errors* (Harvester-Wheatsheaf, 1992) and *The Racism of Psychology* (Harvester Wheatsheaf, 1994). He is currently completing a book on paedophiles.

Graham Murdock is Reader in the Sociology of Culture at the University of Loughborough and a Professor of Mass Communications at the University of Bergen. He has written widely on the organization of the cultural industries and on the mass media and contemporary culture. His books include, as co-author: *Demonstrations and Communication* (Penguin, 1970) and *Televising Terrorism* (Comedia, 1983) and as co-editor: *Communicating Politics* (Leicester University Press, 1986).

Jane M. Ussher is a Lecturer in Psychology at University College, London University. Her research interests are in the field of gender and health, focusing on female reproduction, eating disorders and sexual dysfunction. She is currently carrying out research on female sexuality. Her publications include *The Psychology of the Female Body* (Routledge, 1989), *Women's Madness: Misogyny or Mental Illness?* (Harvester-Wheatsheaf, 1991), *Gender Issues in Clinical Psychology* (ed. with P. Nicolson, Routledge, 1992), *The Psychology of Women's Health and Health Care*, (ed. with P. Nicolson, MacMillan, 1992) and *Psychological Perspectives on Sexual Problems* (ed. with C. Baker, Routledge, 1992).

Paul Wilkinson is Professor of International Relations at the University of St Andrews and Director of the Research Institute for the Study of Conflict and Terrorism. His publications include: *Political Terrorism* (Macmillan, 1974), *Terrorism and the Liberal State* (Macmillan, 1977, second edition 1986) and *The New Fascists* (Grant McIntyre, 1981, second edition 1983). He is editor of the academic journal *Terrorism and Political Violence*, now in its fourth year of publication, and of the symposium *Terrorism and Technology*, published in 1993 by Frank Cass. He has been a regular contributor to the media on aspects of conflict, terrorism and political violence since the mid-1970s, and is editorial adviser to *The Contemporary Review*, consultant to *Jane's Intelligence Review* and editor emeritus of *The Security Handbook*. His recreations are enjoying modern poetry and art, and walking in the Scottish countryside.

Preface

Dissemination of research is a vital part of the scientific process. The mass media represent the gateway to communicating with a much wider audience than is usually reached through the normal academic outlets. Yet so often the interaction between academics and the media can be unsatisfactory or frustrating and even disastrous. Some academics respond to this problem by steadfastly avoiding media contact. This is not the solution. It is far better for academics and media practitioners to be aware of the potential dangers and to work together to the benefit of all concerned. This is particularly important in the case of the social sciences, where research findings often have direct implications for society. The description 'social sciences' is used here in a broad sense, encompassing the disciplines of psychology, sociology, social policy, social medicine, political and economic science and business management. While this book is concerned with the reporting of social scientific research, many of the issues discussed are relevant to the physical and biological sciences.

Media reportage of the social sciences is explored from the point of view of both social scientists and the media. We have personal accounts from social scientists who have 'enjoyed' extensive media contact, along with the views of representatives from radio, television and the press.

We look at the problems inherent in media coverage of social scientific research and outline ways in which to achieve a more fruitful relationship between the social sciences and the media.

Acknowledgements

The editors would like to thank the contributors who helped in various ways throughout the preparation of this book. We are grateful to Reed Health Publishing for allowing us to include an article which appeared in the magazines *Doctor* and *Hospital Doctor*.

We would like to acknowledge the support and encouragement given by our friends and colleagues in the Department of Epidemiology and Public Health at Leicester University and the Department of Social Sciences, Loughborough University. We are particularly grateful to Samantha Buchanan for the considerable secretarial support she has given to this project. We also wish to thank Chris Rojek and Anne Gee for their help throughout the preparation of this book.

We owe many thanks to our partners and families for their support during the preparation of the book. Particular thanks go to Roger Haslam for his computing assistance and general help and encouragement.

Introduction

Cheryl Haslam and Alan Bryman

REACHING A WIDER AUDIENCE

Social scientists often come into contact with the mass media, as both willing and unwilling participants. Such contact can arise in a variety of ways. Research findings may be reported in newspaper articles or social scientists may be interviewees on, or consultants to, radio and television programmes. Another, fairly recent, forum for social scientists is the audience participation programme, where social scientists may be invited to offer 'expert' opinions on the topics under discussion.

It is the role of the social scientist to disseminate research findings and this may include publication and presentation beyond strictly academic outlets. Effective dissemination of research findings is a vital component of social scientific endeavour. In relation to the field of psychology, for example, Canter and Breakwell (1986) argue that the process of explaining psychological issues and concepts to the 'psychologically naïve' is a good discipline in itself. They consider that psychologists have a moral obligation to disseminate research findings to a wider audience.

Making research accessible to as wide an audience as possible is an important objective for the social sciences. Gouldner (1978) states that social science research will always be evaluated by society, not only from the standpoint of its 'correctness' but also in terms of its relevance to society. Through the media, social scientists can bring their work to the attention of a broader constituency of people than can be achieved through the conventional channels such as journal articles and conference presentations. Goslin (1974) outlines the potential audiences for social scientific research: the public at large, policy makers and sponsors of research (including foundations, charities and government agencies).

Weiss (1974) notes that the media are major sources of information to policy makers. The utilization of social scientific research was examined by Wingens and Weymann (1988) in relation to the field of work and education policy in West Germany. They suggest that the social sciences can influence the policy-making process by swaying public opinion and affecting standpoints advanced in public discourse. Politicians and reporters may employ findings from the social sciences to underpin or to substantiate a particular viewpoint. Wingens and Weymann place their assertions in the context of changes in the social sciences over the last three decades. The 1960s has been regarded as the time in which the social sciences offered fresh insights, or as Cherns (1986) put it 'the sun of the social sciences had risen'. Wingens and Weymann maintain that nowadays the social sciences face an 'innovation problem' in that both policy makers and the informed public have become accustomed to the social sciences.

Canter and Breakwell (1986) point to the need for social scientists to reach a wider audience given that recruitment to universities and the allocation of funds for research may often be determined by individuals who are not familiar with the scientific literature. It may be from the media that such individuals obtain a sense of which social scientific issues are important and relevant to society.

Clearly the social sciences need a voice in the public arena in terms of informing the public, policy makers and potential public and private research sponsors. The editors of this book believe that the media have an important role in giving a public 'platform' to the social sciences and in stimulating public interest in social scientific research. This is why we feel that social scientists and media practitioners need to meet (as they do in this book) with a view to establishing some mutually beneficial ground rules.

POTENTIAL PITFALLS OF PUBLICITY

Lack of control

Media attention can enhance a researcher's reputation and may open up a new sphere of contacts. However, the social scientist usually has little or no control over the ways in which findings are reported in the media. Researchers frequently complain about the lack of control and about inaccuracies in reporting (Tankard and Ryan, 1974). Social scientists are used to exerting control in the course of conducting research and writing up results. But when social scientists become involved in a radio or television broadcast or newspaper article, they sooner or later appreciate that the control rests with the producer, presenter or journalist. In a very real sense, the social scientist takes on the role of a 'subject' in the media's data collection (McCall *et al.*, 1984). Such a radical change of position can have a number of unforeseen consequences since the research may be misrepresented or given publicity in outlets which the social scientist would wish to avoid.

Unexpected and uncontrolled media coverage of research may sometimes alter the course of research itself. This need not neces-sarily be a wholly negative experience. Morgan (1972) describes media coverage of a participant observation study of female factory workers in Manchester. In a conference presentation, Morgan discussed the inter-relationships between a working woman's roles in the workplace and home, drawing attention to the ways in which the workplace becomes 'domesticated' and how the social rewards associated with work were at least as important as the paypacket. The research was widely reported and two newspapers printed the names of the factories, causing considerable embarrassment for the researcher. The way in which the factory workers responded to the newspaper reports fell into two camps. Older women who had been with their firm for some time saw the research as a 'betrayal', a mockery of the working class, while younger women felt much more affinity with the reports and saw the press 'scandal' as a welcome distraction.

The press coverage, which rather trivialized the research, unearthed interesting information about the nature of the social relationships in the organizations concerned. Employees res-ponded to the press reports in terms of the meanings they assigned to work and to work relationships. Older women reaffirmed their commitment to work and to working-class values. Younger women expressed their alienation from certain aspects of the workplace and reaffirmed other values, deriving largely from outside the workplace and expressed in terms of youth and youth culture. Morgan concludes the publicity and the 'social drama' associated with it revealed information not only about the community under investigation but also about the research process itself.

Distortions in media reports

Goslin (1974) examines the different types of information that may be channelled through the media. The first comprises general statements about planned research such as, 'Dr X proposes to do a study on. . .'. The second relates to studies underway: 'Dr X is doing research on. . .'. The third discusses findings of a particular study: 'Dr X has just discovered. . .'. The fourth type describes what is known about a particular area: 'research indicates that. . .'. The final, and potentially most problematic, type of information relates to the policy implications of particular findings: 'the implications of these findings are. . .'. Goslin states that much of the controversy that surrounds social science stems from complications in the communication process. While social scientists may be quite clear and accurate in their statements (and the current editors are not trying to suggest that all social scientists are), by the time these statements reach the policy makers they may have become some-what distorted for various reasons:

1 Time constraints under which many journalists work.
2 Pressure on reporters to produce entertaining copy.
3 Absence of communication networks to inform journalists about the range of ongoing research in the social sciences.
4 Inability or unwillingness of social scientists to make their research findings comprehensible to the media or indeed to anyone else.
5 Inability of the media to distinguish between good and bad research – a difficulty exacerbated by the tendency of social scientists to disagree among themselves.
6 The barriers of technical language or 'jargon'.
7 The fact that the subject matter of the social sciences includes concepts with which the media practitioner and the public have had experience, and about which they consider themselves 'experts'.

In view of these factors, it is quite likely that policy makers may be influenced by research that does not fully reflect the conclusions of those who conduct it.

The quest for instant answers

Journalists want instant, digestible answers from 'experts' in the social sciences. Silberman (1964) described the distinction between journalistic and academic aspirations and considered what the two approaches have to offer each other:

> Scholarship has a dedication to the search for truth which the journalist needs; journalism has a passion for the relevant and the immediate which the scholar needs. The journalist is sometimes too impatient with the scholar's concern for substantiation; the scholar sometimes fails to remember what the journalist can never forget – namely, that life can never wait until all the evidence is in, that important decisions must always be made on the basis of incomplete information. (p. ix)

The questions put by journalists are often uncomfortably general to the academic, who will try to answer with appropriate caveats and qualifications. This issue is nicely illustrated by a statement from Bernard Berelson who, after completion of a major volume on human behaviour (Berelson and Steiner, 1967), was asked to summarize the main generalizations about human behaviour. He made three points:

1 No matter what the subject matter of inquiry, some people do and some people don't.
2 The differences aren't very large.
3 It is always more complicated than that.

(cited in Goslin, 1974)

This sums up very well the difficulties social scientists face. Goslin notes that responsible statements made by social scientists must be couched in highly qualified terms, which clearly poses problems for the media. Answers from social scientists which are deemed by the media to be unnecessarily complex or tentative may be subject to 'pruning' which may involve over-simplification or even distortion. Canter and Breakwell (1986) warn that research findings and tentative conclusions may sometimes be manipulated in the interests of their entertainment value. These authors state: 'never take a cherished idea to the media and expect it to be intact at the end' (p. 284). Canter and Breakwell argue that the skill on the part of the academic must be to give the impression of a direct answer whilst redefining the question into a more answerable form.

Perhaps social scientists could learn a trick or two from some politicians!

Inaccuracies in social science reportage

Weiss carried out a systematic examination of media reporting of social scientific research in America (Weiss, 1985; Weiss and Singer, 1988). The investigation comprised a content analysis of all stories that appeared in 10 major newspapers over a five-month period in 1982 followed by a study in which reporters and the social scientists associated with 127 of the stories were interviewed.

Weiss (1985) noted that 75 per cent of the social scientists interviewed were satisfied with the reporting of their work. While they were satisfied with these particular stories they were less happy with the reporting of social scientific research in general. A quarter felt that reporting is generally inaccurate. Weiss suggests an explanation for this discrepancy is pluralistic ignorance – while these social scientists are themselves content with reporting of their work, they are unaware that other social scientists are also content (they feel they must be especially lucky). As Weiss points out, it is usually the horror stories regarding the media reporting of research which tend to circulate among academics. Weiss (1985) and Weiss and Singer (1988) examined the specific complaints about social science reportage:

1 Over-simplification of social science complexities.
2 Undue closure and certainty in the reporting of social science results.
3 Inadequate scrutiny of the quality of social science studies and the expertise of quoted social scientists.
4 Fragmentation, i.e. no attempt to relate an individual story to a body of research.
5 Biased selection from the range of available social science.

Weiss considered the evidence for each of these five specific complaints. As regards the charge of over-simplification, Weiss (1985) quotes one reporter as saying:

When writing for newspapers you have to leave out subtle detail and state positions more dramatically than perhaps you would like. That's the difference between social scientific reports and media reports, because you want people to read what you write. (p. 40)

Weiss states that media demands for brevity, speed and clarity make over-simplification an enduring criticism from social scientists.

On the issue of undue closure and finality, Weiss discusses the strain between the media and social scientists which she terms as the 'tug between finality and uncertainty'. Reporters tend to over-emphasize the conclusiveness of social science research findings, as Weiss states:

The reportorial push for conclusiveness grows out of the conditions of journalistic practice. Reporters strive for impact. They need to make a story get past the editor and into print. They are competing with their colleagues for a limited amount of space and an even smaller amount of airtime. To win this competition, they have to make the story sound significant. They add drama, and they sacrifice the sense of cumulative and collective inquiry. (p. 40)

On the third problem, that of of inadequate scrutiny, social scientists in Weiss's study complained that reporters were insufficiently critical of social science both in their choice of research studies to cover and in their selection of experts to quote. The question of critical judgement is particularly important when the research relates to a controversial area or one about which social scientists disagree. An obvious example would be the environmental and genetic determinants of intelligence or personality, the classic nature/nurture debate. In this sense, social scientific writing is even more complex than science writing. Ironically, while the media perceive science writing as requiring specialist training, the reporting of social science is often seen as something that any journalist can do (Weiss, 1985).

As regards the issue of fragmentation, Weiss and Singer (1988) note that the media have few incentives to review previous research. The media focus on what is 'new' and to expect media practitioners to conduct literature reviews is unrealistic. On this issue one journalist commented: 'Social science is of immense value, but its single pieces are never put together. There are no holistic overviews.'

On the final question of biased selection, Weiss (1985) states that the media tend to ignore all social science work on methods and most developments in theory. Generally they are uninterested in studies that do not have an obvious link to public interest, namely, daily living, economic conditions, social trends or political events. Weiss puts forward several hypotheses relating to media bias and examines the evidence for these hypotheses. They are that the media select: quantitative studies over qualitative studies; findings that support rather than challenge major institutions of society; and liberal-leaning social science.

With regard to the first hypothesis, Weiss points out that reporters, like most of us, have become accustomed to using statistics to lend credibility to a piece of information. She found little evidence to support the second hypothesis, stating that 45 per cent of the stories examined (note the emphasis on quantitative data there) reported social science research that suggests the need for mild-to-moderate institutional change. She did note that reporters appeared to favour more 'liberal' social science with a leaning toward humanitarian issues.

In summing up her findings, Weiss concludes that it is not at all surprising that reporters tend to simplify social scientific research and to give undue finality and certainty to specific findings. To capture public attention, findings must be simplified and made to seem significant, as Weiss states:

> Too many qualifiers and the editor would reject the story or the public would become confused, lose interest, and wonder why the findings are being reported at all. (p. 47)

As regards the taking for granted of expertise, Weiss points out that there is every reason for academics working in reputable institutions to appear qualified to comment on social scientific issues. As for topic selection, people working in the media will naturally select topics that are already in the news and will not have time to review previous work in the chosen areas. Weiss argues that it is the job of the media not to reflect the priorities of social science but rather to appeal to their audience.

A QUESTION OF ATTRIBUTION

It is all too easy for social scientists to dismiss the media as untrustworthy and irresponsible and indeed for the media to regard social scientists as incapable of giving a straight answer. Some suspicion may stem from the different ways in which social scientists and media practitioners approach their subject matter. McCall and Stocking (1982) examine the different approaches of psychologists and journalists. On the issue of topic selection they note that psychologists typically choose topics because of their theoretical importance and for the potential of filling gaps in existing understanding. In contrast, journalists select items that are 'interesting' to large numbers of people. However, many well-known and successful social scientists have made a name for themselves in areas of interest to large numbers of people – topics that touch people's everyday lives. In some cases, these areas will have been selected because of their theoretical salience, but we suspect that some social scientists have 'a nose' for the more widely popular topics which they find difficult to resist.

On the issue of sampling, journalists, because of their time constraints, will simply identify a few key people in an area and seek information from them. The social scientist will usually attempt to achieve a 'representative' sample. Having chosen one's sample, the next stage is the interview. McCall and Stocking (1982) point out that when academics are misquoted following an interview they invariably blame the reporter. While reporters do make mistakes, the way in which social scientists put information across may be ambiguous and offer considerable scope for error in interpretation.

A further dissimilarity in the approach of social scientists and journalists, according to McCall and Stocking, is the format of reports. Scientific articles follow a rigid format reflecting good scientific methodology: introduction, method, results, discussion, conclusions and implications. In complete contrast, journalistic reports are written in roughly the opposite direction. The aim is to grab the readers' attention and motivate them to continue reading the article. In writing scientific reports, social scientists produce numerous drafts and carefully review the piece to check for errors. Journalists do not usually have time for such luxury. When reporting social scientific research journalists may feel that allowing the social scientist to review an article may jeopardize their journalistic integrity, or at the very least, open the door to unwanted censorship.

While there are notable differences between social scientific and journalistic endeavour there are also aspects which overlap.

Weaver and McCombs (1980) examined the trends in American journalism since the 1920s and concluded that, partly as a result of the ever increasing use of political polls, journalism has come to embrace the use of both social science perspectives and methods. These authors note that journalism has gone some way toward achieving Meyer's (1973) request that journalism should become 'social science in a hurry'.

Weaver and McCombs (1980) point out that journalists have changed from being 'passive transmitters of descriptions of specific events' to become 'more active truth seekers' in a transition toward more investigative journalism. This gradual transition has, according to Weaver and McCombs, led to some overlapping in the roles, perspectives and interests of social scientists and journalists and resulted in greater communication between the two. These authors note that journalists are more concerned with the specific, whereas social scientists aim to generalize, but both start from 'an empirical base' in that both search for observable evidence to support conclusions about the nature of social reality.

SOCIAL SCIENCE EQUALS GARBAGE SCIENCE?

As early as 1968, the American Professor of Journalism, Krieghbaum, argued that rising social problems since the mid-1960s brought social scientific research into the focus of the mass media. He states that in addition to the problems of finding proper social scientists to interview and research papers to quote, reporters have three problems to overcome as they try to cover the social sciences: their own scanty background in these fields; reluctance of some editors to recognize the importance of social science reporting; and inability of the public to assimilate results and put them to use effectively and efficiently.

Over two decades later, social science reportage is big business. Social scientific research is widely reported in the media for several reasons. Firstly, it has been suggested that social scientists react more favourably toward the media than other scientists (Dunwoody, 1982; Dunwoody and Ryan, 1985). For example, an American survey found that 50 per cent of physical and biological scientists interviewed had encountered no journalists within the previous year (the remaining 50 per cent had at least one contact). Conversely, 50 per cent of social scientists had talked to at least three journalists during that period while the remaining 50 per cent had 0–2 contacts. (Dunwoody and Ryan, 1985; Dunwoody, 1986).

A second reason why the social sciences are widely reported lies in the fact that editors favour stories relating to the social sciences because they are judged as being more interesting and accessible to the general public (Tichenor *et al.*, 1970; Dunwoody, 1983; McCall, 1988). A final, rather worrying, observation is that journalists favour social scientific research as material for articles because such stories can be quickly put together when they are working to tight deadlines (Dunwoody, 1982, 1983). This latter point would explain the over-simplification of social science research and the neglect of important qualifications and details. As Baruch and Kaufman (1987) note:

> In most popular press accounts of social science research the scientific method and mode of inquiry are treated as nuisances, or at best, as necessary negatives in the pursuit of knowledge about human behaviour. (p. 53)

The social sciences (in contrast to the physical and biological sciences) may receive differential treatment from the media. McCall (1988) suggests that social scientists are often required to generalize from their research results and to comment on areas that their research has not specifically addressed. Some journalists even appear to regard the social sciences as 'garbage science' and believe that no specialist knowledge is required to write on matters relating to the social sciences. Dunwoody (1980) argues that those journalists who could best understand the scientific methodology of the social sciences tend not to wish to write about the social and behavioural disciplines. She quotes a science writer who commented: 'I'm not very well equipped to evaluate sociology, but it can't hurt anybody so I figure it's not going to do much damage if I get it a little screwed up' (p. 20).

However, as McCall (1988) points out, given the often direct policy implications of the social sciences: '. . . getting behavioural science "a little screwed up" may hurt people more, not less, than reporting errors in stories on other disciplines' (p. 92).

The 'special treatment' of the social sciences does not come exclusively from the media. McCall (1988) points out that while the public and newspaper reporters acknowledge that they are in no position to judge the validity of results emanating from the physical and biological sciences, everyone considers themselves a psychologist or sociologist of sorts. Some of the terminology of the social sciences is commonly used in everyday language (though there are often important differences in the meaning which academics and the general public attach to such terms). The result of all this is that the media and the public are often more sceptical or critical of social scientific research compared to the other sciences.

OVERVIEW OF THE BOOK

Given the different priorities, perspectives and methods of the social sciences and the media it is not surprising that problems arise when the two disciplines meet in the name of publicizing research. This book gives a broad set of accounts from social scientists who have had extensive media contact. These accounts cover actual experiences that the authors have had in relation to the mass media, be they good, bad or disastrous. The academics who have contributed to this book have conducted research on a diverse range of topics including: education, stress, football hooliganism, intelligence, risk factors for illness, drug use, performance appraisal in universities, politics, sex, religion, pornography, female sexuality, terrorism and youth culture – a rich mixture of 'sex, drugs and rock 'n' roll' plus much more! We also have chapters from three well-known media practitioners (from radio, television and newspapers) in which they express their views of how social scientific research is portrayed in the media.

Chapter 1 by Robert Burgess gives an account of his experiences with the media relating to the promotion of social sciences for the British Sociological Association. He describes the media treatment of his research on education and, most recently, his work on learning about nutrition in schools, which earned him the title *Dr Din-Dins*. He also discusses the lessons he has learned about issuing press releases through his role as Chairman of the Examination Board for the Certificate of Practice in Estate Agency.

In Chapter 2 Cary Cooper writes of his extensive and varied experience of dealing with the media (including the making of a Channel 4 series). His work on occupational stress and health has received considerable attention from the media. Based on his (mostly positive) experiences with the media, he offers some useful advice for academics.

In Chapter 3, Eric Dunning discusses the media reporting of his research on football. Being regularly called upon by the media to comment on football hooliganism and crowd disasters, he has had a range of experiences in relation to television, radio and newspapers. He draws upon these experiences to provide an interesting analysis of the role of the media in reflecting and shaping public opinion. In particular, he suggests that the tabloid papers play an important role in the construction of football hooliganism as a social problem.

Hans Eysenck in Chapter 4 gives a fascinating overview of the reporting of his work on intelligence, risk factors for illness, and the effects of vitamin and mineral supplementation on children's IQ. He describes the selectivity of the media, the slanting of evidence and the tendency of the media to create controversy in social science.

Chapter 5 by Cheryl Haslam and Alan Bryman describes the consequences of some untimely and unwelcome press interest in two research projects. The first piece of research concerned drug use among medical and nursing students and the second examined performance appraisal in universities. Both of these cases highlight the dangers of reporting preliminary results.

Helen Haste in Chapter 6 explains how she is often asked to comment on issues well beyond the remit of her research interests. She explains how, through her work with the British Association for the Advancement of Science, she has come to be portrayed in the media as an expert on the sex lives of dinosaurs and, perhaps even more worryingly, an expert on the pop idol Madonna.

In Chapter 7 Dennis Howitt gives an account of the 'gatekeeping' function of the media, the selectivity of reports of the social sciences in general and specifically in relation to coverage of a Home Office commissioned review of pornography. While the report on pornography received wide media attention, the actual content of the report was rarely the focus of media coverage. He examines how pressure groups used the report selectively to argue their cases and indeed how some social scientists acted in conjunction with pressure groups to manipulate the media.

Graham Murdock in Chapter 8 gives an analysis of the clash of cultures when social scientists work with the media to publicize research. In this analysis, he draws on his wide-ranging media contact. Some of this media contact has resulted in unfortunate and unpredictable consequences, such as the press coverage in the 1970s of his work on youth culture in which he was portrayed as suggesting that Mick Jagger was a homosexual.

Jane Ussher in Chapter 9 gives a very honest discussion of the reasons why academics work with the media, including the false flattery offered by those in the media and the associated ego boost. She provides an interesting discussion of the 'gatekeeping' role of the media, their tendency to publicize selectively research which supports current thinking. Jane describes a range of personal experiences, including the simplification of her research in the press, the aggression and ridicule she received while taking part in audience participation programmes, and her work (on the other side of the fence) as a radio presenter.

In Chapter 10 Paul Wilkinson discusses the way in which social scientists use the written and electronic media as sources of information for their research. He considers the essential differences between the goals of social scientists and people working in the media. He examines the challenges and pitfalls of contributing to the media with particular reference to the ways in which the media use and abuse academic specialist contributions. Finally he offers some valuable advice for social scientists when dealing with the media.

In Chapter 11 radio presenter Peter Evans offers insights into: the editorial thinking behind specialist science radio broadcasts; the selection principles which operate when choosing social scientific research to feature in these programmes and the treatment of social scientific research in radio broadcasts. He uses actual examples to illustrate these issues and discusses the implications for useful collaboration between social scientists and the media in publicizing research.

Television producer Martin Freeth discusses in Chapter 12 his experience of working with social scientists in the making of documentaries (such as *Horizon* and *Antenna*), studio-based programmes (like *The Burke Special*) and drama documentaries. Martin also describes the occasion when he himself was a subject of a social scientist, Roger Silverstone, who studied the process of making a BBC documentary.

Chapter 13 stems from an interview between Cheryl Haslam and Oliver Gillie, journalist with the *Independent*. In this chapter Oliver Gillie describes his transition from scientist to journalist and explains how his scientific background has helped him in his reporting of the social sciences, particularly in the area of social medicine. He explores the commonalities and differences between the social scientific and journalistic enterprise. Finally, he offers advice to social scientists on how to publicize their work in newspapers.

In the concluding chapter, the editors draw together the themes from the preceding chapters and integrate these with other published work. We examine the implications and offer advice for social scientists in disseminating research in the mass media and for media practitioners themselves in reporting social scientific research findings. We outline ways in which to achieve a more fruitful relationship between the social sciences and the media.

Part I

Social scientists

Chapter 1

If you want publicity. . . call an estate agent?

Robert G. Burgess

When I published my first major empirical study (Burgess, 1983), I was encouraged by my publishers to think about the way in which my research could be linked to a story that would be attractive to the media. The study was of an urban co-educational Roman Catholic comprehensive school and had looked at particular aspects of school organization and also at the education of children who were defined by the school as being of 'average' and 'below average' ability. In this sense, the volume, which was an ethnographic study, provided portraits of difficult situations and disruption in a school and was expected to capture media attention.

It was decided that a press release would be prepared by the publisher and this would be sent together with a copy of the book to selected local and national newspapers, television programmes and radio shows. At this point, my hopes were high. I dreamt of being interviewed by numerous national newspapers, of appearing on breakfast television and of being contacted to appear on the *Jimmy Young* show on Radio 2. Indeed, my major concern was how I would inform friends and relatives that I was to be interviewed on the *Jimmy Young* programme if I was not given sufficient time or warning as to when I would be required. These were just dreams. The day the book was published I recall I waited close to a phone, but there were no calls. Almost a week later there had still been no follow-up, but I was told by the publisher that this always took time.

At last, after a week, the education correspondent on the *Coventry Evening Telegraph* telephoned me. She indicated that she had most of the details on the press release and just wanted to check out one or two things. This was my first real media interview.

It seemed very routine until she got to the question 'And can you tell me, is this a local school?'. At that point my heart quickened. I was concerned that a discovery might be made, but I gave the standard reply that I had promised not to divulge the identity of the school. To my surprise, she did not follow it up, did not ask a further question, and thanked me for the interview. This had been easy but I remained concerned. I could imagine her telephoning various schools rather in the way in which journalists had telephoned local factories in Greater Manchester when David Morgan had reported his findings to the British Association (Morgan, 1972). In this respect, I thought there was a chance that my cover would be blown and the real identity of the school would be portrayed in the press. Two nights later my fears were allayed when a very small column reported the contents of the book, and indicated I was a member of the Department of Sociology at Warwick University. There was no comment, no follow-up and really very little space devoted to it.

I report this exchange as it illustrates my naïvety in handling the press. I had no experience of dealing with the media; I had imagined that journalists would want to publish (indeed sensationalize) what I had written, and that there was a real story. I had little idea that encounters with the media needed to be developed, not only by publishers, but by researchers who need to write press releases carefully and be prepared to answer questions.

Encounters with the media and with journalists take a variety of forms. Since my first experience, I have found that I have been involved with journalists in a variety of different contexts. Firstly, in dealing with issues about the professional state and status of sociology on behalf of the British Sociological Association; secondly, reporting on my research experience and current investigations; and finally, reporting educational developments in my capacity as the Chairman of an Examination Board which was established to devise the first national examination for estate agents.

In each of these situations, my contact with the media has taken two forms: Firstly, where a journalist has contacted me to request information in order to develop a story, and secondly, where a journalist uses a press release to report something in which I have been involved, or follows up a press release through a subsequent interview. It is to these encounters that I now turn.

DEVELOPING A PROFESSIONAL IMAGE

Sociology has not had a good press. In recent years the subject has been portrayed in ways which are far from flattering, whereby journalists have claimed that unemployment is higher among sociologists (when in reality it has been no higher than among engineers). There have been claims that sociologists do very little work and old jokes have been recycled in the popular press to pander to the beliefs of the perceived readership. In addition, sociology has not been assisted by British Telecom's Beatie advertisement in which she finds that her nephew has failed all examination subjects apart from sociology. While this may appear an amusing telephone conversation, by implication it suggests that sociology is somewhat easier than other subjects.

In this respect, the British Sociological Association has attempted to counter this image by appointing a press officer and making links with the media. Indeed, it was anticipated that at the time the Association celebrated its fortieth anniversary there would be many opportunities for good press coverage on the discipline. At the time, I was President of the Association and it was suggested that I should give an interview to a journalist from *The Sunday Times* who wanted to do a story on the discipline and on a profile of sociology over 40 years. I was told that the journalist was interviewing a number of sociologists and that I would be interviewed as a representative of the Association. I spent over an hour talking to the journalist on the telephone. I was asked for statistical information on numbers of students taking sociology in higher education and at Advanced Level. Indeed, I recall looking up information as the journalist impressed upon me how important it was to have accurate evidence. By the end of the interview I thought I had dealt with someone who was taking some care over the material to be published. That was Friday evening.

By Sunday morning I was bitterly disappointed. The article appeared, but under the headline 'The 'ology we all love to hate'. This was followed by a statement about sociology and its supposed development together with a series of comments from a number of people who were antagonistic to sociology. Relatively little space was devoted to sociology as a discipline, the popularity of the subject, the increase in higher education applications and so on. In this sense, I really wondered why the journalist had bothered to interview me, but I felt it was important to continue to develop relationships with the press to promote the discipline and develop its image. Interviews would need to be granted to journalists in the future, but in turn it was important to set the record straight. At one stage I had envisaged writing to *The Sunday Times*, but after some discussion with other executive officers we decided that this would be an empty gesture and would only draw further attention to the original article which might well have been missed by a number of readers. However, I decided that whatever opportunities came my way, I would write up the record of sociology and challenge those myths that surround the subject.

Rather than using the popular press I have used other strategies to publicize sociology. In my Presidential Address (Burgess, 1990) I decided I would talk about sociology in a way which would challenge popular stereotypes of the social sciences in general and sociology in particular. A speech by Robert Jackson (the then Secretary of State for Higher Education) had indicated that it was easy to recognize the 35-year-old taxi driver with a Master's degree in sociology 'clinging to the urban fringe'. In my address, I demonstrated that this was a stereotypical image of sociology and reminded my audience and Robert Jackson that a very significant article had been written by Fred Davis (1959) on the basis of being a taxi driver. In addition, I have also published articles in more popular journals such as *Newscheck* (a magazine that goes into schools and colleges). A *Newscheck* article was written with Margaret Wallis, (Burgess and Wallis 1991) under the title that had been used in *The Sunday Times* 'Sociology – the 'ology we all love to hate?', but we added the question mark and went on to demonstrate that this was not the case. Indeed we showed how sociology has increased in popularity at Advanced Level and degree level and how sociology graduates can look forward to being employed in a variety of occupations. Sociologists need to utilize popular magazines as well as academic journals to portray their subject and to counter negative images provided by journalists who wish to pander to their readers rather than base their reports on evidence.

REPORTING RESEARCH: THE ART OF THE PRESS RELEASE

Another way in which the relevance of sociology can be demonstrated to members of the public is through reports on research activities. Here, it becomes important to communicate research work and research findings in a way that will be accessible to a variety of readers. Local and national newspapers can be assisted in reporting findings by the production of press releases that are carefully designed and targeted in relation to the subject matter of the investigation. In recent years I have been engaged in a variety of topics that link together social and educational research where sociology is used as a vehicle to explore a variety of situations that occur in schools and classrooms.

One project on which I worked was 'Energy Education and the Curriculum'. This was a short-term project commissioned by Hampshire LEA between February and May 1989. The project involved an analysis of the way in which curriculum materials were trialled and used in Hampshire schools. The materials were based around a series of curriculum packs, each of which took a zoo animal as a major vehicle for communicating the material – sun monkeys for infant and first school children, and snow cats for junior and lower secondary school pupils. As far as the project team was concerned, we were engaged in a sociological study of curriculum development which would have links with policy and practice in the Hampshire authority and in Hampshire schools (Burgess *et al.*, 1989). Meanwhile, for the local authority it was an examination of the effectiveness of their materials, and for the schools it was an opportunity to have some feedback on the way in which the project had been handled in a variety of locations. In these circumstances, it seemed appropriate to get some material about the project published in the Hampshire press.

I approached our press officer at the university who suggested I should begin by drafting a press release. My attempt was as follows:

WARWICK RESEARCHERS EXPLORE ENERGY
CONSERVATION IN HAMPSHIRE

A research team led by Professor Robert Burgess, Director of the Centre for Educational Development, Appraisal and Research at the University of Warwick, has been commissioned by Hampshire LEA to evaluate a curriculum project on Energy Conservation that is currently being trialled in sixteen schools in south west Hampshire.

The LEA have devised a cross curricular approach to energy conservation for infant/first school pupils, junior/middle school children and secondary pupils. The authority have devised packs of material that include investigations, classroom and field based activities, pictures, fact sheets and a video. The programme is a framework for enquiry based learning in the schools. The Warwick team will visit schools to see the ways in which the curriculum materials are used by teachers and pupils and the links that are made to the school curriculum and the National Curriculum.

The results of the trialling of the project will be available in May.

When I visited the press officer with my press release, he started to enquire about the focus of the project and what pupils were doing in the schools. I indicated that much of the teaching took place around animals that were in Marwell Zoo (a zoo in Hampshire which pupils could visit and see the animals for themselves). This he found more interesting than any of the social science that I had talked about and he therefore offered to rewrite the press release focusing on the use of animals in the zoo. His version of the press release was as follows:

WARWICK RESEARCHERS LOOK AT EDUCATION FOR ENERGY CONSERVATION IN HAMPSHIRE

A research team led by Professor Robert Burgess, Director of the Centre for Educational Development, Appraisal and Research at the University of Warwick, has been commissioned by Hampshire LEA to evaluate a curriculum project on Energy Education that is currently being tried out in sixteen schools in south west Hampshire. The programme is being run under the title 'ECAMP', which stands for Energy Conservation Awareness/ Motivation Project.

Using imaginative teaching packs based on endangered animals at Marwell Zoo, Hampshire LEA have devised a cross curricular approach to energy conservation called 'Sun Monkeys' for infant/ first school children and 'Snow Cats' for junior/middle school children. There is also a pack with a space scene for secondary pupils. The authority have devised packs of material that include investigations, classroom and field based activities, pictures, fact sheets and a video. All packs are built around exciting real life conservation issues complicated by energy needs.

The Warwick team will visit schools to see the ways in which the curriculum materials are used by teachers and pupils and the links that are made to the school curriculum and the National Curriculum.

The results of the trialling of the project will be available in May.

With the rewriting, the focus had changed. Some of the language of the project concerning cross-curricular themes was now embedded with other evidence about the animals who could be seen in Marwell Zoo, and it was claimed (by the press officer) that they were endangered species. Two weeks later a copy of an article was sent to me that had appeared in the *Hampshire Chronicle*. The article consisted of the whole of the press release presented as five separate paragraphs under the title 'Marwell Zoo is inspiration for project'. It seemed a far cry from the world of sociology and social science, but it did communicate with a local readership in Hampshire, it did demonstrate that researchers were engaged in work that was beyond the 'ivory tower' and would have relevance for policy and practice. I had learned a major lesson, namely that press releases need to be carefully designed because they are often used in their entirety by journalists. In addition, I was made aware that topics which may be of immediate interest to social scientists are not necessarily those that are of interest to journalists and the general public. This is an important feature when preparing material for the press, as more often than not the stories are constructed on the basis of a press release rather than on any subsequent interview or investigation.

INTERVIEW OR INVENTION? THE 'NEWS' STORY

Some topics in social science are instantly newsworthy – at least in the eyes of reporters. In the summer of 1992, details of a project grant that I had obtained as part of the Economic and Social Research Council's 'Nation's Diet' initiative was included at a press launch at the British Association meetings. A Nation's Diet pack including details of the project entitled 'Teaching and Learning about Food and Nutrition in Schools' had been circulated to a range of reporters.

My first press contact on this project was with Dorothy Lepkowska

(Education Correspondent of the *Birmingham Post*). The interview and the article which followed focused on the design of the project and the issues we intended to explore under the title 'Professor in search for pupils with taste?':

School dinners are to be scrutinised as part of a nationwide study into children's eating habits.

Prof Robert Burgess, a professor of sociology at Warwick University will spend two years visiting schools, where he will also look at the role they play in children's knowledge of nutrition.

The study is part of a £1.4 million six-year project which will be the first of its kind to look into the eating habits of children in Britain.

It is being paid for by the government's Economic and Social Research Council.

Yesterday Prof Burgess said he was entering his research with a completely open mind.

He said 'Adults always think children eat what isn't good for them, but I will be seeking to find out whether that is the case.'

'I will be particularly interested to look into the McDonald's culture which somehow sits alongside the healthy eating ethos schools are attempting to transmit.'

'We will be asking children to keep diaries of what they eat throughout the day to find out how far they are influenced by what they eat at school, and at home.'

Experts will sit in on classes where food nutrition is being discussed and will attend special events, such as Food Weeks, organised by schools.

Pupils at four Midland schools – two primary and two secondary – will be investigated in depth, but Prof Burgess declined to say which ones.

'They will be situated in different socio-economic areas so we get a good cross-section of population and identify how culture influences what people eat', he said, 'If children choose to spend their lunch money in the local chip shop instead of in the school canteen then we will follow them to find out what they buy.'

A subsequent article appeared in the *Birmingham Evening Mail* which had made no contact with me and appeared to be little more than a recast version of the story in the *Birmingham Post*:

EXPERT PROBES SCHOOL DINNERS

A Midland academic is joining a nationwide study into children's eating habits by scrutinising school dinners.

Prof Robert Burgess, a professor of sociology at Warwick University, will spend two years visiting schools, to look at the role they play in children's knowledge of nutrition.

The study is part of a project funded by the government's Economic and Social Research Council, the first of its kind to look into the eating habits of children in Britain.

Prof Burgess said 'Adults always think children eat what isn't good for them but I will be seeking to find out whether that is the case.

'I will be particularly interested to look into the McDonald's culture which somehow sits alongside the healthy eating ethos schools are attempting to transmit.'

Nevertheless, at this stage the story was reasonably accurate, apart from the claim that the study would take place in four Midlands schools (as at that stage no schools or areas of the country had been selected) and that I would personally visit the schools (given that a research fellow had been appointed to the project). Indeed, the project was not due to commence until January 1993.

However, the following day I was contacted by Ken Gibson (a Midlands-based reporter) on behalf of the *Today* newspaper and by a member of a news agency. The interviews which followed were both very similar. The reporters did most of the talking, answering as well as asking the questions and giving opinions on my project with which I was invited to agree. At that stage, I was aware that considerable care was required to limit any damage to the study. The story that subsequently appeared in *Today* was written by Nicki Pope (someone with whom I had never spoken, nor ever heard of). It contained a mixture of information and invention including invented quotations:

PROFESSOR GOES BACK TO SCHOOL FOR DINNER

A university professor is to spend two years tucking into school dinners in a study on children's eating habits.

Professor Robert Burgess will visit targeted schools to sample cafeteria food and accompany children on lunchtime trips to the chippie.

The results, part of a Government-backed £1.4 million study, will be used to influence school dieticians' healthy-eating programmes.

Professor Burgess, a sociologist at Warwick University, said he feared a 'McDonald's culture' was developing among youngsters who prefer burgers to meat and two veg.

'The fact is that no one but the children themselves really know what they are eating' he said.

'The standard of school dinners is a total unknown too and I'm sure we will find a wide variety of choices available in school cafeterias.'

'I will be sitting down to eat with school children and sampling what is on offer.'

'We will be finding out whether children are eating sandwiches or cooked dinners or just opting for a packet of crisps in the playground.'

'If children choose to spend their dinner money in the local chip shop instead of in the school canteen then I will follow them to find out what they buy.'

An interesting feature of this story was the way the project had been shifted from being about teaching and learning about food and nutrition to a study on children's eating habits. Central to the story was the image of the university professor 'tucking into school dinners'. But this image was further extended in other stories. The *Daily Express* published a short, inaccurate account under the heading 'Burger-Master' which suggested that I was to be paid £1.4 million (the cost of the Nation's Diet initiative) to do little more than eat school dinners and burgers. However, the *Sun* went further with the following report:

DIN-DINS PROF HUNTS CHIP KIDS

A professor is to share bags of chips with kids for two years – to find out why they prefer junk food to school dinners.

Sociologist Robert Burgess, dubbed Doctor Din-Dins, will visit schools around the country and follow children on lunch-time trips.

The Warwick University professor fears kids are developing a 'McDonald's culture'.

His survey is part of a six-year national study costing £1.4 million.

Here, I was portrayed as someone who would 'share bags of chips with kids for two years' – a topic that Simon Worthington (the *Sun*'s education correspondent, who had never contacted me) had decided was part of the research. Both the research and the research strategy were pure invention. However, it did earn the comment in the *Guardian* diary that I should be congratulated on having my research reported in the *Sun* at a time when members of the Royal Family (especially the Duchess of York's holiday photographs and Princess Diana's telephone conversations) were being widely reported.

Certainly, my experience made me sympathetic towards those at the centre of attention from the tabloid press where stories take on a spurious authenticity. Indeed, I found that later in the week in which these 'research' stories were reported I was called by a reporter at the *Coventry Evening Telegraph*. After a 'serious' interview about the project, she passed me to the pictures editor who suggested that he might get a photographer to purchase burger and chips at McDonalds so that I could be photographed eating it. When I objected on the grounds that this would provide a biased account of the project, his defence was to state that the *Daily Express* had reported I was 'to eat school dinners and Big Mac burgers for a year'. It appeared that for him newspaper accounts provided infallible evidence about research. It was the source of all knowledge.

The publicity from this research has generated much amusement among friends and colleagues who warm to the 'Dr Din-Dins' image. In turn, it has also resulted in unsolicited material from people in Sussex and Paris who have provided school meals menus, while others have written with requests for assistance with food projects and details of any employment opportunities that might be associated with the project. However, for me the message is clear – care needs to be taken in handling the press when project findings are available. The initial press encounter might well set the tone of all publicity and in turn the material transmitted in articles which owe more to invention than interviews.

EXPLORING EDUCATIONAL DEVELOPMENTS

A further area in which I have had experience of the media has been in my role as Chairman of the Examination Board for the Certificate of Practice in Estate Agency (the first national examination for estate agents) that has been designed and established by the National Association of Estate Agents (NAEA). I was invited to chair this examination board in order to put a new examination system in place. In this respect, I was called upon to provide expertise on the organization and administration of tests and examinations. As part of this role, I was invited to participate in the launch of the Certificate which involved a number of members of the Examination Board and officers of the National Association of Estate Agents giving presentations to an invited audience. On the basis of our presentations the Association's press officer took notes which were subsequently used in a press release that was issued locally and nationally. The details of the launch of this new qualification were reported in a variety of local newspapers under such titles as 'The NAEA launches its Certificate of Practice in Estate Agency' (*Estate Agency News*, St Annes on Sea), 'New test of estate agents' (*Watford Observer*), 'Standards set for estate agents exam' (*Dudley News*), 'New exam for estate agents' (*Shropshire Journal*, Wellington), 'Estate agents exam' (*Stanmore Independent*), and 'Estate agency training boost' (*Thurrock Post*). While the headlines were slightly different, the story beneath was virtually the same, as shown in the following:

Pontefract Express, Yorkshire	*Pinner Independent*
Exam to test estate agents	Estate agents exam
The first nationally available professional qualification for estate agency managers has been launched by their national association.	The first nationally available professional qualifications for estate agency managers has been launched by the National Association of Estate Agents.

The new Certificate of Practice in Estate Agency has been devised by the NAEA – representing over 9,000 agents nationwide – as part of its training programme.

It is aimed at all levels of the profession, up to and including managers. Candidates do not need to be NAEA members to take the exam.

According to NAEA President, Hugh Dunsmore-Hardy, the certificate has already been welcomed by representatives of major groups and independent estate agency firms.

He says: 'This new qualification provides the best possible proof of the Association's total commitment to raising the professional standards within estate agency and should help further to improve the public's confidence in estate agents generally'.

The exam is in two parts – with the first covering estate agency practices, legal aspects, valuation of residential property and domestic building construction.

NAEA was established in 1962 and represents more than 9,000 estate agents throughout the UK.

The new Certificate of Practice in Estate Agency has been devised by NAEA as part of its ongoing programme of training and issuing qualifications to estate agents.

It is aimed at all levels of the profession up to and including managers.

Candidates do not need to be members of the NAEA to take the examination.

NAEA president Hugh Dunsmore-Hardy said the certificate has already been welcomed by representatives of major groups and independent estate agency firms.

He added: 'This new qualification provides the best possible proof of the Association's total commitment to raising professional standards within estate agency'.

The exam is in two parts.

The first covers estate agency practice, the legal aspects of estate agency, valuation of residential property and domestic building construction.

The second part involves more advanced estate agency practice, management and marketing, but can only be taken once candidates have passed part one or already hold certain pre-determined qualifications.

The examination board is chaired by Prof Robert Burgess, of Warwick University, while an external examiner, Prof Colin Carnell of Henley Management College, provides a further check on the integrity of the examination.

The second part covers more advanced estate agency practice, management and marketing but can only be taken once candidates have passed part one, or already hold certain pre-determined qualifications.

The examination board is chaired by Prof Robert Burgess of Warwick University, and an external examiner, Prof Colin Carnell, of the Henley Management College, provides a further check on the integrity of the examination.

While the headlines are different, the text varies very little. This was a common experience across all the stories reported across the country. The press release was therefore central in capturing the attention of editors and journalists on local and national news-papers, but in turn little more was done other than slightly to recast some of the sentences in reporting this particular story. The quality of the press release was crucial to attract attention and develop publicity in this instance.

Here, comparisons can be made with our first example from sociology. Both sociologists and estate agents share one thing in common. Both suffer a bad press and both are subject to carica-ture and to mythology. In this respect, both are in the business of countering a negative image, but the evidence I have available would suggest that estate agents are much more successful in gaining positive publicity for themselves than sociologists.

LESSONS TO LEARN

The examples I have provided highlight different dimensions of my experience with the press. However, there are three important issues for us all. Firstly, social scientists cannot just rely on journalists ringing up to enquire about their projects and their profession. It is vital for social scientists and sociologists to get to know journalists with whom they can discuss their research and the qualities of social science. Secondly, it is important that sociologists develop the ability to identify the newsworthy story and to communicate it successfully to the press. Thirdly, press releases are very important in relationships with the media. It is therefore essential for sociologists and social scientists to develop the skills to write good press releases which make their material accessible to journalists, and in turn the general public. All these lessons are important for social scientists to learn. Indeed, the training of postgraduate students might well incorporate practice at writing press releases about research activity and communicating material in an accessible way to a general audience. However, it is important to remember that if we want publicity we need to work with experts to enhance our professional image and report our research. For this we might ask: 'Do we need to call an estate agent?'

Chapter 2

The psychologist and the media: opportunities, challenges and dangers

Cary L. Cooper

THE CASE FOR COMMUNICATING WITH THE OUTSIDE WORLD

Stress is highly topical, not least because many people experience it. During the Thatchery of the 1980s, many people were under considerable pressure. We had to accept a great deal of change, in both the public and private sector. And as we all know, change produces stress. People experience daily stress in their job, in the family and in a whole range of activities (Cooper *et al.*, 1988).

Stress research, therefore, has attracted a great deal of media attention. It is a natural topic and the media are very interested in it. Also, I seem to be one of a small band of academics who are happy to talk to the media. I sometimes feel that writing for academic journals, that is, writing for 90–100 colleagues across the world who are actually interested in your particular piece of research, is not the only kind of contribution I want to make. While we conduct scientific research, I think that it is important that we communicate to people in general about 'our science'. Wide dissemination has pay-offs, not just personal pay-offs in the sense that you get well known, but pay-offs in terms of attracting additional research funds, and demonstrating the applicability of research to the wider community.

I believe it is important for academics to put across their ideas in language which the general public find accessible. Not all academics want to do this, and not all are capable of doing this. It is a skill, though a skill which can be learned. Many academics could learn this skill; some do not wish to, but for me, personally, it is something that I want to do. I aim to communicate not only to my scientific colleagues through the conventional sources such as journals and conferences, but also to the outside world through TV, the press, radio, etc. In addition, the public to some extent are beginning to demand this, they are investing in us, we are in state institutions and taxpayers are paying for these institutions. It is incumbent upon us, therefore, to show that much of what we do is relevant to society.

THE DOWN SIDE

Many would argue that if you are prepared to speak to the media for visibility reasons, or because you enjoy it, then you have to take the good with the bad, the ups with the downs. In this regard, it is worth being aware of the common problems.

No control

A negative aspect of working with the media is the lack of control over the way in which research findings are reported. Taking the different media in turn, I trust radio most, followed by television, followed by the press. But in each medium the scope for control is very limited. With regard to radio and television, much of what you say may be edited, and journalists never show you what they have written. Basically, you just have to trust them. Generally my contact with the media has been most positive. Of course, there have been occasions of distortions of what was said, emphasis on one particular aspect or a statement taken out of context. These occurrences can be problematic, but one has little control over them. If an academic tries to exert control, the media are unlikely to respond; that's not the way they function.

I do not appreciate wasting time apologizing to people for things that I never actually said. I am quite happy to confront and deal with problems arising from something I did say, but so often a comment can be distorted in such a way that there is only the slightest grain of truth in it. Most problems occur where comments are distorted or taken out of context. Sometimes problems stem from not knowing where the material will end up. I think it is very important for social scientists to realize that a story can escalate to many more outlets than they envisaged.

Given the lack of control in the process, social scientists have to think very clearly about what they say. In reality this is difficult to achieve, particularly in interviews. Often at the end of an interview

I find myself thinking 'Oh my God, what if they decide to use that. I am sure they won't, I am sure they will realize that I didn't mean it in that context.' Strangely, in the vast majority of cases one is quite safe. I think the competition between newspapers means that there is a greater danger of the press, more so than radio and television, using the more 'risky' or 'off the wall' comments that you may have made.

Media attention equals second-class scientist?

It seems to me rather sad that in our business the more you talk to the media, the less your academic peers value you. I don't know why this happens, but some colleagues see you as a second-class 'academic citizen'. As such, the only academics who do a lot of talking to the media are those who feel extremely secure in their academic base. This is unfortunate, as it constitutes only a limited number of academics. There are many young academics with interesting things to say to the media who are deterred, in case they are labelled 'not very academic' or worst yet 'popular'.

Many Ph.D. students are conducting research in interesting areas and have very useful ideas to contribute, but they are frightened to talk to the media not only because they are inexperienced with regard to dealing with the media, but also because of what their colleagues will think of them. Such snobbery is really bad news for our business. The bodies which fund research need as much help as they can get in terms of publicity, which can highlight just how valuable our research is to the wider society, if they are to put pressure on government to get more money for the social sciences. So we should encourage not discourage (out of some sense of academic superiority) young academics to interact with the media.

Colleagues often say 'I saw you on telly last night', and certain colleagues will say it to put you down, while other colleagues say it in a more positive and rewarding way. There are some colleagues who are either jealous, envious or threatened by what you are doing, and you have to put up with that. Others think it is a really good thing. Academics generally can be a little narrow-minded and blinkered, and then wonder why money is cut for social science research by the government, and do not see the importance of communicating with the outside world.

In addition, I have had colleagues say to me 'What did you

appear on Radio 1 for?', but consider presenting a series for Channel 4 totally acceptable. There is a real snobbery in the social sciences, indeed, in academic life generally. One can talk to the *Guardian*, the *Independent* and *The Times*, but not to the tabloids; similarly Channel 4, BBC 2 and BBC 1 are fine, but ITV not so fine. Radio 4 is okay but Radio 1 – 'Oh my God!'.

It confuses some colleagues when I talk to all types of media, because I cannot be easily pigeon-holed. Featuring in the *Independent*, on Channel 4 or Radio 4 is not a problem, but when I appear on Radio 1 then people start asking questions. I once appeared on BBC 2 in a programme which was a teenage slot about youth unemployment. The programme was very well done, but some people asked 'Why are you doing a "young persons"' programme like that?'. This is a rather silly reaction, because we have a wide range of constituents out there who are interested in our work.

Putting words into your mouth?

Sometimes the media ask for a comment when they really want you to agree or disagree with *their* comment. Some journalists call up knowing the kind of comment they want from an expert. They call up and say 'So would you say, Professor Cooper, that . . . ?'. The minute you say 'Yes', you have given them what they want. Of course, if you agree with the argument or approach there is no problem. On the other hand, you might say 'No I don't agree with that at all, in fact, I think its quite the opposite', in which case they will either not use your comment or adopt your contrary viewpoint to their own purposes. So, sometimes they lead the social scientist down a particular path. Remember, when people write articles for the newspapers they are always looking for an expert to provide an opinion, and they usually tend to couch it in a particular way that meets their needs. But you don't have to go along with that. Journalists are usually honest, they won't put words in your mouth that are not there if you stand your ground, but they may have a hidden agenda – a point I shall return to later.

Disruption

Sometimes when a big story has broken, the media are desperate for a comment from a psychologist, and I may get over 30 phone calls in quick succession. This can be very tiring and intrusive, because I am doing other things at the time. So what do you do? Should you refuse everybody or should you be selective about whom you talk to? Generally, I try to resist the usual academic snobbishness about the press. Women's magazines frequently want comments from social scientists, but they are much more flexible in their timescales than newspapers. Often a story doesn't have to be in for another three to four weeks. Occasionally they want more than a quick comment, because they are trying to get a lot of information from which to build up an article. It can be very time consuming, and when I am too busy they usually understand and are fairly flexible.

Sometimes I am contacted at home, which is fine as long as it is not intruding into particular family activities, and providing the enquiry is reasonably quick (and from my experience most of them are reasonably quick). They don't really want to spend a lot of time with you, they want to get a quick opinion and then off they go. Newspaper reporters are very resilient; if you're not responsive, they will call somebody else. They call the British Psychological Society or they have a list of psychologists and they work through the list. So if you are busy, they just accept it. I can remember one or two occasions when people have been pushy, but most of the time they are not. Media contact only becomes an intrusion, when people are unable to say 'No'.

GETTING THE RIGHT BALANCE

When I started to do most of my television work, I was a well-established academic, I had published not only numerous scholarly articles, but also a lot of books. Over the years my work with the media has not detracted from my other output. I suspect it could cause problems where an academic gets taken over by the media, and then stops doing the other things that make academics credible.

I do not think academic institutions particularly value media contact *per se*, even though it may give the institution a good gloss. Institutions in general do not regard media contact negatively or positively, although there is a growing appreciation of the benefits in terms of public relations. Outside communication is relevant, it attracts more students, it makes institutions more visible, it even assists in attracting research grants. Obviously, when applying for research funds the most important criterion is to have a good proposal, but having a high-profile institution helps as well. This is particularly important when applying for funds from the private sector – if they recognize that your research is relevant to the community, then they are more likely to be interested.

TYPES OF MEDIA CONTACT

The interview

During an interview itself, there is little sense of having any control over what topics are to be covered. In agreeing to be interviewed, we must be prepared to make ourselves visible, and to some extent vulnerable, often having little idea of what questions will be asked. I have rarely ever had a list of questions given to me on any television or radio programme, and while they may give you a rough idea of where they are going, that may not be the way the interview develops, particularly in radio where it is almost a free-wheeling process.

When a radio or television interviewer throws in a totally un-expected question, I always try to offer an answer. I am not always happy with my response, I may react in a flip way to get out of it. I usually respond, I never say 'No, I refuse to answer that.' I think we have to respond in some form or another. I do not think social scientists should expect that when dealing with television or radio or the press they are going to be given, in advance, a list of questions. Something may happen that you are not going to like very much. They may throw something at you that you had not really expected, but providing it is not a live broadcast, you could request that they don't use it.

On radio, there is usually an informal chat before the actual interview. This may be recorded to enable the technical staff to achieve the right level of recording. Sometimes the informal chat can carry on into the actual interview itself. This can be potentially problematic, as you may not wish them to use some of the things which you said informally. One radio interview I took part in illustrated this problem. I was being interviewed on a popular, national radio programme about a book of mine which had just been published. Before the interview, the presenter and I were chatting informally. He asked me for my opinion on a number of general issues, including my views of a particular celebrity who had made some contentious claims which had attracted considerable media coverage. Unknown to me, the whole thing, interview and pre-interview chat, had been recorded. I had to request that they not use my pre-interview comments in the broadcast – which were irrelevant to the purpose of my interview anyway – and of course, being a responsible broadcasting authority, they complied.

This is an unusual event; in the majority of cases a red light indicates that you are being recorded. Once or twice I have been recorded without my knowledge, but the material was not broadcast, so obviously they were setting the recording level. I have never known a situation where recorded 'off the cuff' remarks in the pre-interview chat have been used in the broadcast. I have enough confidence in the BBC and other broadcasting authorities to hope they would never ever do that.

The television documentary (and more!)

I recently had an unfortunate experience when working with television. I was interviewed for a documentary television programme, a very good programme, and everything seemed fine. Having been interviewed, I was told that the programme would appear in about nine months' time. Some time later, a video came on the market, of which apparently I was the presenter, though I knew absolutely nothing about it!

As far as I was concerned I had been interviewed for the documentary, for which I was paid a nominal fee. During the filming I spent most of the day with the producers and later signed the mandatory waiver stating that the producers have the right to use the material. I did not read all the detail of it, I do not think any social scientist does, we just trust them. It said in the fine print that they could use the material and have copyright over it. They had recorded a lot of me to make the documentary. In the actual transmitted broadcast, they used only a little bit of my interview, naturally with the rest of the programme taken from other material that they had collected. With the remaining material taken from the interview with me, they made a video, unbeknown to me, never cleared it with me, and never asked me for my opinion about it. This became a real problem, because I had been asked to make a teaching video on stress for managers by a very respected company. This company were most surprised when the promotion for this first video (which I knew nothing about) ended up on their desk. This video had on it 'presented by Professor Cary Cooper' on the packaging.

There were two important issues here. Firstly, I never presented anything, I was an interviewee on a documentary programme, nothing more than that, even though the video claimed to be 'presented by Professor Cary Cooper' on the cover. Secondly, this video was released at the same time that I was producing another video. I had signed a contract which excluded me from any similar concurrent projects, so I was called to account. The company I was producing a video for wanted to know what on earth was going on. Though I pointed out that I knew nothing about it, this initially seemed incredible to them. I found the situation horrendous, people were making a lot of money from me and causing me considerable embarrassment. This is not what I call very good practice.

The Authors' Society (of which I am a member) complained to the organization on my behalf. The organization felt that there was nothing wrong with their actions because I had signed the waiver. I was absolutely appalled by this episode, which could have caused legal problems for me, as it appeared that I had broken a contract with another company. Eventually my name was taken off as presenter of the video, after vigorous complaints to senior management.

If a social scientist signs a document for radio or television, they should ensure that the material cannot be used for commercial purposes without their permission. Social scientists can be very vulnerable. In this particular instance, I was advised to take legal action, but I chose to forget it. I chose to think that it was just one aberration.

Reports in newspapers

In all the years I have been dealing with the newspapers, my perception is that 90 per cent of newspaper reports are fairly accurate. Many social scientists, however, do not want to talk to the tabloid press. They are quite interested in talking to the *Independent*, the *Guardian*, *The Times*, the 'respectable' newspapers, but they are frightened of talking to the others. But in the majority of cases, both the broadsheet and tabloid press are reliable, though they may not actually print what you thought they were going to produce.

Reporters have to put a particular slant or orientation on a story. That is the danger, because you do not know what's really going on, primarily because they themselves might not know exactly how they are going to use your interview. They interview you, take notes, interview somebody else, take more notes and then they come up with an idea of the structure of the story. I am not saying that I am always happy to open up a newspaper and find my comments put in a surprising context, but I often concede 'Well, I did say that actually, but that's not what I thought they were trying to get out of me.' I have written complaining to a newspaper on only one occasion, and I got a letter back saying that they had looked into the matter and as far as they were concerned the story was reported accurately. I didn't take the matter any further. My perception is that there have been a number of occasions on which I have been misquoted and it has upset me, but I can understand why they may have misquoted me in the context of what they were writing.

When commenting on research, but not wishing to divulge certain details (such as the name of the organization in which the research was conducted), newspapers, including the tabloids, usually respect this wish. The sanction is that you refuse to talk to them in the future. An important constraint on their behaviour is that it is more important to cultivate a trusting relationship with you and gather future material, than getting one story and then never using you again.

A common occurrence, which can be frustrating, is when a journalist has a hidden agenda. This is the situation where a journalist says 'My story is about X', so I comment on 'X', but they then throw in another linked question and I respond to that as well – and that is what they really wanted. The quality papers do not usually do that, they usually stick with 'your story'. When this problem arises, there is no redress other than to write a letter to the editor. I tend not to bother because it simply draws more attention to the story, and you could be on this kind of band wagon for months.

There are occasions when your comments are taken out of context or misrepresented. But this is all part of dealing with the press. There are potential dangers in it, there are certainly a number of potential traps, and I am learning all the time about identifying them. After a while, though, you think you have been dealing with them for so long that you know all the pitfalls, and then something new comes up that surprises you.

To give an example, a journalist, purporting to be from a

particular newspaper, called with regard to a story he was writing. The following day the story appeared, but not in that newspaper, it appeared in three other newspapers. It turned out that the journalist offered the story to the newspaper he usually writes for, they were not interested, so he sold it on to other newspapers. I was unaware of this practice. None of the other newspapers called me up to ask me about the story, and it was 'sold on' to a range of newspapers, including some tabloid newspapers. Unfortunately, the journalist had reported something that was totally inaccurate. He had called up saying that a study had been conducted in the US on X. He wanted a comment on the study and the British Psychological Society suggested he contact me. The story appeared the next day as 'A STUDY CARRIED OUT BY PROFESSOR COOPER FOUND . . . '. I had not conducted such a study, and also it was about a topic which offended certain people. I started to get angry telephone calls. This episode caused me embarrassment, I was personally upset and angry, and wrote to the newspaper concerned.

The various reports which appeared were totally inaccurate; I had not conducted such a study nor had I made the comments that were reported. When I called up a friend who is a journalist and I asked about this practice of selling on stories, I was told that it is not considered proper practice (particularly for a staff reporter), but it happens. It is a danger when you believe that a report will appear in a particular newspaper and then you see it somewhere else. The inaccuracy of the reporting probably arose as a result of information being passed from one person, who then sent it to others who then failed to seek confirmation. This was a disturbing episode, though such occurrences are, thankfully, rare. Normally the newspapers call back to confirm a story and ask for further comments.

The media reporting of conference presentations

A few years ago, conference presentations relating to research conducted in two large companies received some unfortunate media attention. The conference sponsors requested press releases for the conference papers, which I provided for one of the papers, which concerned research completed some time ago. As regards the other paper, I did not issue a press release because the research was not quite complete. For both papers, I was keen to protect the identities of the companies so they were not mentioned in the press release, and in the conference presentations I and my co-author used fictitious company names. In the particular industry we were looking at, there are only a handful of companies, so it was not that hard to figure out which one was involved. Indeed, a journalist guessed the identity of the company, but I refused to comment.

There was considerable press coverage as it was a very topical issue. The next day the company was named in the press, and I felt I had let them down. How the press came by the name is an intriguing question. It was a three-day conference and the press were present at the social functions as well as the actual paper presentations, and may have come across the information indirectly. It may be that one of us had informally mentioned it. Social scientists need to be very cautious if they want to protect the identity of a company or organization. I do not know how we can overcome this danger, because you are talking to people informally all the time at conferences.

A senior manager of the organization called to register his discontent. I explained that I did not know how it got out, as I had sat through the whole session and my colleague did not mention the name during the presentation. This type of situation creates problems when conducting research in organizations, because you feel that you have let the organization down. It affects your credibility as a researcher, in that organizations may be concerned about leaking details to the press. As it transpired, I was able to demonstrate to the organization that this episode had good PR implications. Few organizations could claim to have addressed issues of shopfloor worker stress by sponsoring a large-scale study.

Requests for comments

Social scientists are often contacted by organizations who have carried out research. These organizations may be commercial or public service. They carry out surveys through independent bodies like Mori, for example, and subsequently want an expert in the field to comment on the findings. So a company may call me up and inform me of the results of a survey and ask if, when they issue a press release, I would be willing to talk about the results to the media.

This service role is an interesting one, first of all because sometimes I'm very interested in seeing the results of these surveys.

A recent poll on working hours among managers was fascinating and my comments on the study were accurately reported. As mentioned earlier, sometimes one can be misrepresented in the sense that readers think that it is your study, when in fact it is nothing to do with you. When asked to comment on a study conducted by another researcher, all I can offer is a comment. It can only be a comment, unless it is based on certain facts that I have at my disposal.

Sometimes I am asked to comment on an issue that nobody has ever studied, and in these cases I put forward several possible explanations for the phenomenon or behaviour concerned, indicating that there is little empirical evidence to confirm or disconfirm my views. The media do not want academics to sit on fences, they hate that. Academics are trained to sit on fences, we are trained never to express an opinion where there is no data to back it up. We are disciplined to keep our opinions to ourselves, even though they sometimes get out. In general, we try to make every statement on a particular form of human behaviour supported by some kind of factual or empirical base. But this is 'unreality', this is not the way the world functions, and certainly not the way the media function. The media do not appreciate academics saying 'Well, on the one hand . . . on the other hand', and putting forward all the caveats that we have to make when we present academic papers or write scholarly articles.

In my view, much social science research, although it is conducted in a way that can be replicated in many instances, still has a substantial subjective base to it. Indeed, social scientists frequently do research on topics that have personal relevance to them. The most important thing, therefore, is to present research in such a way that other people, who may not be so emotionally involved, can criticize it and try to improve on the design.

Presenting a documentary

Presenting the series for Channel 4, *How to Survive the 9 to 5*, was a very new and challenging experience. Before that time, although I had been involved in television interviews, I had never co-written or presented a series. When someone interviews me about, say, the study I did on teachers or doctors, I know the study backwards and can talk about it very easily. But to actually 'present' something on television is quite different.

The producer of the series (who actually had a background in psychology) had seen me often on television, and had rather more confidence in my skills as a potential presenter than I had. Initially, I felt most uncomfortable in front of a crew in the middle of an office wandering through desks and talking. I found it extremely difficult to talk for a set time without the aid of an autocue. Later the producer realized that I needed an autocue, because I was not trained, for example, to spontaneously deliver a 42-second insert between other film clips, while walking through a heavy engineering factory. The material had to be written out and delivered exactly to a pre-set time slot, so it was not my 'normal' style of delivery.

Presenting that programme was the most stressful professional activity I had ever done in my life! It was so different from what I had been used to. Overall, I enjoyed the experience, and the fact that it was produced by a psychologist helped enormously because we worked very well together. Looking back I can see aspects that could have been done better, but in general I was very happy with the final product.

Presenting a series is quite different from being interviewed for a documentary. By virtue of the fact that you are having to make a subject interesting to people outside your field, you cannot explore ideas in too much depth. A particular idea you wish to put across has to be demonstrated in an interesting visual way. For example, it is easy to state 'The relationship between a boss and subordinate is absolutely fundamental to health, the worse your boss is to you and the more s/he de-values you, the more damaging it is to your health' – but to put that on film, demonstrate it and make it interesting is rather more complex.

Presenting the series did give me a lot of scope, and I felt more in control. I was working with the producer, we discussed ideas for filming and presenting, and I was also somewhat involved in the editing. The producer would write a bit, then I would say it to camera and if it did not feel comfortable (because they were not my words), I would rewrite it. The producer gave me a framework, and then eventually sometimes I would just write my own material. It was a good experience from that point of view, but very stressful because although I had more control, I was having to perform in front of a whole crew. When you are performing in front of camera as a presenter, people are expecting you to perform professionally. When you are an academic being interviewed they do not expect you to perform; they expect you to open your mouth and offer a few 'meaningful' or 'unexpected' insights that are relevant to the subject.

The best programme in the series I did was the first one, which we filmed last, by which time I really was more relaxed and skilled. Some of the bits were done without the aid of autocue, but in general I think social scientists need aids in these settings, and should not try to memorize and reproduce the material. Academics tend to elaborate, pontificate and go off on tangents – you cannot do that when presenting on television.

I have also produced little parts of other programmes and have enjoyed that. A breakfast television programme asked me if I would help them put together and present some seven-minute films on issues such as women in the workplace and child care. These were self-contained slots which I helped to create, film and present. It was an enjoyable experience. The thing I like about television is that they tend to get you involved (if you want to be) in all phases of the process, even the editing. Nevertheless, for an academic, I still feel television is an odd medium. Walking between tower cranes on a building site and talking, while everything is going on in the background, is fine for the professional television presenters but challenging (!) for academics, however much television work you have done.

ADVICE TO SOCIAL SCIENTISTS

In radio and in television, providing the broadcast is not live, you can ensure that they don't include things you don't want. Occasionally, after being interviewed for radio and television I have been sent tapes or film for my comments. But often radio and television producers work to tight deadlines. If it is a documentary that won't be out for six months, you might be able to reflect on what you contributed after you did it, and then suggest which parts should be used. You have to trust them, but let them know what you might be worried about. People in the media are not stupid and also they do not want to get into any trouble legally, and they may wish to use you in the future. So be open and honest with them at the time, rather than walking out and later saying 'Oh no! I am frightened that they might use that.' If in doubt, contact them a day later after reflecting on it.

With newspapers, it is a different matter: they call you, the story goes out tomorrow and that's the end of it. I don't think there is any way in which journalists are able to give feedback on what they are going to say. You might request that they fax you what they have written, but it is unlikely that they will meet such a request. They usually write the piece straight away, and send it on to the editor. I do not know what you can do except think carefully about any comments you make. Generally journalists respect your wishes if you ask them not to use a particular comment.

But if you are overly cautious in your comments, they are unlikely to use them. Often journalists want an 'expert's' opinion, a view on a particular topic. For example, early in 1992 the then President George Bush collapsed during a formal dinner. The press asked me a series of questions about the incident such as whether there was a stress component to his condition. One reaction to such an enquiry might be 'How the hell do I know?'. My reaction to that, however, was that I thought he was under enormous pressure. I had just come back from the States, and I knew that public opinion in the US was very negative toward Bush's economic policy. I knew he was in electoral trouble before I left the UK, but had not realized the scale of it until I was there for three weeks. My actual response to the press was that he may have had a stomach bug, which could be partly linked to the fact that his immune system might have been suppressed because he was under so much pressure. So I tried to offer some explanation of why he collapsed. Now, I could have said, 'I don't know', but I decided to express an opinion. I hadn't any evidence, I hadn't seen the results of any medical examination. But I knew he had been under stress from public opinion and forced to go to a public meeting 24 hours after a long flight. Such factors, possibly combined with exposure to a virus, may have caused the problem. Now many academics might feel it is foolish to offer such suggestions to the media. But if we have nothing to say, what are we in the social science business for? If we open our mouths only when we have clear-cut evidence based on a sample of at least 400, on a longitudinal design, using structural equation modelling, then we won't be opening our mouths very often!

When you receive a telephone call from a journalist asking for a comment, it is quite legitimate to ask for a little time to think about it. Take time to consider what would be a reasonable response, if indeed you wish to respond. This is a useful strategy, particularly if you feel you are on unsafe ground and you are concerned about being put on the spot for an immediate response.

Young academics probably have many interesting things to say to the media, and they should not be frightened of doing so. But, as I have outlined, there are inherent dangers in dealing with the media, and relatively inexperienced academics may be more susceptible to these. It is probable that the young academic may be working with some 'longer in the tooth' social scientist who knows the field a bit better, although it doesn't necessarily guarantee that they know the media better. But in a joint study, younger academics or Ph.D. students ought to discuss the best way of presenting results to the media. So they should carefully draft a press release, outlining no more than three main points of the research in simple language. It is useful to put their thoughts down on a piece of paper before they get bombarded by the radio or newspapers.

The following tips might prove useful:

1 Be concise, try not to be frightened of the media.
2 Give them exactly what you want to give them.
3 Do not agree with something you do not agree with, just because that's what they want you to say.
4 Do not be frightened of expressing an opinion.

Sometimes they are going to ask questions that have nothing to do with anything you know directly about, but nobody else knows either, so just consider it 'your professional opinion'. They probably won't come to somebody very young for that kind of comment, basically because they are looking for somebody who has had some track record in the field. They will probably come to the younger person, however, for his or her specific research results.

One of my Ph.D. students recently conducted research on teachers, and a large proportion of her work was exposed to the media. She appeared on television, but beforehand we summarized what she should talk about. She knew exactly what she was doing and had no problems whatsoever. I think the young academics are the ones that really have interesting ideas and are doing some very challenging new research. By definition, a Ph.D. should be original, innovative and at the leading edge. These are the people who should be exposed to the media, but we also have to protect them so that they don't get exploited, or hurt.

To young academics or any academic with little or no media experience, I would suggest starting with lower-risk ventures. In other words, start with local television, radio and the press, as opposed to national broadcasts or national newspapers. Gain experience by a process of gradual exposure, and enjoy learning the necessary skills along the way.

Chapter 3

The sociologist as media football: reminiscences and preliminary reflections

Eric Dunning

The fact that football has been my major area of research for more than 30 years has led me to have considerable experience with the media. I do not attribute this experience to anything other than my choice of subject, particularly the media prominence given to football hooliganism in the 1980s. It certainly has not come about as a result of any 'star quality' on my part. Nevertheless, since my experience has been fairly extensive – with newspapers as well as radio and television – it strikes me that the following reminiscences and preliminary reflections may be of interest to some of my fellow social scientists and – who knows? – perhaps to some media people as well.

My experiences with the media have, I think, implications regarding the way in which knowledge is popularly constructed. They also shed light on the difficulties which social scientists face in getting their message across in a society such as ours with its characteristic media forms and patterns of ownership and control. However, as the reader will quickly see, some of my media experiences have their amusing side and have left me with egg on my face. Others have been rather more revealing regarding the relationship between the universities – particularly university sociologists – and the media. Still others suggest conclusions that are damning, particularly of the tabloid press. Indeed, one of my principal conclusions will be that, while posing as ostensibly neutral reporters of 'the facts', the tabloids play a part of some significance in the construction of problems such as football hooliganism.

I have entitled this chapter, 'The sociologist as media football', in an attempt not only to be mildly amusing in relation to my research subject but more importantly in order to indicate my perceived and factual powerlessness in relation to the media and their personnel. However, since the relationship has not been entirely asymmetrical and tilted in their favour, I shall also attempt to show some of the ways in which my colleagues and I have attempted to use the media for our purposes. In order to convey something of the flavour of my experiences as a 'media football' and how my colleagues and I have begun to learn how to 'kick back', I shall begin by briefly recalling an interview that I recorded for *Channel 4 News* in September 1989.

On the day following the interview, one of my students informed me that his parents had seen the interview, recognized the name of their son's tutor and had immediately rung up to ask why he had never told them that I was blind! Since I was looking downwards to the left and had my eyes closed throughout the interview, their mistake was understandable. What had happened was this. The interview took place at the Central TV studios in Nottingham and I was connected via a British Telecom telephone link to a Channel 4 news reporter in London. On arriving at Central, I had been taken straight to a studio where a receiver had been stuck in my left ear. Unfortunately, it seemed to be defective and would not stay put. A few minutes 'fiddling' by the sound engineers got it to stick but at the expense of a substantial black protuberance out of my ear which led them to ask me to face three-quarters to the left so that the monstrosity would not be visible on screen. I obliged but, to make matters worse, the interviewing reporter came through very faintly which explains why my eyes were closed. I had to concentrate very hard in order to hear what his questions were. I suppose I should be grateful for the fact that the receiver in my ear was hidden so that my student's parents did not ring to enquire whether I was deaf as well as blind!

Over the years, I have become a fairly seasoned television interviewee. This has been the case especially since the Heysel tragedy of 1985 and the consequent upgrading in the status of football hooliganism as a perceived social problem which led to an increase in the media demand for the services of my colleagues and me. In a word, I was already reasonably experienced by the time of my Channel 4 interview in September 1989. Nevertheless, it still proved to be a learning experience of some importance. Perhaps I am a slow learner. Both the Channel 4 and the Central Television people said to me 'Good interview' at the end and I left Nottingham – it was about 5.30 pm, an hour and a half before the programme was scheduled to go out – feeling reasonably pleased with myself and thinking that I had justified my £50 fee. The subject was the announcement of the formation of the Police Football Intelligence Unit for collecting and coordinating data on football hooligans and I thought that I had put across a reasonably good and balanced case. More specifically – with all sorts of caveats about the difficulties of defining football hooliganism and the problems of identifying those who engage most persistently in serious violence – I had argued that a unit of this kind would probably form a useful adjunct to Part II of the Thatcher Government's 'Football Spectators' Bill', the part aimed at preventing known hooligans from travelling to matches abroad.[1] However, I had also argued that Part I of the bill, the part concerned with supporters registering as members of their clubs and requiring computerized all-ticket entry to grounds, was positively dangerous. Indeed, far from representing a means for ameliorating the problem of football hooliganism, I suggested that it was a recipe for turning normally peaceful fans into hooligans and for increasing the incidence of crowd disasters.[2] (Part I of the Football Spectators' Bill was ditched in 1990 following the recommendations of the Taylor Inquiry into the Hillsborough tragedy of 1988.)[3] I also suggested that the problem of football hooliganism will never be dealt with satisfactorily as long as it continues to be seen solely in law and order terms and just as a football problem. Punitive and control measures will have to be allied with measures of a more positive, community-orientated and, above all, educational kind if progress is to be made. The reader will be able to imagine my disappointment when all I was presented as saying was that the sophistication of the hooligans had increased in response to the growing sophistication of the police, and that, up until that point, the hooligans appeared to be 'winning the war'. Such a point makes full sense only if used as a lead into the argument about the need for positive as well as punitive measures. However, everything I had said on that score had been discarded, leaving me just a very brief appearance as a 'talking head'.

I can understand from the programme makers' point of view why so little of the material from my interview was used. They had to put the item together very quickly and, in this case, most of it was already complete when I arrived at the studio in Nottingham. Nor had they discussed with me over the phone in detail what they planned to say. Had they done so, I might have been able to disabuse them of a fallacy which marred an otherwise reasonably good item. They might also have been able to include some of the more positive parts of my case. The fallacy was this: at the start of the item, they announced that football hooligan violence had increased in seriousness and intensity but decreased in frequency and extent between 1985 and 1989. Both parts of this proposition were erroneous. What actually happened over those years was that, as a result of increasing controls inside grounds, football hooliganism had been driven increasingly outside them. Expressed more precisely, it had been displaced to the fringes of and beyond the police and club controls, i.e. into areas where the hooligans perceived the controls as either weak or non-existent.

The national incidence of a phenomenon such as football hooliganism is, of course, notoriously difficult to measure. Nevertheless, all the reliable evidence pointed to its having been displaced between 1985 and 1989 but as having neither significantly increased nor decreased in intensity, seriousness, frequency or extent over those years.[4] In my interview, these were points that I repeatedly rammed home and so the programme makers were presented with a dilemma: either change the earlier part of their item or cut what I had said. With only an hour and a half between recording and transmission, I am not surprised that the latter option was the one they chose. There is, though, another possibility which cannot entirely be discounted, namely that, even though, along with BBC programmes such as *Newsnight, Channel 4 News* does allow some scope for the expression of complex arguments and unconventional opinions, I had been trapped into allowing myself to be used as a 'talking head' in order to reinforce an item supporting the hegemonic view that problems such as football hooliganism can be dealt with only by means of punishments and controls. In a word, I may have been duped. Whether I was or not on that occasion, my first encounters with the media certainly involved the cynical exploitation of my naïvety.

My experiences with the media began in the 1960s and early 1970s. My first brush came in 1966 when, together with my former teacher, the late Norbert Elias, I published an article entitled, 'Dynamics of sport groups with special reference to football'. It appeared in the *British Journal of Sociology*[5] and was the subject of a reasonably accurate summary in *New Society*. I think it was the novelty of two sociologists discussing football that led the summary to be printed, but they were unwittingly preparing a trap for us. I was still an active footballer at the time and had been playing in London for my school Old Boys on the Saturday after the *New Society* piece appeared. When I returned to Leicester on the Monday, I was greeted by an excited Norbert Elias. He had been rung up by a reporter from the *People* who said he was going to write a supporting piece on our article for the following Sunday's edition. 'You see what happens, Eric,' said Norbert, 'when we take care to write clear, understandable language. Our message gets through to a popular audience.' In the event, what the article in the *People* turned out to be was a send-up of what we had written. It poked fun at our jargon and pilloried the preposterousness of a couple of ivory tower academics thinking they might have something to say about the national game. One of our principal arguments was that a football match involves 'groups in controlled tension' and that the controls on violence in the modern game are indicative of the 'civilizing process' it has undergone.[6] What a ridiculous argument, wrote the *People* reporter, when players like Nobby Stiles, the Manchester United and England half-back, have made a career out of kicking other players' legs. With players like him around, it is nonsense to talk about 'civilizing processes' and 'controlled tensions' in the game.

My next experience was even more demeaning. I was working in my room in the university one day in the early 1970s when the telephone rang. At the other end, a pleasant-sounding woman introduced herself as a reporter from the *Sun* and said she had been given my name by the British Sociological Association as someone who might be able to help her. She was, she said, putting together a piece on the multi-sports clubs they have in some continental countries and she wanted to establish why they are a good idea and why we ought to have them in this country. What she wanted from me, she said, was a sociological statement on the functions of sport in order to help her to make her case. Gullibly, I replied that I, too, thought that multi-sports clubs were a good idea and that I would be happy to help her. So, after a minute or two's reflection, I said something about the triple functions of sport, namely its role in the generation of de-routinizing excitement, in the formation and testing of identities, and in the solidification of communal bonds at different levels of social integration. 'Great,' she said, 'just what I need.'

Then came the 'sting'. I use the world deliberately for I was being conned. I ought to have realized that the *Sun* would not be interested in publishing a sociological statement about the functions of sport. However, in those days I was still naïve and I was hooked. 'Actually, I don't like sport very much myself,' she said. 'My husband's a keen rugger player and I'm always telling him it's a childish activity for a grown man to engage in. You won't agree with me, though, I'm sure.' 'Well,' I said, taking the bait hook, line and sinker, 'you're not too far from the mark. You could say that a central element of sports like rugby and soccer consists in the fact that they provide adults with a socially sanctioned opportunity to regress to childhood levels, allowing them to engage in forms of behaviour that are normally taboo for adults, like getting dirty and rolling around in mud.'

'Wonderful,' she said. 'I can't wait to tell my husband.' Then she rang off.

The reader will probably be able to imagine my anger and consternation when an article appeared in the *Sun* next day headlined with words to the effect that:

'LEICESTER SOCIOLOGIST, ERIC DUNNING, SAYS THAT TAKING PART IN SPORTS IS CHILDISH.'

What she was writing about was not multi-sports clubs at all but adults who do childish things; and, to cap it all, the send-up of what I had said to her in all good faith appeared alongside a photograph of the comedian Jimmy Tarbuck making bread 'soldiers' to eat with his boiled egg!

These were the first of my many unsatisfactory experiences with the tabloids. The editing of items recorded for television and radio can, of course, lead to distortions of the total case one wants to make but the possibilities open in this regard to unscrupulous newspaper reporters and editors are considerably greater. They can twist your meanings and attribute to you things you have not said. It did not take my colleagues and me long to decide that our best course would be to refuse to do interviews with them, especially with the *Sun* and the *Star*. As I shall show later, our decision to this effect was reinforced early on in our research by the fact that our findings were pointing strongly to the conclusion that the tabloids play a part of some importance in the construction of football hooliganism as a social problem.

Not all my experiences with the media have been so negative. At the time of the European Championships in 1988, I appeared on *TV AM* and managed, I think, to take the wind out of presenter

Anne Diamond's sails. Also appearing on the programme were
Tory MP Harry Greenway, and Dennis Lillee, the Australian fast
bowler. We were all introduced beforehand over coffee and I
identified myself to Greenway as 'the opposition'. We started to
chat and he said that, in his opinion, this country had begun to go
wrong when sociologists started to rule. He was, I think, voicing the
common Tory equation of sociology with the advent of the 'permissive society'. But whether that is right or wrong, I was furious
and said: 'You and your government rule. I challenge you to name
one sociologist with power comparable to yours.' Of course, he was
unable to oblige and, at this point, a producer came up and asked
us to repeat our 'battle' on the air. 'I'll be happy to if you provide
us with boxing gloves,' I replied. 'No, no boxing gloves,' said
Greenway rather stiffly and, in the event, the hoped for confrontation failed to materialize. He apparently had nothing to offer in
that context save his right-wing, flog 'em and hang 'em sentiments.
He certainly did not know much about football or football hooliganism. Anne Diamond tried to inject an element of controversy
into the item by suggesting that a total ban on football might be a
means of dealing with football hooliganism. 'It wouldn't work', I
said. 'It was first tried in 1314 by Edward II.[7] It didn't work then
and it wouldn't work now. Even if you did succeed in banning the
country's most popular sport, the hooliganism and violence would
surface elsewhere. There's no alternative to dealing with a
problem of this kind at its social roots.' Anne Diamond was visibly
impressed and I was quite pleased with myself, too. I had been up
since 2.00 am in order to drive from Leicester to London and I was
glad to find my memory working so well.

But let me become more serious. In my experience, the scope
for social scientists to get their message across varies considerably
between the media. It tends to be lowest of all with the tabloids
where, as I have said, if one agrees to give an interview, one is more
or less totally at the mercy of unscrupulous editors and reporters.
It is higher with the 'middlebrow' press and highest of all with
'quality' papers like the *Guardian*, *The Times* and the *Independent*
for, even though their reporters and journalists can sometimes get
a complex argument wrong, their practice conforms more closely
than that of any other section of the national press to a norm of
objective reporting. As far as television and radio are concerned,
one's scope tends to be lowest with recorded news programmes
where editing leads frequently to the use of sociologists as 'talking

heads' in the construction of almost invariably ideological arguments which are more or less totally at odds with the sociological
case they want to put.

This can be illustrated by reference to my experience with ITV's
Walden Interview immediately after the Heysel tragedy in 1985. In
the week prior to travelling to London on the Saturday to record,
I spoke several times to a researcher on the phone, sometimes for
more than an hour, plying her with arguments and information.
'Sunday's broadcast is going to be the Eric Dunning show,' she said
in all seriousness. She meant, of course, that the programme
would be largely organized around the results of the Leicester
research. However, that was not to be. On arrival in London, my
colleague, Patrick Murphy, and I were greeted with the news that
Panorama had already done the sort of 'in-depth' programme the
Walden team were planning and that, accordingly, there had had
to be a change of plan. The focus now was going to be on the need
for all-seater stadia as a means of dealing with the hooligan problem. Patrick and I spent more than an hour trying to disabuse her
of this overly simple idea, pointing out, for example, that Coventry
City's experiment with an all-seater in the early 1980s had been
abandoned because the hooligans tore out the seats and used
them as missiles, that sports violence occurs regularly in the USA
despite their all-seater stadia, and that, in any case, most football
hooliganism takes place outside grounds. We finally agreed to be
interviewed on the understanding that nothing we said would be
used in support of the preposterous thesis that a problem so
complex and deep-rooted as football hooliganism could ever be
eliminated simply by changing an aspect of the built environment.
In the event, though, it was precisely that which happened. Patrick
Murphy's interview was not used at all but there were 20 seconds
of me as a 'talking head' urging the need for more than punishments and controls in a programme devoted entirely to the
all-seater thesis, a programme in which Coventry City's experience
was not even mentioned.

Let me return to the main line of my argument. For obvious
reasons, live television and radio tend to provide the sociologist
with greater scope than recorded programmes for getting a point
across. Of course, one remains dependent on the quality of the
questions asked, and programmes such as *Kilroy!*, where one has to
fight for the presenter's attention against all the assembled guests,
are probably the least satisfactory of all. That is the case less on

account of the pseudo-democratic character of such programmes than it is because the presenters tend to search out and focus on the most sensational and sentimental points. Their view seems to be that sensation and sentiment make for good television while accurate sociological diagnosis is dull. Largely on account of the expertise and intelligence of their interviewers, researchers and reporters, radio programmes like the BBC's *Today* and the news programmes put out by the BBC World Service are considerably better as forums for making a sociological point. However, even they come behind recorded documentaries.

In 1984 and 1985, our group successfully collaborated with Thames TV in the making of an hour-long documentary called *Hooligan*. It was mainly about West Ham United's notorious 'Inter City Firm', one of the earliest of the modern, relatively organized breed of football fighting gangs (they took their name from the fact that they pioneered the tactic of travelling to away matches on inter-city trains rather than 'football specials' as a means of avoiding the police). The programme was, I think, a good one but it would have been better had the Heysel tragedy not occurred while we were making it, thus necessitating a remodelling of substantial parts and a degree of cutting of some of the sociological arguments that we wanted to make. Nevertheless, we were still able in that context to achieve a fair measure of control, not only over our individual contributions but also over the form and contents of the programme as a whole. As a result, despite the remodelling and cutting, we were able to make a number of complex points and we did not come away, as we so often do from news programmes, feeling that we'd been forced to over-simplify. Nor, when the final product was broadcast, did we feel we had been stitched up in the cutting room. Our success with this programme had a lot to do, I think, with the director, Ian Stuttard, a man who understands not only the art of making television documentaries but hooliganism and violence as well.

Let me sum up what I think I have got out of my relationship with the media over the years. The first thing worthy of note in this connection is the fact that my media exposure has brought me a degree of national, even international, recognition. I realize, of course, that this has been principally a consequence of the persistence and relative seriousness of football hooliganism as a social problem. However, I like to think that it may also be a consequence, at least in part, of the fact that the Leicester work is based on the 'figurational' approach to sociology advocated by Norbert Elias.[8] One of the hallmarks of this approach is that it involves an attempt to achieve a judicious admixture of rigorous theorizing and systematic observation, and this, I believe, has enabled us to get close to the heart of the issue in a manner that cannot easily be dismissed as an exemplification of either left- or right-wing values. This in its turn perhaps helps to explain why the media have continued to call on our services for over a decade now.

I think, too, that the publicity attracted by our work may have been of some value to sociology generally during the troubled 1980s. In 1988, for example, the Leicester research was used as the basis for an editorial in the *Independent* and it may be that this helped to make it a little more difficult to dismiss sociology as just an 'ivory tower' subject. It is perhaps also worth mentioning in this connection that, when the Thatcher Government came to power in 1979, an attempt was made to rescind our funding as part of a general attack on the old Social Science Research Council (SSRC). However, our research was successfully defended by Michael Posner, the then Chairman of SSRC. In 1985 and 1986, we were even in receipt of funds from the Department of the Environment. There is, I think, no little irony in a group of sociological researchers being employed by a government which had set out to destroy their subject!

In order to conclude this chapter, I shall return to the issue of the tabloid press. As I suggested at the beginning, the Leicester research points strongly in the direction that, far from being neutral reflectors of and commentators on events, the tabloids have unintentionally played an active part of some significance in the construction of football hooliganism as a social phenomenon. This is a rather complex notion, so let me try briefly to explain it.[9]

In the mid- to late 1950s, in conjunction with the 'Teddy boy' scare and the more general moral panic of those years over working-class youth, the media, especially the popular press, began to pick up on and amplify the sorts of violent incidents that had always from time to time occurred at and around crowded football grounds. However, it was when the preparations were being made for staging the World Cup Finals in England in 1966 that the active part played by popular papers in the construction of football hooliganism began to become decisive. The World Cup Finals meant that English crowds were about to come under the scrutiny of the international media and, in that context, the popular press began to focus regularly on what was now routinely being described as 'football hooliganism', depicting it as a threat to the country's international prestige. For example, in November 1965, when an empty hand grenade case was thrown onto the pitch by a Millwall fan during the encounter of his team with London rivals, Brentford, the *Sun* printed the following story under the headline, 'Soccer marches to war':

> The Football Association have acted to stamp out this increasing mob violence within 48 hours of the blackest day in British soccer – the grenade day that showed that British supporters can rival anything the South Americans can do. The World Cup is now less than nine months away. That is all the time we have left to try and restore the once good sporting name of this country. Soccer is sick at the moment. Or better, its crowds seem to have contracted some disease that causes them to break out in fury.[10]

Around the time of the 1966 World Cup, too, the popular press started sending reporters to matches to report on crowd behaviour as well as simply on the game. Not surprisingly, these reporters saw incidents which they could construe as violent since such incidents have always tended to occur at and around football grounds, but the fact that they were now being more regularly reported contributed to the impression that they were increasing at a faster rate than was actually the case. In addition, partly because it helped to sell papers in an industry that was growing more competitive, and partly on account of the intensifying moral panic in the mid-1960s about youth and youth violence generally, the tabloids tended to report incidents of football-related violence sensationalistically. This went hand in hand with a rising use of military rhetoric in the reporting of matches and, more importantly, with the regular publication of 'league tables' of fan violence. As a result of the interaction of all these trends, football grounds began to be portrayed, in a sense even 'advertised', as places where fighting or 'aggro' and not just football regularly takes place and this had the effect of drawing into the game younger males from the 'rougher' sections of the working class in greater numbers and more regularly than before, in that way adding to the already existing momentum for more 'respectable' people to withdraw their support, if not from the game as such, then at least from the goal-end terraces of grounds.

It is important to get this argument crystal clear. I have not suggested that the popular or tabloid press *caused* football hooliganism but rather that it played a part of some significance in *channelling hooligans into attendance at matches*. The plausibility of this suggestion receives support from the fact that the 'Teddy boys' of the 1950s were rarely, if ever, reported as fighting at football. The same holds true for the 'mods' and 'rockers' of the early 1960s. However, for the 'skinheads', who were first given media prominence in 1967, the season following the staging of the World Cup Finals in England, football was a major theatre of operations. It seems unlikely that we are dealing here with a simple temporal conjuncture as opposed to one in which forms of determination were involved.

One further point is of relevance in this connection. A form of what one might call parochially aggressive nationalism is a key ingredient in the behaviour of English football fans abroad. While, again, one cannot say that this is *caused* by the tabloids, it is clear that, with their frequent references to 'frogs', 'krauts', 'argies' and the like, they do nothing to counter the hegemony of parochial nationalism among their readers and may even play a part of some importance in reinforcing it. Of course, to an extent the tabloid press reflects the readership for which it caters. In that respect, its character – indeed, its very existence – has a lot to say about attitudes to and levels of education in this country. As such, it provides just one indication of the mammoth educational task facing British sociologists at the moment. However, if one thing is clear when one contemplates this daunting prospect, it is that one of the prerequisites for success will be an improved use of the media by sociologists.

I hope that, in this short chapter, I may have said something which will help others to avoid some of the traps into which I have fallen. Who knows? With hard work and hard thinking, we may even be able to reach a situation where the media are the sociologists' 'football' rather than vice versa.

NOTES

1 'Football hooligan(ism)' is, of course, a popular rather than a sociological category. It covers a range of behaviour that takes place in a football or football-related context, varying from, e.g. swearing, jostling and pushing, through pitch invasions, to assault, grievous

bodily harm and, on occasions, even murder. One of the difficulties of measuring it stems from the fact that most incidents take place away from grounds and are unknown to the police. Another difficulty stems from the fact that most police arrest figures derive from use of Section 5 of the 1936 Public Order Act ('the policeman's friend', so called because, for its use, victims are not required to lodge a complaint). As a result, many convicted hooligans have done little more than swear in the proximity of a policeman while the more serious forms of violence tend to take place away from the police, usually outside of and away from grounds. What one might call the 'core hooligans' have usually been detected and arrested only through police under-cover operations involving the infiltration of their gangs.

2 The reasoning behind these observations is complex. For present purposes, it must be enough to bear in mind such facts as that computers sometimes break down and that a vandal-proof com-puterized entry system has yet to be invented. Moreover, it does not take a genius to envisage the dire consequences that might easily have ensued in a case of computer failure at an important night match, say an FA Cup Semi-Final replay between Liverpool and Manchester United with an attendance in excess of 40,000.

3 Lord Justice Taylor, *The Hillsborough Stadium Disaster: 15 April 1989, Final Report*, HMSO, London, 1990.

4 There have been two, partly overlapping, cycles of displacement of crowd disorder at English football since the 1960s. The first started in about 1967, the second in about 1984. The first cycle involved the progressive tightening of police and club controls mainly on the goal-end terraces of grounds, the reactive movement of hooligan activities outside to the immediate vicinities of stadia, and the con-sequent extension of controls to such areas. Eventually, the controls were moved to railway and bus stations, 'football special' trains, and, in London, to the underground and main-line stations. The second cycle began when the hooligans caught the authorities 'on the hop' by moving into the seated areas of grounds and travelling on inter-city trains and private transport. This cycle led to the extension of controls into grandstands, e.g. via 'partial membership schemes', the estab-lishment of the national Police Football Intelligence Unit, and an increasing reliance on undercover policing.

5 Norbert Elias and Eric Dunning, 'Dynamics of sport groups with special reference to football', *British Journal of Sociology*, Vol. XVIII, No. 4, December 1966; reprinted in Elias and Dunning (1986).

6 For a discussion of Elias's theory of 'civilizing processes', see Eric Dunning and Chris Rojek (1992).

7 See Eric Dunning and Kenneth Sheard (1979).

8 For an excellent introduction to figurational sociology, see Stephen Mennell (1990).

9 A fuller discussion of this issue can be found in Eric Dunning, Patrick Murphy and John Williams (1988).

10 *Sun*, 8 November 1965. The reference here to South American foot-ball fans was more than a little ironic. In 1964, no fewer than an

estimated 318 fans died in the panic which followed a hooligan-instigated riot at a match in Lima between Peru and Argentina. It is unlikely that the *Sun* reporter did not remember this. He was thus implicitly equating the throwing of a 'dead' hand grenade with the worst recorded football tragedy of modern times. Reporting of this kind acted over time as a self-fulfilling prophecy, contributing to the production in England of kinds and levels of football hooliganism which, in the 1960s, had been characteristic mainly of South America.

Chapter 4

Media vs. reality?

Hans J. Eysenck

Having had a good deal of contact with the media, I have inevitably developed some fairly firm conclusions about their dealings with social scientists. These are based on literally hundreds of television programmes in which I have taken part in Great Britain, Germany, Austria, Switzerland, France, Italy, Canada, the USA, Australia, South Africa, the Scandinavian countries, and unlikely places like Iceland and Morocco. Much the same applies to radio interviews and programmes. As far as the press is concerned, my wife has amassed enough material to fill a dozen large books! What have I learned? The first point, of course, is to realize that it is impossible to generalize. Interviewers and writers range from an enthusiastic *pro* to a viciously opinionated *con*, with impeccably unprejudiced, objective reporters in between. What can be said is that all such encounters raise one's *visibility*, as Mae West used to say: 'It is better to be looked over than to be overlooked!'

Unfortunately, this 'looking over' often gives a completely distorted and inaccurate picture. I have been introduced or written about as the man who invented the IQ (which of course saw the light of day five years before I was born!), the man who proved that intelligence was inherited (which was established long before I became a student of psychology!), or the man who showed that blacks have a lower IQ than whites (another fact established many years before I even knew what an IQ was!). Thus to many innocent listeners and readers I appear to have single-handedly created modern intelligence testing when in reality I never did any work at all on any of these problems.

While it might be thought that all this would heap credit on me (however undeserved), there was also a reverse side to the medal. I was painted as being 'controversial', a veritable maverick, a person whose opinions went against those of all the experts. Exactly the opposite is true. Snyderman and Rothman (1988) have recently polled over 600 experts in educational psychology, behavioural genetics, developmental psychology, etc., on a number of issues which were supposed to be 'controversial'; they found considerable unanimity on these issues.

The survey results reveal that those with expertise in areas related to intelligence testing hold generally positive attitudes about the validity and usefulness of intelligence and aptitude tests. These experts believe that such tests adequately measure most important elements of intelligence, and that they do so in a way that is basically fair to minority groups. Intelligence, as measured by intelligence tests, is seen as important to success in our society. Both within- and between-group differences in test scores are believed to reflect significant genetic differences, for within-group differences, a majority of the variation in IQ is felt to be associated with genetic variation. Finally, there is support for the continued use of tests at their present level in elementary and secondary schools, and in admissions to schools of higher education.

On all these issues I have, in all my writings, been in complete accord with orthodoxy. Why then this caricature that always appears when my name crops up in the media? Snyderman and Rothman analyse media coverage of these issues very thoroughly and conclude:

> Our work demonstrates that, by any reasonable standard, media coverage of the IQ controversy has been quite inaccurate. Journalists have emphasized controversy; they have reported scientific discussions of technical issues erroneously and they have clearly misreported the views of the relevant scientific community as to the interaction between genetic and environmental factors in explaining differences in IQ among individuals and between groups. One would be forced to conclude from reading the newspapers and newsmagazines and watching television that only a few maverick 'experts' support the view that genetic variation plays a significant role in individual or group differences, while the vast majority of experts believe that such differences are purely the result of environmental factors. One would also conclude that intelligence and aptitude tests are hopelessly biased against minorities and the poor.

We have suggested several explanations, for the media's failure in this regard, including the ignorance of journalists and the nature of the news medium. Journalists generally have very little understanding of social science, especially those segments of social science that involve complex statistics; and they are interested in promoting controversy, as we have seen. However, neither of these factors explains why, with such regularity, Stephen Jay Gould and Leon Kamin are presented as mainstream thought in the profession, while those who stress that genetic elements may play some role in measured IQ are characterized as a small minority within the expert community. (p. 255)

All this leaves no doubt that the media are very powerful in producing a certain effect: Eysenck is brilliant but completely unorthodox and alone in his opinions. Now I have made some contribution to the study of intelligence, particularly in relation to the theory of intelligence and its psychophysiological testing (Eysenck, 1985; Eysenck and Barrett, 1985), but these are never mentioned. Thus my reputation for 'brilliance' rests on the erroneous imputation of originality in fields I never contributed to, and my reputation for being controversial on my complete agreement with expert opinion! Curiouser and curiouser.

Another effect of being looked over, added to the visibility factor, is that of being misrepresented. An outstanding example of this is my attitude to the race issue, which has been so completely misrepresented as to turn it almost upside down. I have given a detailed account of this elsewhere (Eysenck, 1990), and will not repeat it here. Let me merely note that I left Hitler's Germany in protest against his racial policies, and was turned into a 'racist' by tendentious and wildly inaccurate newspaper reports. I have tried hard to find psychological methods for reducing prejudice, and believe I have found a method demonstrably better than others that have been tried (Grossarth-Maticek, Eysenck and Vetter, 1989), as well as contributing to the theory of prejudice; also, nobody showed any interest!

Misrepresentation is an important technique which has been of special interest to me, and I have discussed it in some detail elsewhere (Eysenck, 1990). It consists essentially in attributing to the victim views he does not hold, things he has not done, statements which are inaccurately quoted, political views he does not hold, social attitudes he does not share, and general beliefs alien to him. When I write that smoking is one of several risk factors for cancer, but that it usually interacts with other risk factors (stress, pollution, heredity) to produce its effects on health, a statement no knowledgeable oncologist or epidemiologist would disagree with, this comes out in the media as: 'Eysenck does not believe that smoking is bad for you!', to which is often added an insinuation that I am paid by the tobacco industry to say so!

How does this work? Let me give an example. In a lengthy TV interview in Australia, the interviewer suggested that I had been paid by the tobacco industry to carry out my research in stress effects on cancer and coronary heart disease (Eysenck, 1991c). I pointed out that in reality I had never been paid a single penny. He asked if I had not received grants to carry out my research on stress. I said no; I had received some grants for quite different types of research involving measuring differences in the contingent negative variation in the EEG of extraverts and introverts as a consequence of smoking a cigarette. That seemed to settle the matter, but when I saw the programme on TV, there was an afterthought, added after I had left the studio. The interviewer said that I had not been truthful in saying I had not received a grant for my work on stress; didn't I state in my autobiography (Eysenck, 1990) that my work with Dr D. Kissen had been based on a grant? This leaves the listener with the notion of dishonesty and lying. Of course the grant had been made to Kissen, and I was asked by him much later to help him with the construction of a questionnaire, but I received no money and no grant. But of course I had no possibility of replying! Just another example of the dirty tricks department!

Another well-established trick is to select, from a lengthy interview, just one or two sentences which taken out of context, give entirely the wrong idea. In the same programme a severe critic of mine was interviewed, as well as a psychologist in fundamental agreement with me. Oddly enough this follower was allowed only one sentence, which was vaguely critical. He told me later that he had been interviewed for over an hour in which he supported my point of view strongly; the presenter had taken just one sentence which could be constructed to be critical! You just can't win.

Let me now give a somewhat longer example of the vitiating effect of media publicity, and the absolute disdain for factual accuracy accompanying it. At the beginning of 1991 my wife and I edited a symposium (Eysenck and Eysenck, 1991) which reported on some important experiments demonstrating that vitamin and mineral supplementation, administered over three months to American school-children of apparently adequate nutritional status, had produced very significant increments in IQ. This confirmed earlier work by Benton, who had found similar results, as well as rather less well-controlled studies by others, going back to the 1950s. Ours was probably the biggest such study, using three different amounts of supplementation on different groups of children, to see which was the most effective, if any; there was, also, a placebo group.

The results were published just before a special TV programme dealing with them was shown; the presenter had been with us on several occasions to film our discussions and other material. The firm which had provided us with the very complex pills containing the mix of vitamins and minerals (without payment) brought these out commercially at the same time. The actual study was carried out by Professor S. Schoenthaler and his colleagues, all of whom had been working in this area for many years, and had unrivalled experience. The study was supervised by a scientific directorate containing Professor Linus Pauling, double Nobel Prize-winner; Professor J. Yudkin, eminent British nutritionist; Professor E. Peritz, a well-known bio-statistician; and myself. We held a press conference, assuming that our results would be accepted as finally proving the point once and for all.

A press conference preceded the press coverage which followed, and contained all the ingredients which were to astonish us all – a complete disregard of the scientific results, and a concentration on utterly irrelevant details, most of them quite wrongly stated. I will go into these in connection with the newspaper reports, with a brief statement of the actual facts.

We may start with the *Independent*, which carried perhaps the most inaccurate report. Duncan Campbell, the reporter, stated (as did many others) that the symposium had been published in a small circulation journal of no account; he stated 'that the *Independent* could find only one London college or medical school that stocks it: the Institute of Psychiatry, where Professor Eysenck worked'. What can one say, apart from the fact that the truth or fatuity of the experimental results are not dependent on the particular journal in which they are published? Clearly the *Independent* did not look very far; within a few hundred yards of Senate House, the centre of London University, there are four university libraries which take the journal; I don't know how many more do so. As for it having a negligible circulation, I looked at the Citation Index to discover its Impact Factor, objectively established by counting the number of times articles in a given journal are cited in other leading scientific journals; the one we published in came in the top 15 per cent of all social science and medical journals in the field! Thus not only is the point raised irrelevant, it is quite untrue. The attempt is simply to devalue the findings by suggesting that they were published in a low-quality journal edited by one of the authors of the report!

The point is followed by suggesting that the results should have been published in 'one of the world's most prestigious medical journals'; others suggested the *Lancet*, which had published several such studies. The answer, of course, is very simple. Our study occupies 36 pages; the *Lancet* seldom publishes anything longer than three pages. There simply was no chance of presenting our data in sufficient detail in such a journal. Furthermore, our findings concern the psychological fraternity, not the medical; it is wholly appropriate to publish them in the foremost journal devoted to the study of individual differences and their causes. Last, but not least, the *Lancet* had published two articles on the subject which had ostensibly had negative results, but which were so bad that our referees would have rejected them outright. Thus the quality control of the *Lancet* did not inspire confidence.

What was wrong with these two articles? The point is important because many newspapers cited them as counter-evidence against our claim. One of them gave the supplementation for only four weeks, as against our three months, and the general belief is that three months is a minimum period; we tried to get results after four weeks on one of our tests, but could not. Such a test is consequently useless, and cannot count as a negative instance. The other did in fact have a positive outcome, in the sense that the supplementation group did much better than the placebo group; the difference was not significant, however, because of the quite insufficient number of subjects. Obedience to the demands of the statistical theory of 'power' would have required doubling the number involved; failure to do so makes the results quite inconclusive, but much more in line with our findings than the null hypothesis!

Another point often made was the criticism that the commercial availability of the supplementation pills coincided with the TV presentation of our results. It is difficult to see how this was relevant to our experiment, which can be judged only on objective grounds; we had nothing to do with the commercial aspects of the undertaking which were handled by the Dietary Research Foundation. But in view of what happened two years earlier when the equally positive results of Benton were the topic of a TV broadcast (thousands of parents ransacked the shelves of chemists' stores to buy any and every vitamin and mineral pill available!), it would have been totally irresponsible not to have available for sale the particular formula we had found successful.

It was also objected that the drug firm (Booker) had made a minute contribution to the cost of the experiment (less than 1 per cent). Yet it is customary for drug firms to pay the full cost of clinical trials of their new products, and indeed to pay the physicians carrying them out most handsomely; we did not of course receive a penny for our labours! One law for the rich. . . . *The Times Educational Supplement* accused us of endorsing the Booker pills; we never endorsed anything.

The Times, in its report, quoted an inspector of trading standards, as saying that 'the evidence [for our conclusions] should be widely available for independent scrutiny', suggesting falsely that it was not. Other papers made similar allegations; thus the *Evening Standard* alleged that the data 'has [sic!] been concealed from scientists'. The *Independent* stated that Professor Naismith had said that 'the Foundation have refused to allow him or other outsiders access to the results', a statement also quoted by the *Evening Standard*. Quite untrue, of course; the full results were published, and we offered to supply all the details of methodology and results, including the raw data, to anyone interested. Nobody applied!

Some papers, including the otherwise fair *Daily Telegraph*, suggested that the advanced age of some of the team might have made them less competent than they had been; one TV personality pretty well implied that we were ga-ga. It is true that the mean age of the major participants was between 50 and 60, but I had never heard before that the value of a given piece of research was to be judged in terms of the age of the participants! *Nature* and the *Lancet*, two journals which had criticized our research on scientific grounds, published rebuttals by us which seemed to settle the matter; I know of no remaining scientific criticism of our work. Perhaps we were not ga-ga after all!

I could go on for a long time detailing the misrepresentations, inaccuracies, irrelevancies and downright lies which passed for comment in the papers. Some accepted letters pointing out their errors, like *The Times Educational Supplement*, which also published a piece by Professor Richard Lynn in our support. Others, like *The Times*, 'regretted' that they could not find a place for it in the correspondence columns. So much for objectivity, and right to reply! Some, like *The Daily Express*, published libellous nonsense of a kind which hardly needs a reply; they quoted someone apparently without any relevant qualifications as saying: 'This whole thing looks like a device for extracting money from parents' pockets.'

Press and TV commentators might plead that they merely followed a press release by the Medical Research Council which had apparently been drafted in considerable haste, and either without reading our symposium, or after very hurried reading; it is full of factual errors and unworthy of the Council. I have tried in vain to find out who wrote it, whether it was approved by the Council, or whether it was considered by experts in mental testing, statistics and nutrition. I was fobbed off with meaningless replies. But should newspaper reporters simply print variations on semi-official handouts by interested parties – the MRC was responsible for laying down the RDAs (recommended daily allowances) which we had shown to be insufficient? We have been led to believe that reporters are supposed to check sources and facts; no reporter checked anything with any of us! This certainly makes journalism very easy – don't worry about the facts, my mind is made up! It also makes nonsense of the notion of a free press, independent of government and official and semi-official sources.

Is all this serious? Speaking for the participants in this experiment, I would say that we couldn't care less – our scientific reputations are not likely to be touched by this sort of ignorant nonsense. But there is a serious side. The people receive almost their only information about scientific discoveries through the media, and it is a serious matter that they should be so misled. If told lies in this connection, how can they be sure that they are not always told lies? I have always found that when I knew something about a field that was in the news, the news was usually wrong, slanted, and misinformed. That is a serious state of affairs, and not one the media can be proud of.

Consider another point. We have found (and since then there has been much supporting evidence from other sources) that of typical well-nourished American and English children, almost half

suffer from vitamin and mineral deficiencies, and that when these
children are given nutritional supplements, they show an increase
in IQ of 11 points on the average, compared with a placebo group.
Eleven points is a lot of points, and had we been dealing with truly
deprived children in inner-city slums, it is likely that the increase
would have been much larger – possibly between 15 and 20 points.
Supplementation of this kind is cheap, and the educational effects
would be startling – indeed we already have evidence of marked
increases in educational achievement as a function of improved
diet. The social consequences are considerable, and one would
have imagined that newspapers would have concentrated on these,
and on the scientific status of the enquiry, rather than dishing out
meaningless tittle-tattle, usually wrong, about the status of the
journal in which the work was published, or the alleged financial
interests of the scientists concerned! Failure to check sources, to
concentrate on the important aspects of the enquiry, and to point
out the social consequences is inexcusable.

Equally important is the point that parents who want to do the
best for their children should be entitled to be given the true facts
about relevant research. How can they arrive at a reasoned discussion on the basis of the melange of wrong information, slanted
comment and irrelevant brick-throwing that constitutes media
coverage?

What general lessons can we draw? Of course the experiences
just detailed cannot be generalized to all media coverage, but to
judge by comments of many of my colleagues who have had exposure in this field they are only too common. Lack of objectivity,
failure to check simple facts, looking for sensational headlines
rather than truthful summaries, and searching for what is
politically rather than factually correct are faults only too frequent.
The only solution would of course be for each paper to have an
independent adjudicator or ombudsman to judge complaints, and
to award penalty points to erring journalists which, when amount-
ing to an agreed total, would lead to reprimands, fines and finally
dismissal. In addition, editors would be required to print a proper
correction, in a prominent place, allowing the wronged person
adequate space to detail his complaint. The present practice of
hiding away in an unread corner some quaint retraction of the
kind: 'We regret having stated that Mr Smith is an intellectually
backward criminal who sodomized his invalid grandmother. We
acknowledge that his grandmother is not an invalid' is hardly

adequate. But nothing of the kind is likely to happen, and society will continue to be offered the kind of fare, as far as social science results are concerned, which I have indicated above.

What can the individual scientist do? Not much. He or she can holler as loudly as possible; perhaps someone will hear!

Chapter 5

The research dissemination minefield

Cheryl Haslam and Alan Bryman

In this chapter we describe two pieces of research which received some untimely media coverage. The first incident relates to research on drug use among medical students conducted by Cheryl Haslam during 1987–89 at St George's Hospital Medical School, London University. The second piece of research, which was conducted by Alan Bryman, Cheryl Haslam and Adrian Webb at the Department of Social Sciences, Loughborough University, during 1989–91, evaluated staff appraisal schemes as they were being introduced in universities.

DRUG USE AMONG MEDICAL STUDENTS

Background to the project

Medical professionals have always been regarded as a high-risk group for addiction to alcohol and other drugs. A number of factors may contribute to the problem such as high income, easy access to drugs, knowledge of drugs and poor undergraduate education in addiction. Perhaps the most important contributory factor is the occupational stress of medical practice, namely the excessively long working hours and having to deal with illness, death and grieving relatives.

Doctors are trusted to administer drugs, and society becomes alarmed when they are found to use drugs recreationally. One fear is that in addition to causing themselves harm, there may be adverse effects on the quality of care they provide (McAuliffe, 1983a; 1983b), a disturbing prospect when they may hold responsibility for a patient's life.

Much has been written about the excessive drinking, smoking and use of other drugs among students training for careers in the health care professions (Rawnsley, 1984; Lewis, 1986). The concern regarding this issue has generated a considerable amount of research, mainly in the USA, into the non-medical use of drugs by medical students. Very few studies have followed up the student cohorts as they progress through their medical training and professional careers. There is much evidence that students increase their drug use while attending American medical schools (Slaby, *et al.*, 1972; Grotheer, 1973; Kay *et al.*, 1980; McAuliffe *et al.*, 1984, 1986; Maddux *et al.*, 1986) but relatively little is known of the drinking, smoking and use of other drugs among UK medical students.

Survey of drug use among UK medical students

Between 1987–89 Cheryl Haslam was involved in setting up a longitudinal study of the health, lifestyle and drug use of medical and nursing students. The lifestyle of these students was to be compared with that of non-medical undergraduates studying at London University. In November 1988 she presented a review of the literature along with some preliminary findings at a conference at the Royal Society of Medicine in London. The preliminary data were based on the first 200 medical students who had taken part in the survey. In the presentation it was pointed out that from the data collected thus far, few medical students were current cigarettes smokers (7 per cent) while 13 per cent were ex-smokers. There was evidence that smoking decreased as students progress through their medical training. Ninety-two percent drank alcohol, but the average number of units consumed per week was 14 for males and 6 for females (well below the recommended safe limits). Around 30 per cent had tried cannabis at some time in their lives (only around 7 per cent were current users) and 9 per cent had used tranquillizers at some time in their lives.

Immediate press interest

Following the conference presentation Cheryl Haslam was telephoned by a reporter from *Hospital Doctor* and *Doctor*, the specialist publications for hospital doctors and GPs. Although the reporter had attended the conference, she had actually missed the presentation and asked if she could have a copy of the paper. A copy was duly forwarded although it was stressed that these were very much preliminary findings and that the research had a long way to go before any conclusions could be drawn from the survey. The reporter was asked for some indications of what the article would be like before the journals published anything. Possibly due to the time constraints the journalist was working under, she failed to comply with this request. The first thing Cheryl Haslam saw was the following article which appeared in the Thursday 19 January 1989 issue of *Doctor*:

Cannabis rife in UK medical schools

by Nicole Garsten

CANNABIS has been used by more than 40 per cent of final year medical students — a jump from 20 per cent of first years.

And use of tranquillisers leaps from two per cent to 30 per cent during training, research has disclosed.

The root of the problem could be examination stress, said Dr Cheryl Haslam, research fellow in addictive behaviour at St George's Medical School, London.

'Tranquillisers help students to get through exams and to cope with stress,' she said.

Dr Haslam has also described as 'worrying' the amount of cannabis that medical students took.

Her research involved 200 students at St George's Medical School who were asked to disclose their drug-taking habits since childhood.

She has urged medical schools to give students more information about drug addiction.

All students will be questioned further in a follow-up study after 18 months to gauge the direct effect of

medical school and training on drug-taking habits.

US studies have shown that medical students have more drug problems than other undergraduates.

But there have been few UK studies. The last was two years ago, which concluded that British medical students were less prone to substance abuse than other students.

Substance abuse among physicians may well have its roots in medical school and the profession has traditionally been regarded as a high risk for substance use and abuse, said Dr Haslam.

Easy access to drugs, long working hours and a demanding job could all contribute to the problem.

'Given that health professionals are trusted to keep and administer drugs, society becomes alarmed when these individuals are found to use drugs recreationally.

'One fear is that as well as harming themselves, there may be adverse effects on the quality of care they provide,' she said.

Hooked on hash

Figure 5.1 Article from 19 January issue of *Doctor*

A similar article appeared in the 19 January issue of *Hospital Doctor*. A journalist at the *Sunday Telegraph* must have seen these reports because two days later an article appeared in the *Sunday Telegraph* entitled:

'Doctors taking drugs to escape stress'
Sunday Telegraph, 21 January 1989

The piece outlined Cheryl Haslam's research along with a study in Bristol of 500 GPs which showed that many self-treat themselves with tranquillizers. With regard to Cheryl Haslam's research, the article stated that in interviews with medical students a third of final-year students were found to be current tranquillizer users. In fact the survey was conducted using anonymous questionnaires and the rate of *current* tranquillizer use was actually less than 1 per cent.

Immediate impact of the press reports

Following the press coverage the Dean of the medical school was contacted by friends and colleagues who had seen the reports. Not surprisingly the Dean was 'not best pleased' and demanded to know what on earth was going on. The explanation that the reports had failed to distinguish between the percentage of students who had 'ever tried' a drug and those who 'currently use' a drug failed to pour oil on the troubled waters and the following few weeks were, without doubt, the most traumatic of Cheryl Haslam's research career to date.

The Dean received numerous telephone calls from troubled parents wanting to know what their sons and daughters got up to while at medical school. The Senate of the University of London and the General Medical Council demanded explanation of the press reports. Questions were asked in parliament and the issue is mentioned in Hansard. The stress experienced during those weeks must surely have rivalled anything that doctors have to cope with! A vow was taken that in future whenever presenting findings which could in any way be considered to be even remotely controversial, the conference presentation would be closed to the press and journalists would not be spoken to.

Long-term effects of the reports

Looking on the positive side of these events (which is much easier to do in retrospect) the media reports certainly gave the research a high profile. The controversy surrounding the research meant that a longitudinal survey primarily based on one medical school was untenable. Hence the research was extended to become a national study of drug use among medical students. Also, there was certainly much greater awareness of the fact that medical students and doctors were potentially at risk of drug abuse. Subsequently Cheryl Haslam and her colleagues were asked to devise a drug education package to be used with all new intakes of medical students. The package comprised a video, discussion sessions and lectures. The primary aim was to generate discussion and encourage students to consider the potential stresses of medical training and medical practice and examine alternative (drug free) ways of dealing with these pressures.

Looking back on the events, ultimately the press coverage was 'a good thing'. The press reports certainly brought the issue of drug use among medical students to the surface, though undoubtedly the inaccuracies in the reporting caused considerable embarrassment for the medical school, the department and, not least, the first author. On the plus side, press coverage and raised awareness of the topic came to have important policy implications for medical and nursing education.

THE INTRODUCTION OF UNIVERSITY STAFF APPRAISAL

Background

In the past decade universities have had to respond to the government's requirement for greater accountability and efficiency in the use of public resources. This has resulted in universities adopting more commercial or executive styles of management involving a wide range of indicators to monitor individual, departmental and institutional performance. One of these approaches to performance enhancement is systematic staff appraisal, which has recently been introduced in universities for the first time (it was a condition of the 1987 salary settlement). Funded by the Department of Education and Science (DES), the research team conducted an evaluation of university staff appraisal schemes as they began to operate.

The research

The study involved a national telephone survey of all institutions and four in-depth case studies in selected universities. Using questionnaires and interviews with appraisers, appraisees and senior managers, the case studies were designed to establish the aims and objectives of the schemes and the impact of the appraisal process. In two of the four universities, surveys and interviews were carried out both *before* and *after* the first round of appraisal interviews. In the other two universities (where appraisal had been under way for some time) surveys and interviews were conducted after at least one round of appraisal interviews had taken place; hence in these case studies, post-appraisal views only were sought.

Half way through the research project Cheryl Haslam presented some findings based on the pre-appraisal phase of the research (the *before* surveys and interviews conducted in the two institutions) at an occupational psychology conference in Cardiff in Janaury 1991 (Haslam *et al.*, 1991). Specifically the paper gave the historical background as to how appraisal came to be introduced in universities. It described the design of the study, in particular the national telephone survey conducted with Personnel Officers and Staff Training and Development Officers at all institutions across the country (the mapping exercise). The paper discussed the wide variation found between institutions in their response to the need to develop staff appraisal schemes. The session was well attended and the paper was very well received and generated a lively discussion. The presentation concluded that the research thus far had highlighted a range of expectations surrounding the introduction of appraisal.

Press interest

When Cheryl Haslam returned to her department the following Monday there were 'urgent' messages to telephone a reporter from *The Times Higher Education Supplement* (*THES*, now renamed *The Higher*). When the reporter tracked Cheryl Haslam down it transpired that she wanted details of the research. The reporter was extremely persistent but it was explained that as the research was on-going it would be inappropriate to release details at this stage. Also the researchers were not empowered to give any information as the DES had given authorization only for the specific paper that was given at a conference. After the experiences Cheryl Haslam had had with the research on drug use among medical students she was taking no chances. Trying not to appear completely unhelpful, the journalist was told that when the research was finished, providing the DES were willing, we should be pleased to give her details of our findings.

To our astonishment, when the departmental copy of *THES* arrived on the Friday of the same week (11 January), the front page headline stated:

'Appraisal schemes "too soft" DES survey finds'
Times Higher Education Supplement, 11 January 1991

The article referred exclusively to the research being conducted by Cheryl Haslam and her colleagues, and from the detailed quotations printed from senior managers and others who had participated in the study it was clear that the reporter had somehow obtained a copy of a confidential interim report submitted to the DES. However, the stark conclusion that university appraisal schemes were 'too soft' bore no relationship to the conference presentation or anything which the research team had said about the preliminary findings.

Effects of the media coverage

What was particularly damaging for the research was that the *THES* article mentioned the two institutions which had taken part in the first phase of the research. The *THES* report contained some rather controversial statements made by some of the senior managers of these institutions. While it was impossible to attribute any comment to a particular individual, given that there were only two universities involved one could envisage the agitation caused to those concerned. This was most embarrassing for the research team as we had assured those who took part in the first phase of interviews that their comments would be confidential. Certainly the willingness of the senior managers and other staff at these institutions to participate in the second phase of the research had been put in jeopardy. The next few weeks were spent in a damage-limitation exercise. This involved apologizing to the Vice Chancellors, Pro-Vice Chancellors and Registrars of the two institutions and sending a letter of complaint to *THES*. We received numerous telephone calls about the *THES* article from various sources, including participants in our research, to which we replied that we could not understand how the press had come by the information (which, while this must have seemed incredible to many people, was actually true).

The overt problem caused by the *THES* article was obvious when we returned to the two institutions to conduct the second phase of the research. On turning up to interview staff and senior managers for the second time we sometimes encountered individuals clutching a copy of the offending article. Not the most comfortable way to start an interview! The more covert problem was the extent to which the press report and any associated fears about confidentiality inhibited respondents from speaking freely. This effect was impossible to gauge. Certainly no one overtly refused to participate in the study because of the press report. However, a few interviewees countered some of their stronger statements with comments such as 'I don't expect to see this splashed over the front page of *THES*'. When we visited the other two institutions (for our first visit) questions were asked about the report, though the questions were put in an inquisitive rather than suspicious way.

The immediate, short-term effect of the article was that it impeded the progress of the research while we were conducting the damage-limitation measures. Certainly our reputation as trustworthy researchers took a bit of a dent when 'confidential' remarks were plastered liberally over the front page of *THES*. The real sting in the tail was that because of Cheryl Haslam's earlier experiences with the reporting of drug use among medical students she had been especially careful on this occasion. No information whatsoever had been given to the reporter, yet somehow the details were obtained. The only people who had specific details of the research were the DES and a Steering Committee. All credit to the journalistic skills involved in uncovering the information! It is also interesting to note that, as was indicated in a letter to *THES*, an article on our preliminary findings had been offered to them but was declined.

The long-term effects of the *THES* article were thankfully not too detrimental. The research was finished and written up on time. No one actually refused to cooperate in the study as a result of the press report, though, as mentioned above, we will never know to what extent respondents were more guarded in their comments as a result of the untimely media exposure.

On the positive side, the research was given a very high profile. Following the article we were inundated with requests for information about the research findings and our thoughts on staff appraisal in general. It is now well over 2 years since the completion of the project and we still get many such requests for information. But by far the most positive outcome of the *THES* article and the reporting of the research on drug use among medical students was that it gave the editors the impetus to put together this book!

IMPLICATIONS

It is striking that both of these incidents relate to conference presentations of preliminary or interim findings. In each case, the media exposure had some adverse effects on the subsequent stages of the research. There would seem, then, to be a special risk when interim findings are reported, in that it is not just the prospect of misreporting that may cause difficulties but the consequential impact on the conduct of research. In social research, the people you are investigating are able to read the media reports, and this may have an impact on their preparedness to participate (or to continue to participate) in the research. Alternatively, the very feasibility of proceeding with the original design of the research may be affected, as in the medical incident above. The lesson is clear: reporting of interim findings which may attract media attention carries an extra increment of risk to the researcher which is over and above the personal discomfort that is sometimes engendered. So think (at least twice) before divulging those preliminary results.

Chapter 6

Sex and dinosaurs

Helen Haste

I do research in those areas regarded as unacceptable for dinner conversation in Victorian times – politics, sex and (occasionally) religion. As a consequence, I am approached periodically by the popular press to make comments on current events and give an 'expert' opinion on this and that. In fact, my actual research is rather more mundane; it is on the development of moral, social and political values in adolescence, and on social and development issues in gender – including gender and science. Recently, I have become interested in sociopsychological issues in science – which has involved me in work on, amongst other things, metaphors of dinosaurs.

Often, however, the media requests are far removed from my actual research-based knowledge. Then I face an interesting dilemma. Does the credibility that I have presumably established through my serious work entitle me to express publicly opinions based on little more than common sense? Sometimes, of course, I have some acquaintance with the relevant literature. Obviously, the first step in such an encounter is to tell the journalist to 'Phone So-and-So' – the expert. But if So-and-So is not available, or lives in another country, then I have the choice – or is it the obligation? – to be a gatekeeper, to communicate the findings of psychology to the wider world. This will inevitably appear as 'Dr Haste says . . .'. *Bella* magazine and its ilk are not going to say 'We consulted Dr Haste, who tells us that research by Dr Smith has shown. . .'. Even the readers of this book would yawn, let alone the busy housewife relaxing briefly over coffee. But because 'Dr Haste, psychologist' says it, it will have authority and impact, so Dr Haste's obligations are to communicate effectively, even when it is not in her field.

The more often she does this, the more journalists will phone again and again. Dr Haste becomes a conduit, if not a pundit.

This is different from talking about my own research, which has less pitfalls. Then I am in control, and if I mess it up, it is my own professional reputation that is vulnerable. The art then is to present my work, its questions, methods and results, concisely, without jargon, and in a way which makes it interesting to a lay audience. So I must recognize that caveats I want to make about the generalizability of my results probably won't be included in the final version, because the journalist's job is to communicate effectively and hold the readers' interest.

The journalist is a professional, just as much as I am, but she has a different role. And there are different kinds of journalists. The journalist working for the tabloid press has the – often difficult – task of creating a 'story', which probably demands as much gee-whizzery and even sensationalism as possible. There will be rather a large gap between what I as a psychologist think is a good story, from a scientific point of view, and what the *Sun* reader thinks is a good story. If I want to bridge that gap, I have to be very succinct, very clear, and very practical about my findings – and be willing to accept the inevitable distortions.

So are there any pluses, after seeing one's work reduced to a parody of its former self? I optimistically hope that the more psychologists are visibly doing something, the more the press and the public will take psychology seriously and, with any luck, psychologists will be regarded as the proper experts to consult automatically in the areas where they really can say something useful – about education, decision making, management, health. The point is, the tabloid press will demand some expert: rather it be us than Madame Zorro the psychic medium, or even Mr Squeers the ultra-conservative teacher.

But other journalists are the antithesis of the Grub Street hack. These are the professionals who write – or broadcast – for the 'intelligent lay audience'. These people are highly educated, they are craftsmen. Further, they fully understand the gap between what scientists would like to say, but often cannot, and what their readers want to know about. They also want a 'good story' but they want meat in it, and they want accuracy. Their skills lie in putting over complex ideas effectively – skills that we often lack. Some of them even have a background in science. Roger Highfield, a

prize-winning *Daily Telegraph* journalist for whom I have enormous
professional respect, was a practising scientist before becoming a
science writer. But even those from non-science backgrounds
become tuned in to current trends in the fields because they make
the effort to keep in touch with those members of the scientific
professions who are willing to communicate, and to make their
work accessible. I think particularly of Peter Evans, an outstanding
radio journalist from whom I have learned a very great deal about
the art of broadcasting.

It is all about communication. Yet there are still many people
who are suspicious of the press. Indeed, some narrow-minded
academics, scornful of those who wish to communicate to the
wider world, use words like 'trivialization' and 'slumming' and
even, on occasion, 'prostitution'. 'Popularization' is anathema, a
term of abuse rather than a desirable skill. Psychologists in particular – with some notable exceptions – have been reluctant to
talk to the press. There has long been a tension between the 'right'
kind of communication – to one's peers, in a proper scientific
context where all the fine details, and the caveats, can be discussed
– and the 'wrong' kind of communication – to a wider audience,
not regarded as 'professional'.

There are, of course, good reasons for the anxieties that under-
lie this. We work in a terrain which every human being finds
fascinating – and believes him or herself to be an expert already.
So our subtle research often gets the response 'So what?' or 'Fancy
that', both reflecting a reader who is simply assimilating new
material into existing schemata with the minimum of cognitive
disturbance. Not surprisingly, psychologists have felt unloved, misunderstood and devalued, and have retreated in exasperation.
Further, all too much press attention, especially tabloid, has been
on the more physical, sensational or commonsensical aspects.
What I get telephoned most about is 'relationships', self-image or
self-presentation, none of which is my real field, yet all are
obviously of perennial interest to the public.

Such experiences are upsetting because they require a grossly
over-simplified comment and, further, are very unlikely to reflect
the slant of one's own burning interest in the field. So one is always
tempted to turn the question around. If someone phones up and
asks me whether women in a man's world of work feel anxious
about their femininity, I initially want to spell out the many aspects
of the issue, the varied conditions and contexts under which

different kinds of anxiety occur. But while that might have scientific integrity, it is outside the journalist's (and her readers')
schemata and one can actually hear the glaze coming over her eyes
on the end of the phone. When the article comes out, inevitably
she has taken one or two quotations out of context, or has ignored
you altogether and just printed good old common sense.

But whose fault is it? Being lofty about such experiences has
until recently been an acceptable reaction. For psychologists this
was also fuelled in part by anxiety about their uncertain status in
relation to natural sciences. There are, for instance, only five
psychologists amongst the 800 or so Fellows of the Royal Society. A
misconception is abroad that if we communicate too effectively to
the wider world we may demystify our profession, make it too
commonsensical in order to simplify it for public consumption.
Natural scientists, after all, are just as naïve about their own knowledge of human behaviour, and about the subtleties of explaining
it, as any other layperson. They are just as likely to leap to the
conclusion that what we are doing is not very demanding.

So psychologists have to an extent been caught in a trap, not of
our own devising, but perpetuated by us. What is this trap? We
confuse being a popularizer with being a trivializer. The skills
of good communication are neither negligible nor trivial. It is
interesting that outstanding natural scientists are often extremely
effective communicators. Think of such series as the Royal Institution Christmas Lectures for children, or the many excellent
scientists who talk on television or to a wide audience. One should
not exaggerate this, however; plenty of natural scientists are
equally reluctant to speak to a general audience.

For a large number of years I have been closely associated with
the British Association for the Advancement of Science, in various
roles. This organization has existed for 150 years to disseminate
developments in science to the world. Initially it was the place in
which major new discoveries and inventions were announced;
latterly, with the growth of professional scientific societies and the
demand for a more specialized forum in every field, the BA has
served the purpose of bringing recent developments to public
attention in a palatable way, rather than being the forefront of new
communication. As a consequence, a very close relationship has
developed between the scientific press and the BA. A body of
scientifically informed journalists comes regularly to the annual
meeting. In recent years, the British Psychological Society and

other social science professional bodies have increasingly recognized the importance of establishing very good press relations, and
now actively educate their members to communicate with the
media. The British Psychological Society has a very professional
approach to press relations, employing full-time staff. But there
was a time when the Psychology Committee of the BA sometimes
had to exercise tact and pressure to persuade the occasional
speaker that talking to the press was important.

Nowadays, many more psychologists appear on radio and television, and are quoted in popular magazines and newspapers. This
varies; some people turn up reliably in programmes and articles
which bear some relationship to their main research fields. Others
have made the step to becoming, in the best sense of the word,
'media persons' – they are willing and able to talk about any
civilized topic, in the company of other scientists, literary or political folk. They have carved a place for psychologists among the
intelligentsia, rather than merely among the ranks of newsworthy
boffins. One example is Richard Gregory, who frequently appears
on programmes on all kinds of topics, and has indeed achieved the
ultimate accolade of being a *Desert Island Discs* castaway. He is an
FRS and also recipient of the Michael Faraday Award, given by the
Royal Society for outstanding contributions to the public understanding of science.

My experience with the BA has on the whole been positive, and
I have been pleased by the increasing proportion of press coverage
that the Psychology Section has been receiving over the years[1]. The
broadsheet press – and even the tabloids – pay great attention to
the meetings of the British Psychological Society. But my own
personal experience with the press has been chequered. Often, my
work has been straightforwardly reported, an accurate summary of
the paper or the press release – press releases are crucial for busy
journalists. I have had some very enjoyable experiences making
radio programmes in which I was given free rein to express the
complexities of my argument. I have appeared on a few chat shows
where the challenge (sometimes impossible) is to say something
pithy, live, in less than half a minute.

The most demanding was *After Dark*, an open-ended discussion
programme that began shortly before midnight and ended whenever the discussion ran out – we lasted until 2.30 am. *After Dark* was
nerve-wracking. For over two hours one was 'on stage' and completely unscripted; one might be caught chewing a nail, scratching

oneself, or just looking bored. At one point, the camera focused on my red fingernails twiddling with my necklace, while somebody else was holding forth. The delusion for the audience was that they were eavesdropping on an after-dinner conversation. Dangerously, the participants fall into the same delusion, because the cameras are masked and the crew invisible in the darkness. I caught myself about to say something highly indiscreet, before I remembered that over a million strangers were watching.

But I have had a couple of rather bizarre experiences with the press which some people may see as 'Awful Warnings'. In both cases, the coverage was highly successful in that the story made national and international headlines. In both cases, the under-lying story came out of serious scientific discussion, but in both cases the casual observer might have been forgiven for regarding the reporting as a massive trivialization. Each case was an example of Andy Warhol's '15 minutes of fame': my experience suggests that this is quite enough.

In the first situation, I was cast not as a psychologist, but as a dinosaur. I did not even speak; indeed I simulated the mating position of a female dinosaur. The event was the British Association for the Advancement of Science meeting in Belfast in 1987. My late partner, the palaeontologist Beverly Halstead (who was himself a brilliant communicator), gave a serious scientific lecture on the question of how dinosaurs mated. The constraints of great size and heavy armour were confounded by the relatively small size of the orifices; if dinosaurs had reptilian cloacae, as is thought, we know that through dinosaur cloacae passed eggs only the size of foot-balls. It would be quite an art to align each with the other. My brief role was to simulate a female dinosaur, with my leg extended as a tail, while Beverly illustrated the male's problems.

. The tabloids – and the broadsheets – went to town:

'Bonkosaurus',[2] 'How to make love to a hundred-ton girl'[3]

– and so forth. Virtually every British paper covered it, mostly with pictures, and for weeks we were sent international or local versions of the Press Association report. *OMNI* magazine, the American popular science journal, sent over a reporter, Sandy Fritz, especi-ally for an extended interview and did a full spread on the question of dinosaurs mating – which led to some readers ('Disgusted, Omaha') cancelling their subscriptions.[4]

This story divides people. The publicity it gained for a genuinely interesting – and unresolved – question can be seen as a light-hearted but legitimate way to widen public awareness of an issue. For others the conjunction of sex and science – even when the issue is about sex – is problematic and seen as a minefield.

The second situation was somewhat similar. This time my paper was given the hype. Again the venue was the BA, at Plymouth in 1991. At this point I was President of the Psychology Section. My Presidential Address was on social and psychological aspects of metaphor, and I drew examples from gender, history of science and dinosaurs. My argument was that metaphor is an important part of our thinking, especially innovative thinking, and in com-munication. One of my examples was how dinosaurs have entered our language as a metaphor for everything that is extinct, maladap-tive, over-large and inefficient. This was picked up by the *Guardian*.[5]

However, what most of the press picked up was a passing example, an aside, which had taken about five minutes in an hour's lecture, and one paragraph of a 14-page press summary. I argued that our culture deals with the threat of female sexuality by casting women into one of four stereotypes – wife, waif, whore or witch. Wives, waifs and whores all remain in the power of men, and their sexuality is controllable.[6] The witch, however, is threatening because she is sexually autonomous, sets the terms of reference and refuses to bow to male definitions. I used this convenient frame for illustrating the role of gender metaphors in a variety of social and historical discussions. To make the point more vivid, I cited the singer Madonna as an example: she deliberately confuses the roles of witch and whore. She dresses as a whore, feeding male fantasy, while defining herself as an independent liberated woman on her own terms – a witch. My point was that her success partly lies in this disjunction and confusion of two contradictory metaphors.

The press liked this – a lot. The headlines were variations on:

'Madonna mixes up her sex symbols' (*Evening Standard*)[7]
'Madonna is a real witch' (*Daily Mirror*)[8]
'Singer's image causes sex role confusion' (*The Times*)[9]

Most were accompanied by photographs of Madonna. The *Daily Star*, who referred to me as a 'top female shrink', went further.[10] Their headline was 'Whore, witch, waif or whiter than white wife. Which are you?' Their story in fact missed the point about Madonna's role confusion. This story, the wording virtually unchanged, re-surfaced in the United States tabloid *National Examiner* about two months later.[11] Subsequently I did a large number of live radio interviews, including one with a New York station.

The *Daily Mail* negotiated a feature with me, matching famous faces to the 'sexual labels men have given us'.[12] They printed photos of 20 actresses or other famous women. This story has an amusing addition. I made the point in my lecture, even men-tioning a few names, that many actresses have been cast unwillingly in the 'whore' stereotype, and have complained about the limitations of female dramatic roles. In the original list that the journalist Sue Carpenter drew up there were several living women – and the editor withdrew the story, on the grounds that the newspaper might be sued. The story was allowed to run the follow-ing day, with only dead actresses in the whore category. Such are the delicate – and selective – sensitivities of editors.

This experience was salutary. It is a curious sensation to be, even briefly, the focus of a great deal of press attention. What the press picked up was, in my view, very much an aside, a minor illustration of my argument. I had not prepared myself for suddenly being a world expert on Madonna.

Was it trivialization? I remain unsure. It got across the point about the importance of metaphor, perhaps more successfully than any other example I might have used – though I think the dinosaur might have made it without Madonna's competition. It was certainly a lesson in how to get maximum publicity – hitch your wagon to a star, as they say. But the message that I learned from it was positive. Have one clear idea, with a powerful example that appeals to everyone's experience or knowledge, and put it in terms that everyone can understand. Next time I'll plan it; that time was an accident.

NOTES

1 Haste (1990); Haste (1991).
2 *Daily Star*, 29 August 1987, p. 3.
3 *Daily Mirror*, 29 August 1987, p. 3.
4 Fritz (1988).
5 Williams (1992).
6 Haste (1992).
7 *Evening Standard*, 27 August 1991, p. 5.
8 *Daily Mirror*, 28 August 1991, p. 7.

9 *The Times,* 28 August 1991, p. 8.
10 *Daily Star,* 28 August 1991, p. 3.
11 *National Examiner,* 5 November 1991, pp. 6–7.
12 *Daily Mail,* 'Femail', 30 August 1991, p. 15.

Chapter 7

Pornography's piggy in the middle: pressure groups, the media, and research

Dennis Howitt

> At the end of the day, it is difficult to believe that a society can really afford to embrace pornography with welcoming arms since this may serve to legitimise those attitudes which porno-graphy itself may reinforce. The question must be considered to be wider than just prohibition or other forms of control alone, but how to promote those attitudes and values which under-mine pornography's potential influence. (Howitt and Cumberbatch, 1990, p. 96)

This is the final paragraph of our report *Pornography: Impacts and Influences* (Howitt and Cumberbatch, 1990) commissioned by the Home Office. An account of its treatment by the media probably makes little sense in terms of the report's actual content. Under-standing the involvement of pressure groups in determining the media coverage is necessary to make the process clearer.

MANAGING THE NEWS

One elderly and naïve view of the mass media holds them to be investigative organizations, proactive seekers of news. Typical of rhetoric supporting press freedom from government intervention, the notion of the media as public watchdogs still holds a degree of emotive appeal despite the journalistic excesses of many popular tabloids. But, conceptions of the media as fearless uncoverers of 'the truth at any price' not only seem faintly ludicrous to the modern eye but also ignore more adequate conceptions of the news-gathering process. Early sociological accounts of media organ-izations which saw journalists and editorial staff as 'gatekeepers' (White, 1950) did little to refine notions of news gathering.

The concept of news management marked a major change – a theoretical advance (Cohen and Young, 1973; Howitt, 1982). It provided a much more dynamic and interactive view of the news-gathering process in which the media constitute merely part of a complex web of inter-institutional and inter-individual, in-formation 'politicking'. An old adage holds that information is power. Many social institutions, including the police and the army, can wield enormous control over the circulation of information through the news media. The Gulf War of 1991 illustrated this well. Then most of the news was provided by the armed forces at press conferences and most picture footage only possible under the supervision of the armed forces. Very much the same applies to the political control over material obtained in Iraq at this time. Implicitly, if not explicitly, the possession of 'news' carries the power to determine which 'news' will be provided to the media. Also, to a degree, it allows the news provider control over how the news will be presented. Not 'toe-ing the line' leads to a risk of exclusion from the information supply. This is amply illustrated by the parliamentary lobby-system as employed during the Thatcher prime-ministership (Harris, 1991).

PRESSURE GROUPS AND PORNOGRAPHY

Moral crusades have a long history in Britain. Greek and Thompson (1991) describe a legacy of 21 acts of parliament dating back 350 years which could be used to control obscene or porno-graphic material.

It is easily overlooked that social institutions have an important role in the dissemination of social scientific 'news'. Many pro-fessions now have paid or unpaid 'press officers' to publicize their work. However, one should not forget either that many pressure groups, almost by their nature, seek media publicity actively. Social science impinges directly on the activities of many pressure groups (such as Shelter) much as 'hard' science is part of the armoury of other organizations such as Greenpeace, Oxfam, and anti-nuclear groups. Possibly the most public media pressure group in Britain has been the National Viewers' and Listeners' Association (NVALA) under the stewardship of Mrs Mary Whitehouse, the title 'Mrs' being more symbolic than descriptive. In the course of her campaigning career which was well under way in the 1960s, she achieved status as a media celebrity in her own right (see Tracey

and Morrison, 1977 for a discussion of her). But NVALA succeeded most away from the hostile glare of the press in which it
risks ridicule. Greek and Thompson (1991) comment:

> NVALA, however, is at its most effective lobbying behind the
> scenes of the Houses of Parliament, working with sympathetic
> MPs . . . and where possible promoting private prosecutions of
> material. It was NVALA which brought the major prosecutions
> in the 1970s against *Oz* magazine, the *Little Red School Book* and
> *Gay Times.* (p. 24)

Of course, pressure groups use social scientific research selectively
as judged by the best social scientific standards. Certainly, one
would be loath to suggest that they employ reasonable academic
balance and caution. (See, for example, Barlow and Hill, 1985 on
video nasties.) Nevertheless, social scientific data are part of pressure-
group rhetoric. Perhaps the apotheosis of this was the so-called
Longford Committee Investigating Pornography (1972) which
received much media attention despite its *ad hoc* and informal
constitution. This 'report' contained selective discussions of social
scientific findings. Better remembered are the 'investigative' visits
to live sex shows abroad by members which were gleefully photographed and reported by the media of the time.

In the 1980s the work of feminist anti-pornography campaigners
became more and more visible (Cumberbatch and Howitt, 1989).
However, one should be cautious about equating feminism with
the censorship of pornography. Considerable antipathy has been
expressed about such activities and activists by anti-censorship
feminists (e.g. Carol, 1991; Hayward, 1991). Hayward goes so far as
to describe some of the research carried out by one prominent
anti-pornography activist in the campaign as 'a disgrace'. One
needs to be cautious about equating feminism with a commitment
to the censorship and control of pornography.

In the USA, the Minneapolis hearings of 1983 (*Everywoman*,
1988) provided a public forum for a new group of anti-pornography
campaigners with its roots in certain feminist writings (Cumberbatch
and Howitt, 1989). The Minneapolis hearings sought to and did
introduce new legal (albeit unconstitutional) criteria for
pornography:

> Pornography is a discriminatory practice based on sex which
> denies women equal opportunities in society. Pornography is

central in creating and maintaining sex as a basis for discrimination. (*Everywoman*, 1988, p. 134)

The hearings are important to an account of our experiences since they provided a stimulus in Britain to attempts to create new pornography legislation. This led indirectly to our involvement in the public debate.

Themes from the Minneapolis hearings were taken up in Britain by various 'feminist' groupings, especially in the form of the 'off-the-shelf' campaign which sought to have removed from newsagents' displays so-designated pornographic materials. According to Greek and Thompson (1991), the preamble to the bill emerging from the campaign reflected beliefs rather than social scientific evidence:

> This House views with grave concern the continued rise in sales, both covert and overt, of pornographic and obscene material; notes that such publications have a grossly degrading and damaging effect, particularly in the depiction of women and children . . . ; and calls on Her Majesty's Government to initiate an urgent study of the impact of pornography to update and supplement the limited research currently available and thereafter to implement urgently whatever measures are necessary to protect those who directly and indirectly suffer as a result of such perverting influences. (pp. 97–98)

The clarion call for a study of the impact of pornography signalled events which led to our involvement.

JOINING THE AFFRAY

We became directly involved in the debate about pornography late in 1989. Despite having a long academic involvement in mass media research, both together and individually since 1970 (e.g. Cumberbatch *et al.*, 1987; Howitt and Cumberbatch, 1975b), we had had very little involvement with research on pornography other than a single chapter in a mass media textbook (Howitt, 1982), a study of an Andy Warhol film *Trash* for the British Board of Film Censors (Howitt, 1972), and Cumberbatch's evidence to the Williams Committee (1979) based on our book on television violence (Howitt and Cumberbatch, 1975a). However, in 1989 the Broadcasting Standards Council, a government-financed media watch-dog, commissioned us to write a review of research on the effects of mass communication which included a section on pornography (Cumberbatch and Howitt, 1989).

A little later, we were approached by the Research and Planning Unit of the Home Office to review research on the effects of pornography, especially with reference to sexual violence. In January 1990 the contract was agreed and announced in the House of Commons by David Mellor MP, then a Home Office minister. Our report was due by the end of April of that year. This was reported in a number of newspapers which prompted a few pro- and anti-pornography letters to us from members of the public. As well as the usual obligation to sign under the Official Secrets Act, we were contracted not to discuss the report with the media until after its publication. Of course, the report was a major undertaking in the time available especially given that there were at least 200 papers and books on the effects of pornography to be read, evaluated, described and discussed. Furthermore, we were asked to give emphasis to European research. Consequently we wrote numerous letters throughout Europe seeking research evidence, virtually without any success. Pornography research is not an obsession of continental Europe.

We were hardly naïve about the degree of media interest that our work had received over the years. For example, we featured in a half-page cartoon in a national newspaper in the 1970s for our studies of television violence (Howitt and Cumberbatch 1975a, 1975b) and Cumberbatch's analyses of media content (Cumberbatch *et al.*, 1987), *inter alia*. Furthermore, immediately prior to the award of the contract the Home Office had responded 'firmly' to a newspaper feature concerning Cumberbatch's work on the media. Clearly the whole enterprise was 'primed' to be sensitive. Furthermore, we quickly were forcibly made even more aware that journalists could not be trusted to respect 'off the record' comments nor to avoid 'cobbling together' stories through conjecture.

Hostility was the commonest response from most quarters. Not surprisingly, then, the sex magazine industry encouraged readers to lobby the Home Office opposing further legislation:

Dear Readers
I want to draw your attention to a move (by the Government) which unless YOU do something will stop the sale of all girlie

magazines in Britain . . . The rag-bag alliance of feminists, religious bigots, ultra-conservatives and opportunist publicity seekers have decided to mount an attack on the rights of adults to decide how they spend their money. They have persuaded the Government to set up a review of the effect of pornography . . . They have made their voices heard. If you don't show that you are the majority there is a real threat that this magazine (and similar mags) will no longer be on sale . . .
Love
Zeta

(Zeta, 1990)

At no stage did we expect the work to be politically easy or to be warmly welcomed. It would have been foolhardy to ignore the emotive and ideological underpinnings of the pornography debate. Political rows around social scientific reports on the effects of pornography have a long history (Cline, 1974; Commission on Obscenity and Pornography, 1970; Cumberbatch, 1984; Einsiedel, 1988; Eysenck and Nias, 1978; Koop, 1987; Nobile and Nadler, 1986; Van Den Haag, 1971; Vine, 1990; Wilcox, 1987), especially in North America. In Britain, a considerable degree of hostility had been directed against the Williams report (Williams, 1979). Its recommendations were essentially by-passed by the government (Simpson, 1983). Furthermore, part of the Home Office's interest was familiar to us. We were well aware of lobbying of ministers by anti-pornography campaigners and, quite reasonably, we were 'encouraged' to take their comments into account indirectly in our review. As with any other writing, the structure anticipated the most likely criticisms from different quarters. Nevertheless, the casual reader of the report would be unaware of how the report reflects a dialogue between us, the ministry, and pressure group lobbyists on how the research literature should be interpreted. However, officially commissioned reports are written in a context which involves wider concerns than those of the academic community. They need to address a variety of agenda. Nevertheless, the report was our synthesis of the material and contained what we consider to be a fair evaluation of the strengths and weaknesses of the research, though with greater emphasis on the caveats than we would normally include in social scientific writing. Our recommendations for future (largely) policy-oriented research in the British context were also included as part of the contracted requirements.

THEY WOULD SAY THAT, WOULDN'T THEY?

The report's contents were rarely the focus of attention. Presumptions about what the report said were far more important in guiding the response articulated through the media. The earliest signs of this came round about the end of April 1990 when the national media featured articles on pornography, apparently timed to coincide with assumptions about the date of publication of the report. At this time *New Scientist* published an article by 'a specialist in animal psychology' at Aberdeen. This presented a rather selective survey of the evidence on pornography's effects on behaviour (Baxter, 1990). Grossly in error on his description of the basis for government policy, he concluded:

> Taking all the current evidence together, I question whether the British government's policy, established by the Williams Committee on pornography in 1979, is still valid. . . . Do we still know too little about the effects of pornography to seek to control it? I argue that there must come a time when the demand for conclusive proof gives way to 'evidence beyond reasonable doubt'. (p. 41)

By what criteria a lack of reasonable 'doubt' can be established for social scientific data is not made clear by Baxter. Furthermore, his unspecified notions about controlling pornography ignore that British legislation is amongst the most restrictive in Europe. Another publication at this time gave considerable attention to the views of anti-pornography campaigners. It is difficult to believe that this was not timed to undermine the publication of our report though direct evidence for this is, of course, lacking. Baxter has connections with anti-pornography campaigners. He has chaired at least one meeting addressed by Campaign Against Pornography and Censorship associates. But the actual publication of our report occurred several months later. Redrafting to meet ministry requirements was necessary, including on going criticisms raised by lobbying anti-pornography campaigners at the ministerial level. Attempts to undermine our credibility were being made and at least one minister is known to have met with anti-pornography campaigners during the time of the preparation of our report.

This meant that there was a lengthy period during which the media were in a limbo. Telephone calls from journalists were common during this period. While for the most part the press merely 'tested the water' from time to time, the *Daily Mail* seemed to be the most fixated on our report. This newspaper put considerable effort into attempts to obtain advance information about our conclusions. On one occasion a journalist arrived at one of our workplaces, apparently hoping for sight of the report or a clandestine meeting elsewhere to a similar end. When neither of these were forthcoming, he travelled 50 more miles to the other's university to try again.

Indeed it was a story in this newspaper suggesting that the report had been 'shelved' which led to its eventual publication just days before Christmas in 1990. The timing is significant since it was the beginning of the holiday season for politicians and the media. No press conference was organized and our requests for one rejected, putatively at the ministerial level. The reasons for this fell into place with the publication of the report at 11.00 am on 20 December, accompanied by the Home Secretary's press release. It included his statement together with a list of potential journalists' 'questions' plus the Home Secretary's 'replies'. This appeared to structure much of the press's coverage of the report:

> An official report which concluded that rape and violence were not caused by pornography was effectively disowned last night by the Home Secretary, whose own department had commissioned it. (*Daily Mail*, 21 December 1990, p. 1).

> Home Secretary Kenneth Baker has reacted with irritation and impatience to the report sponsored by his own department – before he took over – into the effects of pornography on sexual violence. 'Curiously inconclusive', he called it. (*Daily Express*, 21 December 1990, p. 8).

While this seems a substantial condemnation of our report by a government minister, the Home Office press release paints a different picture from the hostile gloss given the minister's comments by the media:

> There can be little doubt that pornography has an insidious and dehumanising effect on attitudes to women and family relations. Regardless of whether or not it encourages violent crime, pornography degrades all who come into contact with it. That is why the Government has taken such tough action to control it ... I recognise that there are still concerns about other aspects of obscenity legislation. These research findings, which in many

ways are a curiously inconclusive mixture, are published as a contribution to the continuing debate. (Home Office press release, 20 December 1990)

Just why these comments were interpreted as they were by all the media is difficult to explain given the detail of the press release's text. Was it another case of the media creating conflict? One suspects that some Home Office press officer placed such a slant on the press release. Certainly, throughout the period prior to the publication of the report, journalists told us that the Home Office was blaming us for the 'lateness' of the publication of the report, despite virtually all of the delay being on the Home Office's part. Were these signs of the ministry protecting its own back?

Typically, the news reports used comments from pressure groups and other figureheads. Mostly these were predictable: Mary Whitehouse of the National Viewers' and Listeners' Association, Catherine Itzin of the Campaign Against Pornography and Censorship and Michael Hames of Scotland Yard's Obscene Publications Squad. Their comments were also readily anticipated and usually not geared to the report's actual contents. Take, for example, the following comment attributed to Detective Superintendent Michael Hames, who said that:

it was impossible to prove a link between pornography and crime. 'But I can tell you from bitter experience that the sick deluge of pornography is on the increase and so are violent sexual crimes.' (*Guardian*, 21 December, 1990, p. 6)

This was a remarkably disingenuous comment to make in a week when the newly published crime statistics based on police reports had shown a decline in recorded sexual offences! Our report contained what we acknowledged to be rudimentary and tentative evidence against the view that the circulation of pornography was increasing. Hames has spoken on the same platforms as 'moral campaigners' and had written of the relationship between soft pornography and violent crime for popular newspapers (Greek and Thompson, 1991). Other comments were also deficient in preparation or accuracy. For example, when Mary Whitehouse commented:

the report was just a waste of public money. 'This is just another of the highly controversial reports that get us nowhere.' (*Daily Telegraph*, 21 December 1990, p. 3) she was probably misled by the claims that the report had cost about two-thirds of a million pounds. A self-serving error on the part of one newspaper, this figure multiplies the sums involved by a factor of about a hundred!

Bandwaggoning the story in order to publicize one's own organization was also detectable. For example, we heard one radio interview with the clinical director of a clinic for sex offenders. Having claimed to have read the report, he went on to contend that we had merely rehashed old material, ignoring the need to understand how sexual offenders process pornography. Or in a letter written by the director of the same clinic:

> the report has again become stranded in the 'cause and effect' debate and failed to address the use of pornography as a tool of the sex offender. . . . As the only residential centre for the treatment of sex offenders we are daily made aware of how the sex offender uses pornography to support his distorted thinking in 'normalising' his abuse and as an aid in the 'entrapment' of his victims. . . . We need to extensively research the impact of pornography on the offender before we conclude the debate . . . (*The Times*, 31 December 1990, p. 13)

In fact, our report recommended this as an important area needing future research and also discussed the limited research evidence available on the matter! Any of the early comments which appeared in the media attributed to pundits are also unlikely to have been based even on a cursory reading of our rather lengthy report. Indeed, sometimes the media used comments made in another context prior to the publication of our report almost as if they were said of the report. This clearly does not apply to several journalists who wrote fairly precise summaries of it.

The press's treatment of the report varied markedly. It was virtually ignored by the tabloid newspapers such as the *Star* and the *Sun*, while the *Daily Mirror* devoted little more than a column inch to a brief few words. The so-called quality papers such as the *Daily Telegraph*, the *Independent*, *The Times*, and the *Guardian* tended to give fair and precise profiles of the report's contents. The true vitriol came from the *Daily Express* and the *Daily Mail* which regarded the report with manifest hostility:

> A report by two university dons commissioned by the Home Office claims that there is no evidence to link pornography and

sexual crime. You have to be in an ivory tower to believe that. (Editorial, *Daily Mail*, 21 December 1990, p. 6)

This exercise has been a waste of time and money. Mr Baker's robust response at least suggests reassuringly, that no one in his department will be misled by it. (Editorial, *Daily Express*, 21 December 1990, p. 8)

It could be suggested that these newspapers were also bandwaggoning the report. Thus the *Daily Mail*'s attack provided a vehicle for the newspaper's current editorial stance against pornography. Similarly, in what initially appears to be a spirited defence of us against the Home Secretary's putative comments, a closer examination of an editorial in *The Times* reveals the primary intent of attacking the Home Secretary on crime rather than of promoting our report:

No sooner had the Home Office published its report challenging the assumed link between pornography and sex crimes yesterday than the home secretary, Kenneth Baker, ambushed it. . . . Pressure to ban pornography is a reaction to a form of crime which creates fear in and for the most vulnerable members of society, women and children. The concern is largely a displaced anxiety arising from the failure of the penal system to tackle the correction of sex offenders more successfully. (Editorial, *The Times*, 21 December 1990).

There was some, but relatively little, response from the general public, all inspired by the newspaper stories about our report's content rather than the report itself. A favourite was the anonymous correspondent who clipped one of the more hostile press reports and wrote on it:

What barmy buffoon gave you the job then?

MORE AND MORE 'EXPERTS'

Within two months of the publication of our report, a press conference was held in the Jubilee room of the House of Commons, apparently organized by the Labour member of parliament Dawn Primarolo, and Catherine Itzin of the Campaign Against Pornography and Censorship, though the press release was apparently issued by the Campaign for Press and Broadcasting Freedom. This conference attempted to counter the conclusions of our report and, of course, to gain the attention of the media. A number of individuals were promoted as speakers including Jo Richardson, the Labour Party's spokesperson on women, Teresa Stratford, vice-chair of the Campaign for Press and Broadcasting Freedom, Elizabeth Carola, co-ordinator of the Campaign Against Pornography, Liz Kelly of the Child Abuse Studies Unit at the Polytechnic of North London, Maureen O'Hara of the Children's Legal Centre, Ray Wyre and Trevor Price, directors of the Gracewell Clinic/Institute, Abigail Morris of the Campaign Against Pornography and Censorship, Clodagh Corcoran of the Irish Campaign Against Pornography and Censorship, and Tim Tate author of *Child Pornography* (1990). Not surprisingly, these were, by and large, stalwart anti-pornography campaigners including some associated with the 'off-the-shelf' campaign. The event seems to have been a little chaotic. One reporter told us that she found it difficult to extract a coherent argument from the organizers. Newspaper coverage was not too complimentary:

> Dr Catherine Itzin . . . told a Commons press conference: 'I could not make head or tail of the Home Office report.' She said that the United States, Canadian and Australian governments had accepted the negative effects of pornography. . . . At the somewhat confused press conference, long on anecdote and short on organised research, campaigners from various groups demanded more studies into the use of pornography by sex offenders, its role in child sexual abuse and its effect on attitudes and behaviour . . . (*The Times,* 21 February 1991, p. 10)

Once again, much of this is what our report recommends! The press conference also provided the opportunity to circulate an extremely hostile review of our report by a Canadian psychologist, James Check. Significantly, Check was amongst a number of North American academics approached by Dawn Primarolo for comments. For the most part they were known to be actively anti-pornography – Diane Russell who had written extensively on sexual violence was probably by far the best known of them (Russell, 1980; 1988). It has to be remembered that our report was made available on only 20 December but by 14 January 1991 Check had written a 15-page, single-spaced critique of our report which had been sent to him by Dawn Primarolo on the 27 December! It is largely irrelevant here that Check's review largely confused our views with those of authors

we were reporting, claimed we had written things we had not, and
asserted that we had not written things that we had. A snippet of
Check's comments will dispel any impression that they might be a
social scientist's dispassionate and objective comments:

In a word, this report is rubbish. (Check, 1991, p. 1)

One aspect of all of this stands out: the involvement of social
scientists in pressure-group politics and attempts to advance their
cause through the national media. Many of those disparaging our
report were trained social scientists themselves. Mike Baxter is a
psychologist at the University of Aberdeen, James V. P. Check is a
psychologist at York University in Canada, Catherine Itzin is a
sociologist and honorary research fellow in the Department of
Sociology at Essex University, Liz Kelly is a research fellow at the
Polytechnic of North London, Diane E. H. Russell is a sociologist
at Mills College in California, and James B. Weaver III is at Auburn
University in Alabama.

A degree of networking exists even among this small number of
people. For example, as has been mentioned, Itzin, Kelly and
Weaver shared a platform chaired by Baxter at Edinburgh's International Festival of Science and Technology in 1991. This occasion
allows a different strand to emerge in the equation between the
social sciences and the media. Here we have examples of how
social scientists co-act with pressure groups attempting to manipulate the media – if one likes, news management by social scientists.
Important questions arise, of course, about the nature of a social
science hitched to the needs of pressure-group politics. There is
nothing new about social scientists disputing the conclusions of
other professionals, but to use the national media as a vehicle for
political action is not particularly common. Further, to publish in
sources which are not accessible to reply is a problem. By presenting an imprecise and crude attack on our report as if it were
the careful and considered assessment of an independent 'expert'
is to abuse the best ideals of social science.

This strategy was extended during the spring and summer. A
Home Office minister was sent Check's comments on our report
together with brief comments from Weaver and Russell. In addition a nine-page letter commenting on our report was included
written by Itzin and sent on academic letter head addressed to
Dawn Primarolo MP, almost as if this was to be seen as an
independent academic comment! In fact it was one activist writing

to a close collaborator. Within this lie the seeds of a major dilemma – that of separating the social scientist from the activist. Can it be proper to exchange hats like this? Interestingly, in *The Times* of 20 April 1989, Ronald Butt describes how the moving spirit of the Campaign Against Pornography is a journalist, Catherine Itzin. Although there is no particular difficulty in researchers being activists involved in pressure groups, it is a problem when the dual allegiances are not made clear or, even, when they are manipulated. Declaration of interests by social scientists as an ethical formality might be the appropriate safeguard. The BBC's *Public Eye* programme got excited by the claims of the anti-pornography lobby though seems to have lost interest after seeking clarification.

CONCLUDING COMMENTS

The question arises as to who or what was the 'piggy in the middle'? Seemingly there are several piggies and several middles. Arguably, the media were the piggy since they had to negotiate the claims of pressure groups and those of ourselves. But is that adequate? The media by perhaps valuing and seeking conflict can hardly be an innocent victim – few of the media chose simply to summarize our report without recourse to the views of their chosen pundits. Were we piggies in the middle? Yes and no. To the extent that we knew that there would be some sort of row no matter what the report's conclusions suggests that we jumped and were not pushed. But much of what happened was out of our control – the relationship between the Home Office and the media for example. We certainly had no warning of the Home Secretary's press release which we did not get any opportunity to see prior to its issue. Furthermore, we were stuck between the press's attempts to obtain knowledge of the contents of the report or even merely 'our views' and the strict obligation to the Home Office not to discuss the matter with the media. We had discovered prior to accepting the contract that journalists could not be trusted to keep to bargains over not reporting what was 'spoken off the record'. This had resulted in one of us being 'called up to the ministry' for 'discussions'.

The curious thing as we see it is that the report was not a vindication of pornography though this has been how the 'liberal' voice on pornography has presented it. We had expected that anyone reading the report could find in it considerable evidence and comment making an anti-pornography argument, despite the fact that we were less than convinced that the available research provided satisfactory, in-depth, evidence of causality. Possibly the pressure-group lobby had shot itself in the foot somewhat by providing a commentary about what they believed we would write. This was an ongoing process, as we have seen, from the time that we were awarded the contract. They had set their own agenda which they would have found difficult to depart from. It is note-worthy, then, that Clare Short MP in her book *Dear Clare* reviewed the report in terms which found resonance with her own anti-pornography views and campaigning:

> Interestingly, the report was widely misrepresented in the media as claiming that there was no link between pornography and sexual violence. In fact the report says that it is not possible from the available research to decide whether or not pornography causes sexual violence. It also adds that claims that pornography is beneficial in creating outlets for men who might otherwise engage in sexual violence are also unproven. The report con-cedes that many women do find pornography distressing, and that women staying in hostels as a result of domestic violence frequently had partners who use pornography heavily. The report also admits that some sexual offenders used pornography heavily . . . including in their preparation for their offence . . . . Despite these conclusions the *Sun* rang my researcher to ask whether as a result of the findings of the report I intended to call off my campaign against Page 3 pornography. I didn't bother to return the call: those who are determined to mis-represent even a Home Office report are unlikely to quote what I say fairly. (Short, 1991, p. 27)

The irony is that Short's anti-pornography associates were largely responsible for creating the climate of hostility.

Chapter 8

Tales of expertise and experience: sociological reasoning and popular representation

Graham Murdock

There is no doubt that sociologists have become more publicity conscious of late. Partly this is a defence, an attempt to demonstrate relevance and utility in an era of shrinking resources and greater competition for grants. But it is also indicative of a new responsibility, a sense that those of us who live off public funds should be accountable for the ways in which we spend them. Having one's work featured in the major mass media is a way of satisfying both criteria with the minimum of bad faith. But coverage is not always an advantage. It can equally be a problem. It depends on the conditions which produced it. In thinking about this it is helpful to distinguish between publicity and access.

Publicity is the result of accidental, unplanned, or uncontrolled visibility. It can be particularly problematic if it occurs at a sensitive stage in the research or pre-empts the scheduled release of results. It may be the product of a leak, whereby internal documents, working papers or draft reports find their way into the public realm. Or a conversation may be used in attributable form because a researcher failed to insist that it was 'off the record'. Equally, unanticipated media interest can cause problems at the other end of the research chain, as I and a colleague discovered when we gave a speech to the Annual Meeting of the British Association for the Advancement of Science in the early 1970s.

The paper reported findings from a national study of teenage culture and its relation to schooling (Murdock and Phelps, 1973). Among other things, this had involved in-depth interviews exploring pupils' involvement in music and subcultures and their feelings towards a range of stars and celebrities. As the work progressed we noticed that working-class boys consistently attacked singers such as Mick Jagger as 'girls', 'queers' and 'wankers'. This prompted us to modify our original focus on the connections between musical taste, school career and class location, by adding an argument about the role of sexual identities. The central emphasis, however, remained firmly on the links between class and subculture. These dynamics were being fiercely debated within cultural studies and the sociology of youth at the time so we expected a lively response from the research community, but the volume of press coverage came as a surprise. We should have known better. After all, we had dealt with two terms in youth culture's holy trinity of 'sex, drugs and rock 'n' roll'.

The following day a number of national dailies led their reports of the conference with a precis of our paper. Though they all carried the argument about sexual identities, the 'qualities' generally retained our emphasis on class. The *Daily Telegraph* headline for example, read: 'Mick Jagger and John Lennon a "middle class taste"'. Even the *Sun* refused to focus solely on sex, preferring the familiar language of the pop industry with the headline; 'Kids who voted Jagger a Miss'. Overseas coverage was a different matter, however, as we found out when cuttings from foreign newspapers began to arrive in the office. For the most part, class took second place to sex, as in the story carried by *Dagbladet* of Oslo headed: 'Mick Jagger og John Lennon unmandige og homoseksuelle', complete with a photograph of Jagger wearing a hat with a flower, pouting at the camera. As researchers with a particular interest in the mass media we should have predicted this. But knowing something analytically never quite prepares you for the actual experience. In retrospect, it was clear that there was very little we could have done to prevent it. A determined journalist can always find another 'angle' in even the most carefully worded paper or press release, one that fits their brief rather than yours. In this situation, 'dissemination of results' is altogether too anodyne a phrase to capture the clashes of interest that occur when researchers' desires to put their case across in ways that do justice to their work collide with the popular press's premium on entertainment.

In contrast, access is the product of action which researchers initiate and over which they attempt to retain a degree of control. Being interviewed and providing on-the-record comments fall into this category. It is a contractual arrangement whereby research findings or scholarly expertise is exchanged for public visibility. Even so, the results may not always be exactly what the researcher had in mind since the terms of the bargain always favour journalists and programme makers, not least because they retain the right to edit contributions.

Contests between conflicting criteria of professional judgement are fought out on the battlegrounds of linguistic and visual signification. Sociologists face particular problems of language since so many key words – class, culture, community – are in common usage and have to be carefully qualified and defined before they can be used with any degree of precision. Alternatively, sociologists can seize the initiative and coin new phrases. This immediately opens the way to accusations of using jargon. Some specialist terms are certainly clumsy and inelegant and ought to be buried, but others are indispensable to clear expression. Unfortunately, some editors fail to see the difference.

I encountered this in its most adamant form when I received the proofs of a piece I had written for a weekly magazine and discovered that the sub-editor had changed the phrase 'social structure' to 'social shape'. I immediately rang the office to insist that the original line be restored. She refused, claiming that this was exactly the kind of sociological jargon she was heartily sick of, and that anyway 'shape' exactly fitted the line and since it was about to go to press it was too late to change it. I explained that 'social shape' was meaningless whilst 'social structure' at least had some general currency. Tempers flared and the deadlock was only broken by the intervention of the editor, who decided in my favour, but not before he had given me another lecture on academic pigheadedness. Even where authorial rights go unchallenged and a piece appears exactly as written, control over the public presentation of the arguments can easily slip away as the original story is taken up by other media, and moved from the 'posh' to the popular end of the market.

In the spring of 1979, I and a colleague wrote an article for one of the journals sponsored by the British Film Institute, reviewing the state of debate on the links between television and delinquency and raising questions about the status of the research evidence supporting claims for a direct causal connection (Murdock and McCron, 1979). We ended by arguing that the terms of the debate should be widened beyond the concentration on the 'effects' of televised violence to encompass other, less obvious, connections. We suggested that the possible links between property crimes and television's celebration of consumerism in advertising and game shows would be a particularly fertile area for exploration. A short-ened version of this piece was also published in *New Society*, a magazine that successfully addressed both academic and general readers (Murdock and McCron, 1978). We saw this as a way to give our arguments greater currency, but the fact that it came out before the original piece meant that they entered the popular domain without the careful caveats of the full version.

The popular dailies were quick to pick up on them. The *Sun*, for example, carried a story headed: 'Danger of the TV quiz shows', that began: 'The real villains of telly violence may not be the tough cops like Starsky and Hutch . . . but prize-filled quiz shows, claim two experts.' The term 'may' did at least indicate that we were pointing to a possibility not stating a case. However, the argument enjoyed a surprising longevity and surfaced regularly for some years. In the process, suggestion hardened into assertion. Hence, by the time the *Daily Mail* came to cover the British launch of one of the most famous American game show formats, *The Price is Right*, in February 1984, the paper's television correspondent could write that 'Sociologists Graham Murdock and Robin McCron claim that give-away shows equate success and happiness with possessing ex-pensive goods – and that this leads to crime and violence'.

This movement through the circuits connecting minority- to mass-audience media marked my arrival as an 'expert' on the question of the links between television and social violence. My name had clearly found its way onto the card indexes that tell television researchers who to ring for background information, a usable quotation or an appearance. During the second half of the 1980s I was involved in a number of programmes on this issue. I have chosen three as a way of exploring the relations between sociological reasoning and popular representation.

Television occupies a uniquely privileged position in the orchestration of social debate. It is the major site for explorations of the state of the nation and the main public forum for discussions of governmental performance and policy alternatives. Debates centre around the competition between a range of dis-courses, each of which offers a distinctive way of talking about and looking at a particular domain of social life or political action. The stakes in this contest are threefold: visibility – to be seen and heard; legitimacy – to have one's claims treated as credible, authoritative and worthy of respect; and precedence – to set the agenda and terms of debate.

From a very early point in its formation, public service broadcasting has defined the field of 'political' debate as more or less coterminous with the reach of the major parties and pressure groups. Consequently, the presentation of debates has revolved around the struggle between three main sets of discourses: the discourses of government, concerned with defending current policies and advancing new proposals for legislation; the discourses of parliamentary opposition, concerned with criticizing current policies and proposing alternatives; and discourses of advocacy, concerned with pressing the claims of particular interest groups. These discourses in turn draw on a range of sources to support their own claims to legitimacy and to call their opponents' claims into question. Two are particularly important for the present argument: discourses of experience and discourses of expertise.

Discourses of experience are grounded in the micropolitics of everyday life. They express the 'common sense' of 'ordinary people' and base their claims to legitimacy on the supposed authenticity of direct experience. Their articulation within the broadcasting system takes the form of personal testimonies – tales of knowledge and judgement gained in the school of hard knocks. In contrast, discourses of expertise set out to distance themselves from 'what everybody knows' through a variety of rhetorical manoeuvres. These centre around the presentation of two key figures: the 'scientist' and the 'intellectual'.

The discourse of scientific expertise advances claims for the autonomy and superiority of 'scientific' knowledge by way of two main devices. Firstly, it counterposes the selective and anecdotal evidence derived from grounded experience against the systematic and generalizable nature of research 'findings'. The notion of 'findings' is crucial. It conjures up a world of pre-existing 'social facts' waiting to be uncovered by the correct methodological equipment, like a metal detector locating objects buried on a beach. Secondly, the disinterestedness and facticity of this knowledge is played off against the subjective and partisan nature of political discourses that the speaker wishes to challenge or discredit. The plausibility of this second claim depends on how far hearers subscribe to what we can call the Mary Poppins view of the university researcher. In the same way that Mary, in the children's story, had a magic umbrella that allowed her to float high above the rooftops of London and look down on the ebb and flow of everyday life far below, so 'scientists' claim to have a conceptual and procedural umbrella that enables them to rise above the confines of mundane perception and the dirty business of political in-fighting.

This claim rests on the absolute dichotomies between facts and values, knowledge and experience, analysis and empathy, that lie at the dead heart of positivist conceptions of science. But many sociologists, myself included, refuse these divisions, seeing research as an endemically social practice whose results depend on the particular strategies of inquiry and representation which are mobilized. From this perspective, sociological reasoning cannot claim any special exemption from the play of power and interests and must include itself within the scope of a critical sociology of knowledge. This position detaches sociological researchers from the figure of the 'scientist' (in its positivist forms) and repositions them as 'intellectuals' – men and women of ideas – whose claims to a hearing rest not on the facticity of their findings but on the coherence, authority and explanatory power of their arguments. How these two contrasted images of the academic sociologist are mobilized with the television system can vary considerably, as we shall see presently.

The ideal of public service broadcasting has always placed particular emphasis on providing viewers and listeners with the access to the information, analysis and debate that they need to make rational choices on contentious issues (Murdock, 1992). From the outset this was an avowedly paternalistic project, a matter of giving discourses of expertise the widest possible currency. As Charles Lewis, the BBC's first Organizer of Programmes, argued in 1924:

> Its unique position gives the public an opportunity they have never had before of hearing both sides of a question expounded by experts. This is of great general utility, for it enables the 'man in the street' to take an active interest in his country's affairs. (quoted in Smith, 1974, p. 43)

Almost immediately, however, this top-down model was challenged by programme forms which allowed the 'man in the street' to talk back and testify from experience. The balance remained highly uneven, however. Experience might provide material for debate but analysis was generally the province of expertise. Recently, with the rise of participatory talk shows there are signs of a reversal. The new televisual populism which celebrates personal testimony and common sense is steadily eating away at the foundations of paternalism.

Because they have always been a central arena for the contest of discourses, current affairs and documentary programmes have long enjoyed a special relationship to the viewer-as-citizen within the broadcasting system. How this contest is organized in any particular instance will, however, depend crucially on the programme's form and the production team's relation to the political and economic forces operating inside and outside the organization. In approaching the mediating role of programme forms and formats we need to ask two questions: how many discourses are allowed into play within the programme and how are they treated? Most current affairs programmes deal with more than one discourse, but they do so in a variety of ways, ranging from the relatively hierarchical to the more or less egalitarian. Several dimensions of organization are worth noting.

Firstly, there is the issue of how much time each discourse occupies. Secondly, there is the question of priority and centrality. Two discourses may enjoy equal time but one may provide the organizing rationale for the programme, setting an agenda for debate, and leaving the second in the position of contestant or challenger. Thirdly, there is the issue of legitimacy. How far are a speaker's claims accepted and how far are they questioned or undermined? Visual images play a key role in this process.

Most work on discourse, including most writing on television's handling of social issues, treats it as a purely linguistic phenomenon, analysing the utterances of participants and interviewees and the questions and comments of the programme's presenters. This misses the obvious but decisive point that television is also a visual medium. Arguments and debates therefore proceed along two dimensions: the voice track which operates as a sequence of turn-taking and the image track which works by juxtaposition and association. In most cases what can be seen on the screen serves either to anchor and confirm what is being said or to bolster the speaker's claims to legitimacy. But images can also undermine a speaker's credibility or provide an ironic counterpoint or critical commentary.

Traditionally, intellectual expertise is signified by having the interviewee appear in a book-lined room, indicating accumulated knowledge. Production teams will sometimes go to considerable lengths to bring this cliche into play. One of the first interviews I ever gave on national television took place in the flat of the programme's young female researcher. From the director's point of view this had two major advantages: it was free and it was near the studio. The problem was that there were no academic books in the house. I was eventually photographed against a background of paperback crime novels, carefully photographed so that the titles were out of focus. Viewers could see that they were books but they couldn't quite make out what they were about.

Other directors, however, refuse this image, seeing it as over-used, too static and too reminiscent of the monk's cell. They favour the grit and movement of location shooting. They prefer activity to contemplation. They like to see their 'heads' talking against a backdrop of street life signifying that the speaker is 'in touch' with the flux of everyday experience. But life has an unfortunate habit of invading art.

Several years ago I was asked to contribute to a BBC current affairs programme on the future of the quality newspaper press. In place of the stock interview, the director decided to shoot in a small newsagent's shop near to Television Centre in West London. I was to walk to the rack with the presenter, pick up a copy of the *Independent*, start to read it whilst commenting on its relative success in the market, and then turn and pay at the counter. The shop was cramped and since the crew more or less filled it, it had to be emptied and locked before we could begin filming. The owner had been assured that it would take only a few minutes, but setting up the shots proved problematic in the limited space. The camera-man, who had flown back from a war zone the previous day, began to make ironic comments, *sotto voce*. Outside a crowd was gathering on the pavement wanting to buy the early edition of the evening paper which had just arrived. Not unreasonably, the proprietor demanded to reopen the shop and we retired back to the studio where the director reluctantly settled for a back-up interview. Ironically, the only room available at short notice was panelled in wood in a passable imitation of popular visions of a university senior common room.

One way to avoid the hazards of location filming, whilst still presenting academics as connected to the world, is to show them surrounded by the new tools of their trade: desk-top computers, video cassette machines, modems, and CD-ROM equipment. As we shall see presently, conspicuous displays of technology can play a key role in anchoring claims to 'scientific' expertise.

The impact of these dynamics was brought home to me through my experience of participating in two major prime-time programmes on the television and violence debate, *Open the Box* on Channel 4 which was first transmitted in June 1986, and an edition of *Panorama* which went out in February 1988. Television had been a consistent target of attack for the moral right that formed part of the coalition supporting Mrs Thatcher. They particularly objected to what they saw as the overly permissive attitude to the portrayal of violence and of sexuality and saw these representations as playing a central role in encouraging violent crime. They bolstered their case with evidence from laboratory experiments and surveys which purport to find a direct causal link between viewing violence on screen and behaving violently, and on the strength of this evidence called for greater controls and censorship. Their campaign met with a degree of success. Despite the unreliability of the evidence of ill effect (see Murdock, 1984), concerted lobbying produced the Video Recordings Act which instituted statutory pre-censorship of all video cassettes intended for public circulation. Pressure was later to lead to the creation of the Broadcasting Standards Council, a new oversight body charged with keeping a watchful eye on matters of taste and decency in television programming. But one major campaign failed. This was the lobby to change the terms of the obscenity law and to apply it to broadcasting as well as to printed matter.

It was against this background of concerted right-wing pressure for greater controls over film and television production that the two programmes were planned and put together. They both set out to interrogate the claims that the New Right were making. I had developed my own critique some time before in a number of publications. My position revolved around two basic arguments. Firstly, that research had not succeeded in establishing a direct causal link between viewing violence and behaving violently in everyday life and that there were particular problems with the studies most often cited in support of this contention. Consequently, if a case was to be made for greater censorship and control it would have to be argued on moral and aesthetic grounds. It could not be supported by appeals to 'science'. Secondly, that the mechanistic forms of censorship being proposed by figures like Hans Eysenck were bound to reduce artistic freedom to an unacceptable degree since they focused solely on the nature and degree of the violence being portrayed and took no account of its role in the development of the narrative or of the authors' intentions.

A colleague and I outlined these arguments in our 1979 article for the British Film Institute's journal, *Screen Education*, which had gained a certain currency within media studies and among the Institute's staff. Consequently, when they set out to collaborate on a series of programmes on television and society, entitled *Open the Box*, I was in their line of sight. As the old adage has it, who you know (or who knows you) is as important as what you know. There is no doubt that personal networks often play a key role in securing access, but they don't necessarily guarantee sympathetic treatment. This will depend on how a contribution fits in with the production team's developing ideas of how the programme should be organized, both argumentatively and visually. These conceptions in turn are shaped by the team's overall position within the organization and the pressures and opportunities that this entails.

Channel 4's remit expressly directs it to provide space for voices and experiences that are underrepresented on the main channels and to develop innovative forms of presentation. This gives programme makers a licence to explore minority viewpoints, including those attacking established orthodoxies, and to experiment with the relations between voices and images. The *Open the Box* team took full advantage of these opportunities. In the case of the programme I was involved in the provocation began with the title, 'Sheer Filth', a phrase taken from a speech that the Conservative Member of Parliament, Winston Churchill, had made supporting a Bill to amend the obscenity law and extend its provisions to television. The programme opened with a voice-over of Churchill putting his basic argument:

> The increase that one has seen in crimes of violence is most disturbing and cannot be separated from the rising tide of obscene and violent material that is thrust before young people and before society as a whole.

The programme aimed to deconstruct and discredit this position. When my participation was first mooted I met with the producer and researchers and talked for some time about how they saw the programme. The fact that their views coincided with my own on a number of key issues led me to think that I had a fighting chance of getting at least some of my points across.

The programme's basic argument – that the links between

violence on the screen and real life violence were problematic and contestable – was incorporated into the way the key location sequence was organized. This was filmed in the back room of a terrace house in South London, with French windows opening onto the garden. The main participants were a professional stunt man and stunt arranger and a special effects expert. They were shown setting up a shooting and talking about their trade. When everything was ready, a woman burst through the French windows and shot the stunt man, spraying fake blood around the room from a series of vivid bullet holes across the chest. Clips of the meticulous process of fabricating violence were interspersed throughout the second half of the programme, leaving the final shooting to provide a dramatic ending and a visual reminder of the programme's basic argument.

This use of images to underscore key points was characteristic of the programme's general presentational style. It assumed that the audience was visually literate and could follow the logic of juxtapositions and overlays without instructions. Accordingly, there was no presenter to link the various segments and no 'voice-of-God' commentary to nudge viewers towards a preferred interpretation.

This technique was used to particular effect in a sequence where I read a passage from *War Without Frontiers*, a thriller co-written by Douglas Hurd. At the time the programme was first transmitted he was Home Secretary with responsibilities for both broadcasting and law and order. He was therefore a particularly appropriate peg on which to hang the argument about the problems of state censorship raised by the proposals to amend the obscenity legislation. Added to which, the chance to puncture his pomposity was irresistible.

The segment began with a close-up of the book's cover with the sentence 'Soon to be a major TV series' clearly visible. This was followed by a sequence of me talking direct to camera

> It's going to be difficult to imagine, if the Bill goes through, how he will handle some of the key scenes in the book. Let me give you this one for example; 'The body was suspended from the chimney pot, blackened and smouldering. Kemble whimpered, swore in terror, grunted four letter words.'

At this point, a still of a newspaper story headed 'Hurd given reassurance on TV violence' appeared on the screen. My reading then resumed: 'Spreading towards him was a river of blood. Her body arched up convulsively then slithered to the floor and lay twitching like a dog in a dream.' This was immediately followed by a still of a press story headed 'Hurd urges clean up' and a clip of Winston Churchill on television condemning Derek Jarman's film *Jubilee* for its excessive violence.

At one level I was pleased with this outcome since I had been able to put one of my main arguments across in a forceful way. But at another level I was uneasy. I had appeared in the room where the stunt men were preparing, and in the final cut clips of me speaking direct to camera were interspersed with sequences of them talking and working. By situating me within the world of the programme team and, by extension, the television professionals, any distance between my position and theirs had been erased.

If 'Sheer Filth' illustrated the temptations of intellectual incorporation, the *Panorama* programme, 'Violence on Television' made nearly two years later, pointed up the dynamics of exclusion. The political context was similar. Debate about the ill effects of screen violence had gained new momentum following the shooting of 16 people in the small town of Hungerford, and the widespread rumours that the assailant, Michael Ryan, had been wearing a headband in the style of Sylvester Stallone's highly successful film hero, Rambo. The government had announced the setting up of the Broadcasting Standards Council, and renewed attempts were being made to amend the obscenity law. Against this background the programme set out to evaluate the evidence of a clear connection between television and violence.

I was approached and decided to participate, mainly because the presenter was to be Kate Adie, a reporter for whose integrity I had the highest respect. It was arranged that we would film an interview at the University. The researcher had originally asked if it would be possible to do the interview in my laboratory. I explained that I didn't have one and that I worked in a rather different way, so we agreed to film in my office. When the camera crew arrived it was evident that my room was far too small and we transferred to a colleague's office. While the crew were setting up and ensuring that I would appear in front of shelves containing the requisite number of impressive looking books and papers, we ran through the questions that Kate Adie had in mind. It was clear that her agenda and mine diverged at a number of points. She was particularly interested in children, a group that I have never worked with, but I was confident that there was sufficient common ground between us to allow me to make most of my main points. The interview went well from my point of view. It was reasonably long and relaxed. I was able to raise what I saw as the key issues and I was confident that at least some of the main points would appear on screen.

When I saw the finished programme I was dismayed and angry. None of my major arguments had survived the editing process. I appeared only once, talking about children, a topic I had been reluctant to be drawn on. On viewing it again two things became clear. Firstly, the programme's argumentative structure left no room for the issues I wished to raise. Secondly, my remarks had not been anchored by a convincing image of authoritative expertise. I presented myself as an 'intellectual' when what the programme's strategy of persuasion called for was a more obviously 'scientific' social researcher.

Mobilizing prevailing conceptions of 'science' was crucial to the programme's ability to convince critics that it had considered all the available evidence and weighed it with due impartiality. This was particularly important given that senior members of the government, including the Prime Minister, had taken a particular interest in the issue of television and violence, and that both *Panorama* and Kate Adie had previously been the target of attacks from the Right, alleging partiality, lack of balance, and anti-Conservative bias.

The programme opened with a 'typical' family, the Bartletts of Birmingham, watching and talking about television, with the mother claiming that in her view there was indeed too much violence on the small screen. She was followed by Paul Johnson, the writer and journalist, who supports her case. He chooses to appeal to the discourse of everyday experience rather than the discourse of scientific expertise claiming that:

> the level of violence on television is far too great and ought to be reduced. Now I cannot prove that because I don't think the research can establish it one way or another. But that is the general impression of the overwhelming majority of ordinary people and I think on this sort of issue, the majority of ordinary people are almost certainly right.

The claims of common-sense thinking are then interrogated through an analysis of the press coverage of the Hungerford shooting and five other major stories. In each case it is revealed that there is no firm proof of influence from television. Having proved common sense unreliable, the programme turns to 'science'. The pivotal sequence begins with Kate Adie asking in voice-over: 'So is there any way of calculating or proving how TV influences the viewer about violence? Is there any conclusive scientific evidence about violence on TV and its effects?'

We first see a row of young people watching television with sensing pads attached to their hands and then cut to a close shot of a needle tracing a pattern on graph paper feeding through a machine. We are clearly in a laboratory, the locus *par excellence* of 'scientific' endeavour. Adie's voice over confirms this: 'Over 500 reports have been produced on the subject and academic research goes on, as here at Aston University, where "guinea pig" viewers are wired up to monitor reactions to screen violence.'

We then cut to an interview with Dr Guy Cumberbatch of Aston, pictured against the background of continuing activity in the laboratory. As anyone familiar with the field would know, Dr Cumberbatch is a trenchant critic of the methods employed in the '500 reports' who views the case for a causal link between television violence and violent behaviour as not proven (Cumberbatch, 1989). Although he begins his interview by emphasizing the inconsistencies and contradictions in the research evidence, his caveats are undermined by the imagery of the laboratory which surrounds him. The sub-text is clear – researchers may not have established conclusive connections yet, but they press on, and if they do succeed it will be thanks to the patient application of the kind of 'scientific' procedures you see here.

Within the emerging, more commercially oriented television system, however, the standard current affairs form typified by *Panorama* is steadily losing ground to the new participatory talk shows. The privileged status accorded to the researcher as 'scientist' or 'intellectual' is much more precarious within these programmes, for two main reasons. Firstly, expert speakers are deprived of the visual props that normally underpin their claims. They share the studio with a 'live' audience and are often members of that audience. This has a levelling effect. Secondly, the populist ethos which informs these programmes accords equal status to discourses of experience. The BBC morning discussion programme, *Day to Day*, is a good example.

In February 1987 I was asked to take part in an edition devoted to the television and violence debate, prompted by a new push from the Moral Right to have the obscenity law amended. Although the invited participants, a cross-section of politicians, lobbyists, researchers and television executives, sat with the general audience we were set apart symbolically by the job titles that appeared at the bottom of the screen whenever we talked to camera. The programme opened with a spokesman for the National Viewers' and Listeners' Association being invited to state the case for an extension of the Obscene Publications Act. I was then asked to comment, captioned as a 'Media researcher', to indicate my expert status. I raised questions about the value of the 'scientific' evidence for direct links he had cited, proposed that it was not sufficiently solid to resolve the question, and argued that issues of censorship had to be decided on moral and aesthetic grounds. Directly I had finished, the compere turned to the studio audience with the words: 'What do the audience feel? We've got a lot of people here who are experts on television. You watch television a great deal. Do you think there's a link?' This immediately undercut any special status I might want to claim for my expertise, grounded in knowledge of the relevant research literature. Within the programme's populist framework it appeared as no more plausible or relevant than the common sense of the regular viewer. We were all equally expert.

As this instance and the others explored in this chapter, show very clearly, when social scientists meet the media what is involved is a collision of professional cultures, each with its own procedures and preferred forms of representation and argument. In order to understand this and be able to work within it, we need to do away once and for all with the 'bucket' theory of mass communications which sees the press and broadcasting as simple containers for moving meaning from the seminar room to the living room, and to see them instead as complexly structured cultural fields on which contests of social and political discourse are continually played out. In short, we need a fuller sociology of the shifting relations between sociological reasoning and popular representation.

Chapter 9

Media representations of psychology: denigration and popularization, or worthy dissemination of knowledge?

Jane Ussher

INTRODUCTION

Consorting with the media should carry a government health warning. Any academic who embarks upon the media circus is treading a perilous tightrope. On the one hand, the media men (sic) – initially flattering, almost seductive, but ultimately scathing and dismissive, desirous of expertise to fill column inches, to fill radio or TV minutes, whilst ultimately despising and deriding. On the other, learned colleagues – questioning the very notion of 'media simplification', ever ready to give examples of the (ex) colleague who had a 'worthy' research record, but spoilt it all (and any chance of the elusive professorial chair) through the cheap peddling of mass-market knowledge, selling their discipline for a handful of silver. To be described as a 'media psychologist' is one of the lowest forms of insult. Sexy simplification may sell newspapers or spice up an otherwise dull Radio 4 documentary, but it is the death knell for a serious academic career. And quite right too we might say – or is it?

As one who has both been bitten and betrayed by media involvement, experienced the (metaphorical) seductions and subsequent rejections of media representatives, yet still continues to have involvement in this potentially dangerous – yet fascinating – game, I am struck most strongly by the question of: Why? Why is it that academics, serious scientists and scholars, experts within their own fields, become involved in the world of the media? Why is it that they risk the approbation of colleagues, endure humiliation, broken promises and evidence of the trivialization of their research and expertise, and yet continue to play the game? Is it a wish for the proverbial 15 minutes of fame (*à la* Warhol), or the more worthy aim of disseminating knowledge to a wider audience? Is the current trend for academics and media representatives entering into an unholy alliance a good one?

These questions have no simple answer, and answers will necessarily be heavily biased by the experiences of the individual addressing them. With that caveat in mind, I will attempt to arrive at a balanced conclusion using my own chequered media confrontations, and the case of psychology in the media, as examples. However, I should say at the outset that even addressing this issue opens up a Pandora's box of complicated relationships, of complicities, and of compromises, which normally appear to remain unspoken. Because of this, I have found this account one of the most difficult things I have ever written. Perhaps it reveals too much, or makes impossible the avoidance of the reality of the iniquitous exchange between academic psychology and the media.

REACHING A WIDE AUDIENCE

The most benign explanation for the current explosion in academic interest in the media is the fact that this public exposure can ensure that academic research reaches a far wider audience than will ever be reached through publication in even the most eminent journal. If research is interesting, or has important applications, should it not be publicized outside the proverbial ivory tower? As research is invariably funded out of the public purse, is there not an argument that the public have a right to the fruits of the hard-won knowledge? Equally, researchers may want to influence policy – and therefore want their research findings publicized. Or they may work within a particular ideological framework, and wish to state their (well-substantiated) views in the media in order to influence public opinion, or to counteract competing ideologies. Those researchers who proffer research which counters sexist or racist assumptions are the most obvious examples.

My own impetus in discussing female sexuality with journalists was partly prompted by the frequent representation in the press of the comments of a male psychologist who espoused very reactionary sociobiological views about female sexuality. He argued, for example, that women were chosen as mates on the basis of their child-rearing potential (wide hips, youth) and implied that men were 'programmed' for promiscuity because of the evolutionary drive to 'implant their seed' in as many women as possible. The opportunity to counter this view with a feminist interpretation of female (and male) sexuality was naturally welcomed.

There is also pressure from individual institutions, and from professional bodies, for a 'high media profile'. Universities employ press officers specifically to raise the profile of the organization, and encourage individual staff to discuss their research with the press. The British Psychological Society (BPS) has a press committee and an active press office, which gives out the names of individual psychologists to any member of the press who telephones, aiming to raise the profile of psychology in the media. They are very successful. Psychology conferences invariably receive excellent media coverage, helped by the professional press releases prepared by the BPS. Psychologists are turned to at every opportunity, their research publicized, or their 'expert comments' reported on a range of matters psychological (and many matters not). Media training is undertaken by many, in order to improve their appearance on television and radio, enabling mastery of the all important soundbite. Psychologists now regularly write for women's magazines, host problem pages, or publicize potted versions of current psychological research. In this vein, psychological knowledge can reach millions.

Equally, perhaps it's obvious what other personal reasons motivate individual academics, or social scientists, to talk to the media. It's clearly not money, for contrary to popular belief, academics are very rarely made rich by media involvement – a radio interview with the BBC will net only between £25–£40, and then only if individuals specifically ask to be paid. It's ego. Individuals can work for years on a piece of scholarship or research and receive little more than a nod of approval at an appraisal meeting, or the grudging acceptance by one's peers of an interesting concept or study – underlined by the comment that it is certainly flawed, of course. Years spent on a piece of work can end with rejection from an academic journal, one's whole *raison d'être* questioned to the core. Or, if published, research may be read by only a handful, if that, the achievement of yet another addition to the ever-scrutinized CV seeming to be the main achievement or purpose.

This bleak, but perhaps not unjust, portrayal of the life of an average academic stands in stark contrast to the potential for reward, praise and dissemination of ideas through the media. One newspaper or magazine quotation or article may be read by millions. One television or radio appearance can reach large tracts of the population. And the irony is, one is far more likely to be taken seriously. How many individuals have found that students, friends or parents believe that their work must be really important (implying that *they* are really important) because it's reported in the papers? Peers may scoff, but Mum and Dad are likely to be impressed. It's a sad indictment of the invisibility of academic study that the achievement of a research degree will be seen as less impressive than a two-inch column in a national newspaper.

But is all this exposure of psychologists and their expertise so unproblematic? It is certainly at a price, both for the individual and potentially for the discipline – a price which perhaps rightly deters many from entering into any dialogue with the media, and which may act to denigrate the profession through popularization.

AIMING AT THE LOWEST COMMON DENOMINATOR

In any media representation of psychology there is inevitably simplification and categorical presentation of argument. There is no room for qualifications or caveats, or for the view that research has not yet reached a final answer on a given subject, if it ever will. The media analysis is short, simple and unequivocal. It is also catchy: potentially subverting a serious research finding into something which appears banal, common sense, and is easily derided.

Research can also be distorted – the expert has no control. For example, I presented a paper at a recent BPS conference on constructions of male and female sexuality (Ussher, 1992a), which received wide media reporting. In a nutshell, the paper examined the influence of dichotomous and derogatory discourses associated with female sexuality on women's identity. Through drawing analogies between academic texts and public pronouncements from the nineteenth century, and extracts from interviews carried out with men and women more recently, it was argued that the sexually active woman has consistently been positioned as 'mad or bad', a positioning which acts both to control women and to condone male sexual violence. Through presenting the results of a recent study on female survivors of sexual abuse, it was argued that many of the beliefs held about female sexuality by non-abusing men were core beliefs of men who sexually abuse children, and therefore that these beliefs were of key concern to those attempting to understand sexual violence towards women. In the media the conference paper was represented thus:

'Women's sex terror for men'
Birmingham Evening Mail, 11 July 1992

'Double standards in sex attacked'
Daily Telegraph, 10 July 1992

'New Man still an old-style sexist'
Guardian, 11 July 1992

'Fast girls make their lovers run off faster'
Daily Express, 13 July 1992

'Scared blokes stick to slag tag'
Sunday Mail, Glasgow, 12 July 1992

Perhaps unsurprisingly I would question whether these 'sexy' headlines were a fair representation of what I would consider a serious topic. They were certainly a gross simplification. And what of the men and women I interviewed on whom the arguments in the conference paper were based? How would they feel on reading the simplified headlines, particularly the men on being uncategorically positioned as 'old-style sexists'? I would be wary about recruiting interviewees in the same location again.

I was intrigued that none of the media reporting examined the issue of sexual abuse, clearly delineated in the press release. It obviously wasn't 'sexy' enough, or perhaps too depressing. I was also disappointed, naïvely probably, that none of my argument concerning the effects of this misogyny on women's sexual identity was reproduced. The discussion of the paper was not only simple, but trite. I was embarrassed that many of my colleagues had seen (and commented upon) it.

SELECTIVE GATEKEEPING

What is illustrated by the above example, and by the reporting of only particular forms of research, or particular views, is the important role the media play as gatekeepers for dissemination of knowledge. Sex sells newspapers, so I shouldn't have been surprised (which I was) by the mass coverage of my recent paper. But it isn't *all* research on sex which is newsworthy. At a previous BPS conference (Ussher, 1989b) I presented a paper on gay and lesbian sexuality, which received not one mention in the press, despite the fact that other papers in the same symposium were reported. Gay and lesbian sex is clearly not an issue deemed to be of concern to the British public. Equally, I have been carrying out research for years on menstruation, and on women's mental health, reporting the results at conferences where press releases have been prepared, and received no press coverage. Perhaps it is because research reporting that there is no evidence for a performance decrement in the premenstrual phase of the cycle (Ussher, 1992b) is not of interest to the press: they prefer the more traditional line that women are victims of their raging hormones, popularized by the likes of Dr Katrina Dalton, who *is* frequently reported. This is obviously frustrating, as one side of a hotly con- tested argument is presented to the public, potentially impacting upon women's attitudes and expectations associated with menstru- ation (see Ussher, 1989a; Nicolson, 1992). A cynical interpretation would be that the media gatekeepers are interested in perpetuating misogynistic assumptions about female psychology. A more innocuous analysis would suggest that no news is bad news: a study reporting *no* changes across the menstrual cycle is just not news, as it is categorized as a non-finding. (The same rule applies in academic journals, where statistically non-significant results are less likely to be published.)

This gatekeeping also acts to ensure that only particular forms of psychological research come to public attention, distorting the very perception of what psychologists do in the public view. Would recent developments in neuro-psychology, memory research, vision, or in language be seen as newsworthy? Colleagues who work in such areas don't report being hounded by the media in the same way as those working in areas such as the psychology of women or sexuality. Yet some would argue that these are areas of leading- edge research which deserve more prominence. Is it that those working in this type of experimental research are less able (or willing) to make the gross generalizations the media require? Or that their work is less easily trivialized, less able to be reduced to the level of gross simplification? Perhaps this public (mis)perception of psychology (as not a science) is irrelevant. It is only the successive years of undergraduates who flock to study psychology in the hope of understanding 'what makes people tick' who feel short-changed by such misrepresentations.

This issue of 'gatekeeping' is more commonly discussed in relation to the role academic journals play in selecting research to be published (Harding, 1986) or the role those developing curricula for undergraduate teaching or professional training play in defining the discipline (Ussher, 1992c). Yet the media are clearly of equal importance as gatekeepers of research and determinants of which research influences policy. For as Barbara Tizard has argued:

> For central and local authority policy makers, the educational supplements, but more important the quality press and the media generally, are probably the main gateways. The researcher whose ideas do not pass through these gateways has little chance of making an impact. (Tizard, 1990, p. 438)

Research which confirms the current zeitgeist will be reported; that which does not will be ignored (Kitzinger, 1990; Tizard, 1990). Tizard offers as an example of this the promulgation of research which supported the notion that pre-school education had beneficial effects, and the complete marginalization of research that suggested a more complicated association between positive benefits and type of nursery, as the latter did not conform to the ideology of the day – that pre-school education was unequivocally good. So academics may actively wish to promote their research to a wider audience, but find that they have no takers.

This selective gatekeeping also operates in the selection and editing of 'expert comments', where psychologists (amongst others) are not reporting upon their own research but commenting on events of the day, or on other research findings. The most common form of academic involvement with the media, it is probably also the most questionable.

'TOP PSYCHOLOGIST SAYS'

Journalists wishing to support a particular line, or wishing to pad out a story, turn to the experts. Selecting from a carefully elucidated argument, juxtaposing it with the comments of others, it is easy to find instances of 'top psychologists' making banal comments in the national dailies. Yet as with research, only the comments that agree with the current 'party line' will be printed. I was once telephoned by a national tabloid on the subject of a survey on date rape which suggested that a high percentage of female students had experienced rape or attempted rape. I strongly agreed with the findings, arguing that previous research certainly supported this claim. However, the journalist who talked to me said that she knew that she wouldn't be able to use my comments as the (male) newsdesk wanted an 'expert' to disconfirm the findings, not support them. They clearly didn't want to publicize anything which deviated from the line that rapists are deviant monsters, and that rape is an unusual act that happens to women out alone in the dark – not an action of a man who knows the woman (as is the case with over 70 per cent of rapes). So the story never ran.

But the converse can also happen, as being quoted in the newspapers can have a snowball effect. As news is rarely new, and invariably recycled, radio and TV stations, newspaper and magazine offices are filled with individuals scouring the previous day's or week's newspapers and magazines for worthy snippets to fill the airwaves or empty columns. PR companies are paid a fortune to both create and peddle 'news', hoping that a finding quoted once will set off the media circus. A brief quotation in a national newspaper can lead to repeated requests for interviews and comments: a queen for a day!

But if there was any risk of the sudden fame resulting in an over-inflated ego, there is another side to this. Being positioned in the media archives as an expert on a given topic can be the cause of endless phone calls on topics ranging from the sublime to the ridiculous. As an expert on 'psychology of women', recent requests for quotations included: 'Why did Fergie have her hair cut?', 'How can we cope with the office Christmas party', 'Why do women wear sexy underwear?', 'Why do women shave their legs?'. I hasten to add that I declined to comment – but it isn't always easy to do so. Journalists are clearly trained very effectively in extracting information, and will not always give up easily, particularly if they are on their tenth (or more) phone call on the same subject. Sometimes there is an acknowledgement that the topic in question is ridiculous, and an admission that the request for a comment is insulting. A recent encounter involved a serious request for a psychological analysis of the reported 'craze for toe sucking in sex', which I greeted with incredulity and laughter. The journalist laughed too, and admitted she felt embarrassed asking anyone for a serious discussion of the subject. What would she have thought had I addressed the issue? Whilst I am loath to admit it, in the past when asked to comment on similarly ridiculous (and completely unpsychological) subjects, I (naïvely) have.

The salutary lesson was learning that both the professional body to which I belong, the British Psychological Society, and the university in which I work, collect all press cuttings of members. So an off-the-cuff comment on the weighty subject of whether Charles and Di will ever reconcile their marriage (which I *didn't* do) will almost certainly be read by both professional colleagues and employers. The advice meted out by the Director of Information of the BPS, Stephen White, to imagine your academic colleagues sitting in the room when you partake in a media interview, is clearly one of the most important pieces of advice that can be given. Cringing at the thought of colleagues reading comments made to those in the media clearly means they shouldn't have been made.

DERIDING THE EXPERT

The initial experience of engaging with media representatives is not entirely unpleasant. The initial contact is always polite, flattering, bordering on the obsequious at times. Journalists phoning for an 'expert comment' will be civil, almost deferential, and never disagree. If television is involved no expenses are spared in the seduction. First-class train fares paid, taxi from door to door, overnight stays in expensive hotels, effusive greetings on arrival at the studio. Compared with the drabness and penury of today's academic world, it can feel exciting and breed a false sense of self-importance.

But afterwards, it changes. The deferential journalists will quote out of context, or discard your carefully chosen words into the bin. (Or alternatively, make up their own: I was once quoted in a woman's magazine commenting on a female phobia of which I'd never even heard.) Following the TV appearance, no taxi home, no flattering comments or confidences. A hurried handshake in thanks is hard won. Once the slot has been filled, the expert is no longer needed, and is discarded without thought or care. It is a testimony to the deep desire to appear on the flickering screen or in the newspaper pages that the same said experts will put themselves through the humiliation time and time again. If they refuse, there is always a ready and willing supply of 'top psychologists' waiting to fill the spot.

The experience of TV in itself can be an exquisite form of humiliation.[1] The audience participation chat show, such as *Kilroy!* or *The Time the Place*[2] is the worst. The expert is set up. The people are there to deride and decry the very notion of expert opinion. Personal experiences are held up as evidence of a given theory, a given view, and if the expert attempts to put forward a view based on any form of meta-knowledge, a view based on research or theory, they are laughed out of court. For example, I once appeared on *Kilroy!*, discussing the subject of working mothers. My argument, for which I was specifically invited, was that there was no research evidence that women would cause any harm to their children by working outside the home and using nursery facilities, and that in fact the research suggested that employment was a major factor which protected women against depression. Uncontroversial perhaps – but no. I was faced with an audience made up mainly of mothers who did not work in paid employment outside the home, and who presented a united and morally righteous front. (I was also faced with the Nolan sisters.) In this arena I put forward my argument, and was derided with laughs and jeers. I was asked repeatedly whether I had children, and when I replied that my argument was based not on my own experience, but on research, laughter was the reply.

What is happening here?[3] The very function of the expert is to provide a foil for the more 'real' views of the audience, the representatives of the public. The power is certainly to the people. And whilst I felt I did not let the (academic) side down, and have appeared on a number of such programmes in the past, the experience was both humiliating and degrading, and could not be recommended to anyone. In addition, in being pitted against the public, invariably women, it directly undermined one of the basic premises of my academic research: that it is feminist, and thus working *for* women, and that subjective experience is valid and legitimate. Any illusions I might have had as to the worthiness of my pronouncements on topics as diverse as the validity of premenstrual stress (PMS) as a syndrome, the difficulties of working mothers, or the potential damage inherent in representing women as naked pin-ups in the media (topics I have been invited to make 'expert' comment on) were quickly shattered by the complete rejection of my comments by large sections of the studio audience. Whilst I wouldn't take part in these programmes again, it was a salutary lesson, and one I have certainly learned from. I'm much more wary about adopting a pious position through making claims about the value of feminist research in serving women's needs.

FALSE FLATTERY

But the media representatives themselves are often no better. Whilst the flattery wears thin, and disappears after the moment of use is over, it rarely erupts into the aggression or outright derision experienced in the television audience participation situation. At least not in a direct face-to-face confrontation. Yet the existence of what can only be described as open contempt on the part of certain media representatives towards 'experts' was made patently clear when I worked on the other side of the fence, carrying out interviews with fellow psychologists and members of the public for a BBC radio series. Any illusions I might have harboured about media respect for academics, or acknowledgement of hard-earned learning, were wiped out. Psychologists who frequently consorted with the media were referred to as 'media tarts' – by the self-same individuals who would phone them for a quotation or a last-minute appearance to fill a radio slot. Individual psychologists (and psychiatrists) were described as 'full of waffle', 'inefficient', or 'bullshit merchants', then turned to the next day and unashamedly asked to take part in a programme. Pleasure seemed to be gained from deliberately leaving an individual waiting for the powerful producer to decide whether or not he or she would be used. One person was contemptuously described as 'hanging on by his finger nails' as the producer prevaricated about his continuation as a regular on the series. He was eventually dropped.

Those interviewed were hardly treated any better – but were never heard to complain. Interviews were set up to support a particular argument, and a well-meaning psychologist asked to expound upon her or his views with the foreknowledge (of the producer) that only one fiftieth of what they said would be used. I felt uncomfortable at colluding in this process through encouraging discussion of issues I knew were never going to be used, and indirectly deceiving my colleagues. One individual agreed to be interviewed on her current book, but was going to be broadcast speaking only about a previous piece of research which was the focus of the particular programme. She gave a long interview, made a couple of asides about the previous work, and only the latter comments were used. Equally, a carefully prepared for interview fitting into an overall rationale for a series may be discarded at a moment's notice – regardless of status, or effort involved in taking part in the interview. I persuaded colleagues to give up their time (unpaid) and go though the nerve-racking experience of talking on the radio to find that their interviews were rejected, without explanation. In one case I interviewed a clinical psychologist working in the area of AIDS, and a man whose partner had died of AIDS and, without explanation, the interview was not used. One rejected interview was with an eminent psychology professor, whom I shall be extremely embarrassed to face when I next bump into him at a conference.

This last-minute chopping and changing and rejection is a common occurrence. My own protestations at the iniquity of the situation were met with disdain, if not outright hostility. How dare the media master be challenged by a mere (female) psychologist, inexperienced in such matters? Perhaps this is why 'experts' whose interviews are rejected in this way don't complain, why we don't hear of such common occurrences. Individuals assume it is their own personal failings which determine their rejection – not the whim of a distant media man (sic). Why broadcast our failures to our colleagues; keep quiet and forget the whole sorry episode. My own complicity in this charade left more than a bad taste in the mouth. The openness with which the ploys were discussed before the interviews made me more determined to be wary when I was next on the other side of the fence, being interviewed rather than being the devious interviewer. There is clearly a belief that being given air space, or mentions in a newspaper, is so flattering that any liberties can be taken. Perhaps we deserve it, for we both partake as an audience and, if asked, will engage in the humiliating ritual.

The same disdain was also applied to myself, liberally. Putting aside the fact that I was expected to drop all other commitments and put 'the programme' first (regardless of my having a full-time job), the fact that the agenda was continuously changing, that I was expected to know how to interview on radio, how to write and prepare links without any advice or instruction, the derogatory nature of the whole experience is best exemplified through a description of an incident where a programme was being finally put together and recorded.

Picture the scene: I am sitting in a studio alone, with a series of microphones, and a script. Through a glass screen are four men: two producers, two engineers. They can hear me, I can't hear them – an interesting power imbalance. My job is to read out linking comments which are juxtaposed – with split second timing – with snippets from the interviews I have been doing. Ninety minutes after I should have been being recorded, I am still sitting in the studio. That I have other arrangements is clearly irrelevant (a row with waiting friends was the end result). During this period, whilst my own anxiety mounts, and I console myself by deciding that this could be a scene in a training video concerned with how *not* to treat people you want to perform well for you, I can periodically see the four men laughing raucously and visibly making comments in my direction. Wondering if I am developing paranoia, and asking myself what on earth I was putting myself through this charade for, I felt both vulnerable and ridiculous. If I had any delusions about my credibility or status as a serious academic, they were being rapidly eroded.

When my moment finally came, I was told to read my links, and could see a row developing through the screen. There was disagreement about my intonation. I was made to read the first line again, with different emphasis on particular words. Then the second producer intervened, and I read the same line, again, going back to the original intonation. By this time I had almost forgotten how to speak, and felt both stupid, incompetent and wholly inadequate. When I was released from the ordeal an hour later I vowed that this would be my last dealings with the media. I'm afraid to say I've gone back on my word.

WHY?

Why academics are vulnerable to such derision within the media is perhaps a more interesting question than why they want to appear. One hypothesis is that journalists are treated to such simplistic analysis of issues, or to academic arrogance, that they feel that their intelligence is being insulted. It is certainly the case that many academics will treat a media request with hostility or arrogant dismissal. Or perhaps it is the very reliance of the media enterprise on experts which breeds resentment and encourages misrepresentation of views or outright rudeness, particularly if the same journalist feels that he or she could represent a given topic more accurately, or intelligently – and certainly more quickly than the ponderous academic. It may simply be the contempt for learning endemic in Britain in the 1990s, juxtaposed with the power of the media which can topple cabinet ministers and determine the outcome of general elections. Psychologists are smallfry in relation to these wider powers members of the media appear to have attained. Is it any wonder we are used and abused without regret?

CONCLUSION

In summary, dealing with the media is beset with pitfalls and potential punishment – both from unsympathetic colleagues, and from representatives of the media themselves. It is questionable whether the media is an elusive creature to be courted, each media approach or appearance a further notch on the proverbial bedstead of expert-academic achievement, individual recognition within the media as a reflection of great knowledge or importance; or conversely whether it is an exemplar of all that is bad about popularized intelligence, agents of the media uniformly to be mistrusted as charlatans out to trick or to trivialize. The truth, if such a concept is allowed in this post-modernist age, is probably somewhere in between.

The risk is clearly that individuals – or even the whole discipline – will be misrepresented and misused, that psychology (or any other discipline for that matter) and the individual psychologist are positioned as trite and trivial. One potential benefit is wider dissemination of psychological knowledge: good journalism or serious broadcasting can do much to translate difficult psychological concepts into a language accessible to the lay person. This inevitably leads to a raising of the public profile of the profession. For the individual, the benefits include a short-lived ego trip. Whether these are worthy aims is a question open to debate. But what is patently clear is that any involvement with the media entails a potentially pernicious exchange, where the 'expert' has most to lose, and those in the media have everything to gain. Is the prediction for the future that psychologists who engage with the media will of necessity develop the skills now displayed by politicians, where every question is met with the same, set, answer, and the media is used as a PR tool? Or will we retreat to the ivory tower, and satisfy ourselves with dissemination of knowledge through academic channels, where simplification is not an issue? I know which route I would choose.

NOTES

1 I must thank Sonia Livingstone for bringing many of these issues to my attention in discussions for her book *Talk on Television: Audience*

Participation and Public Debate (Livingstone, S. and Lunt. P., in press). Having been interviewed for the book, I became aware of the degrading process I had willingly engaged in.

2 Experts are placed within the audience, which consists of a group of invited individuals who have a view on a subject, and other members of the public invited because of the location of the programme. The experts can speak only by putting up their hand, along with any other member of the audience, and therefore have no privileged position. However, they may be called upon at any moment by the host to give their view, and are thus in a more vulnerable position than other members of the audience.

3 See Livingstone and Lunt, (in press) for an analysis of the use of the expert in audience participation programmes.

Chapter 10

Contributing to broadcast news analysis and current affairs documentaries: challenges and pitfalls

Paul Wilkinson

In the most obvious sense, most social scientists meet the media every day of their working lives. In order to study any aspect of social behaviour adequately, whether it be the role of the family, trends in organized crime, industrial relations, or the work of international organizations and national governments in attempting to resolve international disputes, scholars need a plentiful supply of information in a clear and readily accessible form from sources which can be readily checked and corroborated. Many social scientists are reluctant to admit that they rely at least to some extent on media sources for this kind of information. Why should this be so?

One fundamental reason is a form of guilt-complex. Unlike historians, who readily utilize contemporary media sources whenever they are available, in the course of their research, and make no secret of the fact, some social scientists apparently believe that their purity as scientific investigators will be lost if they expose themselves to the contaminating effects of reviewing and evaluating materials from the printed and electronic media.

Some of the academics' contempt for the mass media and the journalistic professions may seem well merited, especially if one has in mind the British tabloids with their notoriously prurient and sensational characteristics. But it would be grossly unfair to stereotype the entire British print and electronic media on this picture of the tabloids. There are print media of high quality, including daily journals of record such *The Times*, the *Guardian*, the *New York Times* and the *Washington Post*, which have a well-earned reputation for accuracy and integrity in the reporting of events and for balance, responsibility and rigour in editorial analysis. Similar variations in the quality of electronic media coverage can also be observed. It would clearly be folly for social scientists to disdain media sources in general on the grounds that the worst of the mass media are at worst sensational and pornographic and at best highly unreliable and ill-informed.

Some academics undervalue the media as an information source because of their woeful ignorance of the way in which media organizations actually function. It is too easily assumed that even the quality newspapers are disinterested over their own performance in the matter of accurate reporting, or that the newspapers simply recycle reports from their rivals and from the news agencies. This entirely overlooks the fact that in pluralistic open societies with free media there is intense competition among the printed and electronic media. High-quality journals of record will, by definition, take considerable care to investigate all their stories thoroughly before publication and will take great pride in getting the facts right and in exposing the inaccuracies of rivals. Moreover, there are the huge pressures of the market. Readers are unlikely to continue buying a newspaper of record which is consistently found to be full of factual inaccuracies, and a journal which is unable to sell sufficient copies will eventually founder.

It is also alleged that media sources are too corrupted by bias to make them of any value to the social scientist. But the truth is that all kinds of sources used by social scientists are affected by bias: interviews by bias of both interviewer and interviewee; opinion polls by the bias of those polled and those designing or administering the questionnaire; participant observation by the beliefs, attitudes and values of the observer, etc. Memoirs and biographies, essential sources on the careers and personalities of key individuals involved in politics, administration and the key professions, are notoriously coloured by bias. Academic books and journal articles, though generally eschewing political party bias, often display bias in favour of particular theories, schools of thought and selected works in their field. It is realistic to accept that some degree of value-impregnation and bias is inescapable in the whole spectrum of literature on social behaviour. But if we face up to this and learn to recognize the value preferences, judgements and biases of our sources this can actually enrich our understanding; it certainly does not mean we can afford a wholesale dismissal of the sources. The important thing is, as far as media sources are concerned, to learn to distinguish between editorial comments and *opinion* on events and issues and the factual content of media reports which can be objectively validated, e.g. did such an event occur? If so, when and where? Who was involved? Precisely what happened? What did participants/eye-witnesses actually say about the event? etc. etc.

The quality media in democracies generally handle this distinction with a fair degree of professionalism and rigour. It is hence a relatively straightforward matter for the experienced and alert reader to distinguish between basic factual reporting and editorial opinion. Not surprisingly, there is generally a very high degree of convergence on basic factual matters among journals of record. For the social scientists, therefore, often the greatest interest in comparing media coverage of the same issues and events is to identify and analyse the very diverse opinions and editorial judgements expressed on the same event/issue within the pages of rival media, or even, on occasion, in the pages of the same newspaper. Bias of all kinds, far from being a reason for discarding media sources, should be recognized as crucial data for the social scientist in its own right and therefore an added reason for using media sources extensively.

Last but not least, the social scientist often discounts media sources for reasons of expediency. Searching the media sources, particularly on national and international events and issues, is a huge, time-consuming and expensive task. It is a sad fact that research libraries in universities and institutes, even in the wealthier countries, have been so constrained by smaller library budgets that many have reduced their holdings of journals of record. Even specialist libraries such as the Chatham House (Royal Institute of International Affairs) Library press-clippings service have been drastically reduced. Very few departments of politics and international relations possess major press archives, and few have the resources to employ staff, albeit on a part-time or temporary basis, to maintain a press-clippings library, even in major fields of research interest within the Department. Most universities, however, do now have facilities for taping electronic media items for research purposes.

At this most basic level social scientists need to meet the media frequently enough to monitor their reportage and comment relating to their field of research. This should involve as wide a spectrum of appropriate publications and electronic media productions as possible to ensure a balanced and comprehensive picture of the relevant coverage. If academics do not have the advantage of this regular reconnaissance and assessment of the media sources they are likely to be severely disadvantaged in personal encounters with media professionals, through their lack of awareness of the style and quality of the various individual media sources and of their weaknesses and strengths in the academic's particular field of interest.

It is easy enough to carp at weaknesses in the coverage of particular printed media. Bias, inaccuracy and unreliability are all too evident in some publications, even the major broadsheets. It is also a frustrating feature of even the high-quality media that they do not adopt the apparatus of citations and sources customary in academic books. Frequently they appear to depend heavily on anonymous sources, sometimes on information which has been obtained by dubious or even illegal methods. However, as argued above, media sources are by no means unique in having major disadvantages.

The rigorous social scientist will be aware of these weaknesses and of the danger of depending exclusively on media sources. On the other hand, social scientists are foolish to ignore or neglect the media or to treat all media sources with a kind of ivory-tower disdain. In many fields of social scientific enquiry there is simply no real substitute for the media as a source of basic information about numerous events, statements, comments and trends which are simply not made known by any other means. This is as true for economists studying trends in Stock Market prices and trading and criminologists researching sentencing trends as it is for political scientists studying the behaviour of political parties and elections.

The author's own field of research has been international terrorism and the international community's responses to terrorism. He vividly recalls an occasion at a major international simulation in the Middle East of an airliner hijack in which a leading American participant learned about the importance of the media the hard way. As chairman of the US government team for the purpose of the simulation he was supposed to be guiding his colleagues to a decision as to the next step, following a hijack of a US airliner by a Middle Eastern terrorist group. Each team involved had the world media coverage beamed to them via a loudspeaker system. The US team chairman became annoyed at the constant sniping of the international media, complaining of US 'inactivity' over the hijack. After 30 minutes he got so irritated that he ordered that the loudspeaker 'broadcasting' the news be disconnected. As a result he missed the key fact that three US passengers had been killed, and this was the *only* source of this information. Not surprisingly, the USA team lost control of the crisis completely. Often the news media are first with key items of news. Often they are the *only* source of key news information. Social scientists underrate the role of the media as a basic information source at their peril.

Yet recognition of the relevance and value of media sources in many fields of inquiry into social behaviour does not mean that well-trained social scientists and historians rely solely on such sources. For example, the trained academic criminologist brings to his/her research a detailed knowledge of the relevant scholarly literature, including the products of the latest research, together with other invaluable assets, such as experience of field work, survey material, archival knowledge, historical, political and cultural knowledge, etc. which can be matched by only a tiny minority of exceptionally highly qualified specialist freelance writers and media professionals, individuals who often combine professional academic work with part-time work in the media. It would be a great mistake to expect even the more experienced journalists designated 'special correspondents' on particular countries/ topics to be equipped with the same kind of range and depth of knowledge. Most have not been trained to do anything other than be efficient journalists, competent no doubt at reporting events accurately and providing daily or weekly updates, but largely ill-equipped to provide longer-range analysis and authoritative historical interpretation. To cite an example, it was one thing to write reports on the contents of the START 2 Treaty signed in Moscow in January 1993, but quite another to assess its significance in contemporary international history and the future of American–Russian relations. It is foolish to complain about this: professional news reporters have no more wish to provide academic theories and conference papers and monographs than scholars wish to write daily news coverage.

Many of the misunderstandings regarding the relationship between social scientists and the media stem from a failure to understand the crucial difference between the professions involved. Undoubtedly the professional ethics of both Academia and the media have in common a dedication to professional objectivity and factual accuracy. But beyond this there are significant differences. Journalists are expected by their employers to capture attention, to boost circulation and to amuse, titillate and entertain. Scholars, on the other hand, are committed to the acquisition of knowledge for its own sake, to the formulation and testing of new hypotheses and the development of fresh models and theories which are the vital stepping stones for the advancement of science.

'"COME INTO MY PARLOUR" SAID THE SPIDER TO THE FLY . . .'

If the above gives a broad picture of the way in which most social scientists encounter the media most of the time, we must now consider the somewhat smaller but significant number of social scientists who meet the media at closer quarters by accepting the invitation to contribute. It is important to consider any such request with great care, reflecting on the disadvantages and risks involved as well as the advantages. Involvement with the media can be intensely frustrating, time-consuming and disruptive, even destructive of good academic work. Many university vice-chancellors and heads of department positively encourage their colleagues to contribute to the media, believing that such publicity will be likely to benefit the university. But it is wholly misguided to pressurize or browbeat scholars into entering the alien world of the media. There is no evidence whatever that media participation significantly enhances the bulk of the universities' two major tasks, research and teaching. True academic reputations cannot be created by media puffs. Many academics may not fully appreciate the risks involved. The media have their own agenda. They will not be unduly worried about taking an academic comment out of context and exploiting it for their own purposes, sensationalizing snatches of an interview, or manipulating statements made to the print media or electronic media to create their own stereotypes and media myths.

Young social scientists unfamiliar with the workings of the media may not appreciate that the media are not a suitable vehicle for complex theoretical and technical debate. Broadcasters usually want brief 'soundbites' to explain relatively basic ideas of developments to a popular audience, lending the weight of their academic authority. In one sense this is a challenge to the academic's powers of concise, clear exposition to a popular audience. It is hard to deny that much of this work is very boring and often banal. It is certainly not what social scientists are trained for. Why should they

be? The truth is that only a minority of social scientists have both
the taste and the talent for this type of work. Their contribution is
neither more or less valuable than that of those specially gifted at,
say, research administration and the securing of research grants. It
should be regarded as just one element of the distribution of
auxiliary tasks among Academia. Those who affect to despise colleagues who contribute effectively to the media are often simply
expressing their snobbery towards the media, or sour grapes, and
this is clearly very silly. But it is equally foolish to pretend that
media skills should be especially highly rewarded or the key
criteria for academic promotion.

KNOWING THE 'RULES OF ENGAGEMENT'

Ironically it is highly doubtful whether the social scientist considering contributing to the media will find much helpful information
in the literature of media sociology. Much of this literature has
been compiled by sociologists of the neo-Marxist school preoccu-
pied with the idea that the media are instruments of ideological
control in the hands of the ruling class, and that most academics
who contribute regularly to the media are part of this instrument
of ideological manipulation and repression, 'articulating the
official perspective'.[1]

Few of these media sociologists appear to have any working
knowledge of the way in which the complex organizations and
processes of media production actually operate. As the media
themselves do not offer any guidelines for academic contributions
it may be helpful to the social scientist who may read this if the
author tries to distil from his own experience some of the basic
'rules of engagement' that should be borne in mind:

1 Preserve your academic independence at all times. Your value as
  a contributor lies precisely in your independence from vested
  interests and in your academic knowledge and objectivity. Governments, corporations, political parties and other powerful
  interests all have spokespersons and substantial programmes of
  public information. The media can generally get quotations or
  interviews from such sources without difficulty.

2 Be prepared to stand the heat of controversy. When I was
  invited to give an expert opinion on the security implications of
  the Air India airlines bombing in 1985, when 329 lives were lost,

I criticized the airport security authorities in Canada and the airline for the laxity of their procedures. There was only polite interest when I made these comments on BBC radio and TV. But when I gave a strong critique of British, American and German aviation security in the wake of Lockerbie it attracted wide attention and heated debate. In the following 18 months media interest was revived and intensified by the testimony at the Fatal Accident Inquiry into Lockerbie, where I was the only independent witness on aviation terrorism and security called by members of the Lockerbie families group. The resulting international media interest was often extremely wearing and intrusive. I well recall my wife being telephoned in the early hours of the morning by an Australian radio station. 'Hello, its Sydney here', said the voice. 'But we don't know a Sidney' said my wife, still half asleep. Academics who contribute to public debate on matters of international media interest need to face the fact that they will be placing an additional burden on their families and colleagues as well as themselves.

3 Make sure that your media editors/interviewers tell the public who you are and what you do. It may seem too obvious to need stating, but you do need to ensure that your name, institution affiliation, academic position and discipline are stated correctly in the programme/newspaper in which your contribution appears. The fact is that the media get these details wrong on countless occasions.

4 It is also important to ensure that your media editors/ interviewers know your precise area of expertise. Try to ensure that you are not asked to contribute on matters outside your field of specialism. If this does happen in, say, a live broadcast interview, immediately point out that your own expertise is not appropriate for the matter raised. If your advice is sought by the media organizations on a matter outside your specialism, advise them to get in touch with an appropriate specialist.

5 There is a special category of broadcast programmes to which this strict requirement obviously cannot apply. If you accept an invitation to contribute to a panel discussion on issues of the day, such as BBC Radio 4's *Any Questions* or Radio Scotland's *Headlines*, make sure that you clarify the basis of your participation before the programme. If you have been invited to

contribute a particular viewpoint or political party perspective this should have been properly agreed in advance. Some media people have a tendency to pigeon-hole contributors into right and left categories. If you want to appear simply as an independent contributor make this clear to the producer at the outset, and do not allow yourself to be 'typecast' by an ill-informed or presumptuous presenter. Independent-minded academics can make a useful contribution by challenging standard nostrums of the major political parties. Certainly most of the audience seem to appreciate a change from the usual party mudslinging! But some members of the public have become so used to dreary Conservative versus Labour routines that they cannot escape the mental stereotypes. Following an appearance on *Any Questions* when I had critized a number of government policies in the course of the debate, I was astonished to be assailed as 'a socialist' by a member of the audience. Friends of mine who belong to the Labour Party were very amused. It is hard to escape the stifling Manichean two-party tyranny of much British public debate on social and economic issues.

6 If you are not familiar with the publication/programme seeking your assistance it is a good idea to check it out. Find out what you can about its reputation for quality, accuracy, reliability, etc.[2] It is important to be sure that the media opportunity being offered to you is worth accepting. It would be professionally damaging for you to become involved with a shoddy, corrupt or manipulated media organization. On the other hand, there are media organizations with which it is a sheer pleasure to work. There are many broadcasting stations which produce balanced and interesting programmes on quite low budgets and which show unfailing courtesy and professionalism in the way they deal with contributors. I recall how, in the middle of a live telephone interview with Angela Rippon on LBC several years ago, my labrador let out a deafening bark. Showing great presence of mind, Angela Rippon said 'I hear you have your own built-in security!' and calmly went on to the next well-aimed question. *That* is professionalism.

Over the years I have also gained a great respect for the American quality newspapers' standards of accuracy and the skilful and rigorous way in which they use specialist knowledge. Newspapers like the *International Herald Tribune* and the *Wall*

Street Journal set a very high standard in international coverage. I have never once found them to be inaccurate or unfair in their record of interviews I have given. They are also genuinely interested in the free expression of opinion. Alas, the same cannot always be said for some of the major European newspapers. On one occasion before the collapse of the former Soviet Union, a leading West German newspaper refused to print an article commissioned from me on the grounds that it might give offence to the Soviet leadership, because it advocated that Mr Gorbachev and his colleagues adopt the commonwealth model in relations between Russia and the other republics. It is important to know when to say 'No'.

7 Social scientists dealing with the media for the first time should also be vigilant in avoiding any statement that could conceivably fall foul of the law. Avoid comment that might be the subject of a libel action. Always remember to refrain from commenting on a matter which is *sub judice*, i.e. the subject of pending or ongoing legal proceedings.

8 It is always a good idea to be thoroughly well briefed on the *format* of any broadcast programme to which you are due to contribute. It is relatively easy to familiarize yourself with the format of the quality print media. If you are asked to provide a 700 word article for the *Guardian* for a particular section you know how and where it will appear. In the case of a broadcast programme matters may be more murky. Is the programme to be pre-recorded or live? If you do a pre-recorded interview will it be used in full, in edited form, or as part of a 'collage' of comments? How much time is being allotted relative to other contributors? If it is a discussion, are all the panellists to be in the same studio? Who will be the other participants? Who will chair the discussion? Will there be a live audience? Is there a 'phone-in' involved?

9 Last but not least, beware of placing absolute trust in media personnel. Do not be taken in by the 'matey', informal Christian-names style of media people. The media world is an even more ruthless competitive jungle than Academia. Media people are subject to pressures of ambition, commercial greed, and *sometimes* (though rarely) the political machinations of outside interests or colleagues. Do not entrust media people you hardly

know with confidential or sensitive information 'off the record'. Many modern media people regard 'off the record' as a signal to publish. Media big shots are quite ready to throw you to the wolves if backing you as a specialist contributor becomes inconvenient for them.

I would conclude by suggesting that if these basic rules of engagement are followed the social scientist will be able to meet the media on his/her own terms and retain academic integrity. However, it is easier to enunciate these general guidelines than it is to follow them strictly. The social scientist needs to be mentally alert and vigilant in all dealings with the media jungle. As in all forms of jungle combat, if you get tired and careless over basic matters of self-preservation you may be lost without trace. Good luck! You will need it.

NOTES

1 For examples of this genre see: Philip Schlesinger (1978); Peter Golding and Philip Elliott (1979); Stan Cohen and Jock Young (eds) (1973).
2 The quickest way of gaining information of this kind is to request a copy of the journal (or tape of the programme) for which your contribution is requested before deciding whether to accept the invitation.

Part II

The media

Chapter 11

Productive partners – the view from radio

Peter Evans

There are at least three reasons why social scientists should be aware of how the media work. The first is academic. Media communication is itself a thriving and productive branch of social and behavioural science. The second reason is pragmatic. By knowing more about how the media operate – the editorial processes involved in translating the output of research into programme material – the individual social scientist or department is better placed to make a media impact, if that is desirable. That brings us to the third reason, an economic one. It is now obvious to all but the most recalcitrant ostriches that media attention is worth having. It raises the profile of a department in a cost-conscious competitive milieu. It enhances the marketability of a discipline by telling the world that this or that research is a Good Thing.[1]

On the other hand, there is, in the folklore of Academia, a persistent media nightmare which runs something along these lines. A bright young researcher in, let us say, the aetiology and control of riotous crowd behaviour is one day sitting in her office planning a conference paper when a telephone call comes from a local radio station. At the other end is someone called Suzy who works on a morning programme with a DJ called Steve and they would both dearly love our researcher – Dr X – to contribute to the programme. Tomorrow morning. Surprised, flattered and intrigued that the local radio audience of this small university town should be interested in the dynamics of dangerous crowds, Dr X agrees. The next morning she finds herself in the radio studio reception where Suzy says: 'Nice of you to come. Steve knows all about you. He's very nice and intelligent. Nothing to worry about. By the way, do you have any expenses?'

Within ten minutes Dr X is behind a microphone and in front

of Steve, her head full of data, hypotheses, concepts and research possibilities related to her specialism. She is, in short, ready. But is she? Steve, it seems, is that morning basing his music and interview mixture not so much on the expected theme of crowd control in general but on football hooliganism in particular. What is more Dr X is not his only guest. There is also the manager of the local football team who, it quickly transpires, is in truculent mood, anxious to dispel any thoughts that anyone might have that his supporters are unduly violent or that his team sets a bad example.

Within minutes a clash of wills ensues, putting the hapless Dr X in a classic No Win nexus of trying to defend opinions that she really does not endorse against an 'adversary' who holds all the cards – namely the sympathy of the presenter and his audience. The opportunity to air some interesting new research degenerates into a nightmare of embarrassment. As she leaves the studio Dr X has in her head two words: 'Never again'.

To what extent is this fictitious example representative of how radio might treat the social scientist? In order to answer this question it is necessary first to define 'radio' here.

There is in the UK a plethora of radio outlets – national, regional and local. The BBC has one network while the independent sector – which is financed by advertising revenue – has another, confined to a series of geographical regions or towns.[2] Across this thriving buzz of stations and programmes there is considerable variation in tone, level and ambition in the material broadcast.

The BBC for example regularly delivers high-level talk and analysis on science, medicine, the arts, economics, current affairs and many special interests. Often the producers and participants in such programmes combine general broadcasting skills with specialized knowledge of their subject areas. The BBC Radio Science Unit for example – which produces *Science Now, Medicine Now, The Parts, Blue Skies, Science Friction, Formula 5* and many *ad hoc* documentaries for Radios 3 and 4 – is staffed by physicists, zoologists, biologists, engineers and the like and uses the freelance services of distinguished academics in fields such as genetics, neuroscience, mathematics and developmental biology. This is very much a specialist unit.

Elsewhere the broadcaster simply has to be a generalist – a bit like a reporter on a local newspaper – ready to turn his or her hand to anything that might crop up in the course of local events: sport, health, show-biz, politics, publishing – the list of possibilities is endless. Therefore it makes little sense to treat radio as an undifferentiated whole. In considering how social science might benefit from radio exposure, one has to be specific about type of programme, level of audience, editorial stance and the professional skills of the broadcaster.[3]

EDITORIAL THINKING IN A SPECIALIST PROGRAMME

Clearly a good outlet for the work of the social scientist would be a programme such as *Science Now* on BBC Radio 4 or analogous programmes regularly broadcast in the BBC World Service, namely *Science in Action* and *Discovery*. How do these strands select and subsequently treat items chosen for inclusion?

Science Now is weekly. This means it has editorial affinities with weekly magazines in printed form. It blends items of varying degrees of actuality or newsworthiness – a term which has a particular range of meanings in the academic context. Some will be highly current – echoing events of the day – others will be more reflective, or quite unrelated to current events, like a feature article in a newspaper or magazine.

For example, the *Science Now* broadcast on 7 March 1992 (and repeated on 10 March) contained an extended 'feature' on the topic of sex research. The provenance of the components of this package of information sheds light on the editorial thinking of the production team.

It began with a producer finding out that the editor of a new book critical of the late Alfred Kinsey was to be in the UK around the time of publication. He arranged for an interview which turned out to be primarily a swingeing attack on one of the founding fathers of sex surveys. That in itself would have made an interesting item but it was clearly very one-sided so the producer attempted to arrange a counterbalancing interview with the Director of the Kinsey Institute. She declined the invitation but sent instead a long letter containing a number of rebuttals.

At this point there was something of a pause because the producer still felt that the item he now had was mono-dimensional. What, for example, goes on in Britain nowadays by way of sex surveys, if any? What status does Kinsey have among contemporary researchers? And so on.

To meet the first question he approached a British researcher tracing patterns of sexual behaviour in the context of sexually transmitted diseases, chiefly HIV infection and AIDS. She commented on Kinsey but broadened the discussion out to include historical comment and the need for greater scientific rigour in how we measure sexual behaviour.

Shortly after conducting this interview the programme presenter happened to go to Chicago for the annual conference of the American Association for the Advancement of Science. There, an American sex researcher was discussing his own work – with considerable graphic detail and delicacy – which was a natural candidate for a conference report. At the same time the presenter asked the researcher to comment on the Kinsey allegations, which he did most eloquently.

The final outcome as transmitted – which took some months to generate – was an eclectic, informative and entertaining package of material on sex surveys ranging from the late 1940s to the early 1990s, with a variety of voices and perspectives. There were deliberate editorial decisions taken to achieve this, laced with a little serendipity that comes from being in the right place at the right time.

Certainly the package as broadcast was different from the item originally envisaged, namely an interview with an author about his new book. In fact you might argue that it was the lack of a balanced response to the original interview which triggered off new thoughts on how it might best be used.

This example also gives some insight into the network of information that sustains a programme such as *Science Now* or *Science in Action*. In answer to the question: 'Where do the programme items come from?' we can look to a variety of sources.

There is a range of formal sources such as journals, press releases (on new technology, research, conferences, publications, etc.), government or other institutional reports, all of which are widely circulated. All programme makers receive vast amounts of printed material, routinely disseminated through mailing lists, inviting them to meet so and so or attend such and such. Judgements are usually made quite rapidly as to the potential in such material.

Then there is the informal or personal source. Having broadcast four or five interviews every week for many years, the *Science Now* production unit has built up a huge web of contacts. This can operate reactively or proactively. Suppose, for example, a need arises for someone to comment on a current event with a scientific slant – an earthquake or a volcanic eruption, say. A telephone call to a known, experienced contributor will usually produce the required interview. Conversely, that same individual might think – in the light of some event – that the Science Unit would be interested in having a contribution from him/her, or a member of the department, in which case it is he or she who initiates the contact.

SELECTION PRINCIPLES: IS 'NEWSWORTHINESS' NECESSARY?

Given the range of sources we have been discussing – which may be swollen by such inputs as freelance reporters with interesting items to sell – on what grounds is a piece of research deemed worthy of broadcasting? This is a question which often puzzles outsiders, who fail to see any 'logic' or 'rationale' in the selection process taking place in a given programme. This is especially the case if they have, on the strength of hearing an item, approached a producer with a similar story only to be told 'This is not really for us'.

Again we can gain some insights by looking at a number of editions of *Science Now* to see how and why certain items were picked up and broadcast. In doing so, we shall be exploring the much-used but highly elastic term 'newsworthiness'.

Example One: Topicality – current and historical

On 31 March 1992 *Science Now* broadcast an interview with David Cornwell, a senior prison officer and behavioural scientist, on the subject of the 25-day siege at Strangeways Prison, Manchester, in 1990 – the longest in British prison history.

Dr Cornwell had been called in as a negotiator during the seige, during which time he had had to develop some novel negotiation strategies. Now, two years later, he had encapsulated those strategies in a paper delivered to the annual conference of the Criminological and Legal Division of the British Psychological Society. So, there was 'news value' of two kinds in this research. Firstly, it was being aired in the same week as the edition of *Science Now* that carried it. Secondly, it harked back to a graphic and easily remembered event which had received widespread media attention.

Accordingly, the item began with a montage of radio 'actuality' – that is, on-the-spot recorded material – starting with some piercing sounds and fading into the voice of a radio reporter at the scene saying 'This bizarre combination of noises from the police heli-copter was used against the prisoners on the roof during the mid-afternoon . . .'. This brief, evocative picture then gave way to the programme presenter giving place, date, facts about the Strangeways riot and siege. He then introduced the negotiator, David Cornwell, into the story and went on to mention the BPS conference paper. Within a minute or so of programme time, the importance – both historical and academic – of the research had been pressed home by a brief reconstruction of the scene at the prison at the time of the seige. Here was an obvious 'peg' and the programme producers neatly hung the research paper on it.

Thus, two time-scales were brought together to potentiate each other, thereby generating a higher level of news value than an unillustrated interview on the subject of the conference paper could have had.

Example Two: Opportunism

In July 1992 the Ciba Foundation in London organized one of its distinguished, closed scientific meetings on a topic of unusual interest to a committed, intelligent, lay audience such as *Science Now* enjoys. The theme was 'Consciousness' – a longstanding bone of contention among philosophers which, latterly, has been receiving attention from other disciplines too: social and behavioural scientists; neuroscientists; animal behaviourists and psychiatrists, among others. With great imagination and insight the Ciba Foundation's confer-ence organizers had invited around 30 leading consciousness researchers. It amounted to a widely interdisciplinary collection of individuals, pretty well all of them household names to science broadcasters.

The meeting took place over several days, ending the day before *Science Now* is recorded for weekend transmission. Taking one look at the programme, the unit editor, programme producer and presenter immediately decided to scrap the usual magazine format for that week and produce an instant 'special' on the topic of consciousness.

It was both a logical and slightly rash thing to do. The logic was that a group of excellent interviewees was under one roof, avail-able for interview and addressing a fascinating topic. On the other hand, it is not without some reservation, if not trepidation, that

one contemplates making a Radio 4 programme on a philo-
sophical minefield. No sooner do academics begin talking about it
than the ordinary listener could be lost in a tangle of semantic
knots and technicalities.

In the event, the programme turned out to be challenging but
highly comprehensible. In parts it was extremely entertaining. To
achieve this, however, required intensive and extensive editing of
the raw material. The programme duration was around 29 minutes
including the presenter's studio links of approximately 6 minutes.
That means that 23 minutes were given over to the voices of the 8
contributors – around 3 minutes, on average, for each. Yet each
interview, in its raw state, ran for six or seven times that duration.
There was nothing in the raw material that was, strictly speaking,
irrelevant; but it did reach levels of complexity that would have
baffled a lay audience.

In order then to represent each person's views on the subject of
consciousness it was necessary to capture the quintessence of what
he or she had to say – to abbreviate, simplify, precis and all the
while remain comprehensible. We shall be coming back later to
the strategies employed by the media for translating technical or
academic information into programme terms. For the moment,
though, let us take this programme as a classic example of oppor-
tunistic broadcasting – knowing when an interesting group of
people are going to be in one place and making sure one is there
to exploit their willingness to take part in a programme.

There is an obvious lesson here for social scientists. When
organizing conferences, seminars, discussion meetings and the
like they should consider the media possibilities of the event. A
telephone call to the relevant editor or producer would confirm
their expectations or doubts. If the signs are positive, this should
be followed up by a brief, explicit and clearly written description
of the event, together with the key participants, being sent to the
relevant programme offices. The telephone and the fax machine
make all this vital preliminary information giving very easy.

Example Three: Timing

There is an understandable and widespread dislike in the media of
being seen to be 'following the herd'. All newspapers, magazines,
television and radio programmes want to be distinctive in their
coverage. And if they cannot be unique they like to be differ-

entiated by being first. This poses a serious problem for, say, the learned society or university department with a good 'story' to tell. On the one hand, the wider the exposure the happier the originators are. On the other, it may be better to grant some degree of exclusivity to encourage a chosen media outlet to give the item a lot of space and publicity: quality as opposed to quantity coverage.

At the end of January 1992 a report was published on the effectiveness or otherwise of so-called subliminal messages as embedded in audio tapes.[4] Subliminal auditory tapes were being increasingly marketed in the UK, along US lines, on the grounds that they could confer all kinds of benefits: improved learning and memory; better eating or drinking habits; self-assertiveness; relief from anxiety, and so on. Clearly an informed report on such a topic would be an attractive item for any journalist – radio or print. On the other hand, it would be undesirable for a programme such as *Science Now* which is broadcast on Saturday and repeated on Tuesday to be carrying an item that everyone in Fleet Street had worked over throughout the preceding week.

As it happens, *Science Now* was – though not exclusively – first in the field with the report being published at the very end of the week. This seemed by the way to have little deterrent effect on print journalists during the following week. They still ran the story. But it did mean that Britain's regular weekly radio science magazine programme was encouraged to feature it. Had the report been issued several days earlier or later the subliminal tapes item may have had a hard time justifying its inclusion.

The last example brings us to the question of 'newsworthiness' and precisely what it means in a scientific context. News, as it is generally perceived, is what is happening. It is about last night's election results, this morning's earthquake, the day's big football match. The time of news is 'Now'. Consider now a typical science news story, such as a leading discovery in the journal *Nature*. It appears in, say, September, having been submitted several months earlier and undergoing the usual peer review. It describes a research project begun 15 months earlier than this. Already the normal journalistic view of news is being modified. Perhaps the results as published are in fact six months 'old' by now. What is more, perhaps these results are the most convincing to emerge from a research team which, in fact, has been working in this same area for 10 years. To the academic community then the *Nature* article, though important, is by way of confirmation of a longstanding hypothesis. The hypothesis, the experiments and those conducting them have been around for some years.

Now in such cases it is perfectly satisfactory for the science journalist to take as the news peg the fact that 'Such and Such has just been published in the journal *Nature* . . .'. Likewise the news connection could come from the fact that 'Thus and so was reported at a recent conference . . .'. In May 1992 the Yale University social scientist Professor Paul Kennedy gave a one-off lecture at Imperial College, London, on 'Demography, Technology and the Future of the World'. It was an entertaining and erudite lecture, comparing circumstances at the end of the eighteenth century when Thomas Malthus was looking with alarm at the rate at which the world's population was expanding to those of today where, again, the existence of too many people threatens their own survival. In the eighteenth century, technology, in various ways, turned out to improve matters. Can we expect the same thing to happen today?

Professor Kennedy ranged wide over the globe in his analysis and speculation, putting forward the view that, without international cooperation on the grand scale, technology will not easily solve the problems of the world's hungry and expanding populations. It was a view with which one might have been familiar having read his published work but that did not invalidate the potential in the lecture for an attractive item for *Science Now*. Yes, there are hungry people in the world. Yes, we do have remarkable technologies on tap. What are the prospects for making one serve the other?

So, in summary, for the media, in a sense, all science can be made 'newsworthy' at any time. It can be especially alive when, say, a social scientist is commenting directly, in the light of his or her research, on a contemporary event. But it can be made relevant by sound journalistic techniques of finding a credible news peg. In this respect it may be worthwhile for the social scientist with a story to tell to provide some pointers as to what that news peg might be.

The crucial question to enter the head of a radio producer offered any item is: 'So what? Why should I (that is, my listeners) be interested in this?' It behoves the researcher to think a little about this in advance. It is not enough simply to justify research on the grounds that it is 'extraordinarily interesting' or 'another piece in the jigsaw puzzle'. Of course that is so. But this is not sufficient to key it into the lives and experience of a lay listener.

HOW DOES RADIO TREAT SOCIAL SCIENCE?

When an item for a radio programme is selected, what then happens to it? What is the process by which, say, an academic conference or journal paper is converted into something that will appeal to a general audience?

Even as we pose the question, we become aware that there is a widespread sentiment abroad that the serious researcher needs to 'be careful' of the media. We all know someone (or someone who knows someone) who claims to have had a difficult, if not catastrophic, time like the fictitious Dr X whom we met earlier. Again, some examples drawn from a broadcast programme may shed light on this.

On 21 December 1991 *Science Now* devoted a whole issue to the Winter Conference of The British Psychological Society, held at City University in London. It was a programme made very much 'on the hoof'. The producer and presenter had seen the draft conference programme in advance and formulated some ideas as to which papers might make interesting items. However, in the hurly-burly of a conference, where speakers come and go, have other business to attend to, are enjoying meeting old friends and so on, it is difficult to do too much planning in advance.

Instead of having the quiet comfort of a studio too, the programme maker often has to conduct interviews in noisy corridors or Press Rooms – with a fellow journalist standing by to carry out another interview with the same interviewee immediately afterwards. In other words, these hectic circumstances seem, on the face of it, conducive to things going a bit awry. You might expect, for example, that interviews carried out in this manner are peremptory or, worse, superficial – tending to miss the point.

In the programme in question there were five main interviews (together with a little montage of 'psychological jokes' from various individuals right at the end). Of those five, one had been pre-recorded before the conference started because it required some extra technical work, integrating the interviewee's voice with some archival material – namely the recorded voices of Margaret Thatcher and John Major. The other four, however, were recorded very much on the spot. Helen Petrie from Sussex University discussed the sex-role stereotyping associated with common names. Kate Thirlaway from the University of Swansea described her findings on the relationship between physical activity and mental health and mood. Professor Hans Eysenck summarized his paper on personality type and susceptibility to disease. And Dr Donald Broadbent encapsulated his thoughts as given in the first (eponymous) D.E. Broadbent lecture on the links between behavioural science and other disciplines. The pre-recorded interview, by the way, was by Peter Bull from York University on the topic of politicians' interview styles and strategies.

Now, clearly none of these interviews – average duration say four and a half minutes – would tell the whole story. They would have to be quite ruthlessly selective in the areas they covered. On the other hand, they did give each interviewee some scope for explanation and elaboration. Helen Petrie (sex and names) was able to talk about how she became interested in the subject; put across all her main findings; comment on the social pressure that affects choice of names and even slip in a word of advice for parents-to-be. Peter Bull's paper on political interview styles was also well represented – having the added advantage of taped examples. This was an interview that made little room for theory or background. It simply catalogued Dr Bull's observation of the strategies adopted by public figures for avoiding answering the question. The language was totally without technicality. Anyone – with or without a social or behavioural science background – would readily understand it. Yet it excluded nothing substantive from Dr Bull's research findings.

Likewise the discussion with Kate Thirlaway on physical activity and mood. Here again there was no theory or background – except for some clarifying words on what is meant by 'mental health' – simply the results of the study in plain language. The second half – like Helen Petrie's – was a bit prescriptive when the interviewee addressed the question of 'What level of activity would you need to maintain to keep on a reasonably even, cheerful keel?'.

The final two interviews were quite different in character. Both Hans Eysenck and Donald Broadbent were not so much giving papers reporting on a recent research project as distilling some of the wisdom of a lifetime's distinguished work into the space of 60 minutes. What is needed in an interview here is some kind of generalized statement (and elaboration) of the underlying theme of the lectures and some vivid examples to give colour and flesh to this generalized proposition.

This is what the interviews contained. Hans Eysenck, having talked generally about the link between repressed emotions and propensity to illness, cited the example of a cohort of 100 people who were divided into a therapy and a control group. Those given help with coping with stress were, after 13 years, shown to be markedly less susceptible to cancer. Donald Broadbent illustrated his ideas on 'complex systems' – namely human beings – by an extended analogy between the way people operate internally and the way a well-organized firm operates – making the comparison even more telling by showing how things can go wrong (at Chernobyl or with the *Herald of Free Enterprise*) if a layer of the optimal structure is missing.

What lessons can we draw then from these examples? Firstly, radio tends to treat social and behavioural science – or any science come to that – fairly concisely. Interviews tend to deal in facts – conclusions, results, implications – rather than theories and abstractions.

Secondly, radio needs 'pictures'. A good interview will, by analogy or metaphor, conjure up an image in the head of the listener. This requires the interviewee to think hard about reducing down a difficult concept into everyday or graphic terms. Now many academics become uneasy at the thought of 'over-simplifying' their work. One can understand their fears but these are based on a misconception of what the media are trying to achieve. No radio producer would pretend to do absolute justice to a 10 year research project in the space of four or five minutes of air time. What radio aims for is a skeletal idea, fleshed out where appropriate to aid understanding and to relate the idea to the audience. Imagery is invaluable for doing this.

Thirdly, and lastly, radio treats social science not as academic discussion but as part of its overall output. The tone and turn of phrase of the Senior Common Room can seem pompous within a media context. Theoretical niceties can seem pedantic. It is necessary for the academic to recognize that a radio interview involves changing role. The audience is no longer a captive cohort of undergraduates or a motivated assembly of peers but an arbitrary group of listeners who can and will indicate their boredom by turning to another station. They will be committed to learn only if the 'teacher' is committed to enthuse and intrigue.

PROSPECTS FOR SATISFACTORY COLLABORATION

Let us conclude by returning to the hapless Dr X. She has declared

'Never again!'. What can we do to persuade her that her prospects for interacting with the media are not so gloomy as she
imagines?

We can begin by pointing out that we live in an imperfect world.
There are sub-standard broadcasters as there are second-rate academics. It is in the nature of things that somewhere, somehow,
some things must go wrong. However, the number of occasions on
which researchers feel that a broadcaster has fairly and squarely
'got it wrong' is probably far smaller than we imagine. More often
the media are reproached for not allowing enough air time for all
the dots and commas of a subject to be filled in. Unequivocal
inaccuracy is really quite rare.

But there is a much more positive reason for Dr X not to give up
on the media. The social sciences undoubtedly have an enormous
potential for radio. The social scientist's stock-in-trade is people
and their behaviour, interactions, organizations, expectations and
ambitions. The range of research that social scientists undertake is
breathtakingly wide – and most of it is either directly relevant or
can easily be made to appear relevant to the general audiences that
radio commands. What is more, those general listeners, although
untrained in social science, are not unintelligent. They are certainly often highly motivated and enthusiastic about speech-based
programmes that test their wits and expand their horizons. Analysis
of audience reaction to *Science Now* in recent years suggests not
only that this *prima facie* 'technical' programme is highly popular.
It also shows an interesting demographic trend towards drawing its
audience from an increasingly broad social spectrum.

One can make of this what one will but one conclusion might
well be that, for all the more lightweight output of national and
local radio in the UK, there is a definite and perhaps growing need
for intellectually challenging speech programmes. Social scientists
can surely contribute towards meeting that need.

NOTES

1 There is a fourth and more altruistic reason too: the intrinsic desira-
  bility of disseminating scientific knowledge to the public at large. The
  foundation of a special committee (COPUS) and the establishment of
  Britain's first professorial chair in the public understanding of science
  reflect this preoccupation.
2 By 1993 the number of BBC local radio stations was approaching 40
  while the independent sector was in excess of 70. A new independent

national station, Classic FM, had been launched with another, analogous to the BBC's Radio 4, promised for the following year.
3 The individual academic or department should not necessarily be alone in this assessment. University press, public affairs and/or information officers can often provide experience and hard data on who is doing what in radio and television.
4 BPS (no date).

Chapter 12

Television's dangerous liaisons

Martin Freeth

The scene: a rice paddy field in the Cagayan Valley in the Phillipines. I am trying to set up a filmed interview with Dr Jim Litsinger, a scientist from the International Rice Research Institute. Exceptionally, and uncomfortably for a BBC television producer/director, I am being observed. The sociologist, Dr Roger Silverstone is quietly collecting the material he will later turn into the book *Framing Science: The Making of a BBC Documentary*. But he is observing significant interactions and relationships which I do not notice, or which I take for granted. As he sees it: 'The crew arrives . . . they bring their equipment, silver cases with cameras, lenses and recorders. . . . They bring something else: a private, indefinable, encapsulating culture, as powerful as a force field, a way of being based on their confidence as professionals.'

When Roger sees me in action, he sees a manipulator at work, but in his view I have little choice because I have been allocated all the cards: 'A film-maker may believe, or expect, that his dealings with his subjects are dealings between equals. In some, perhaps limiting, cases, this may be so – for example in a live transmission with a professional or experienced performer. But in every other case it cannot be so.' Here, in this battle of wits in the rice field, Jim Litsinger and I have very different agendas: 'Litsinger answers. He answers as a scientist. He talks of the knowledgeable but confused farmer. He talks of the potential and the limitations of research now being undertaken.'

As a producer, I want Jim to express his criticisms, which he had so readily expressed during dinner the night before, of the widespread expectation that all scientists need to do to feed the world is to trick plant genes. Above all, I want him to express his passions: about the need to respect the feelings of the local people and farmers, and not to play into the hands of large landowners who want nothing but profit; about the urgency of the situation world wide; about his pleasure as a scientist when he sees a flourishing plot of a new variety, growing out there in the real world.

The problem for me is not that he wants to be truthful and express some of the real complexities of the Cagayan story (after all, I can always edit out some of the complexity) but that he is, when the camera is running, somewhat diffident and low key. Eventually, under pressure of film costs and fading light, I lose patience and say what I really mean. As Roger describes it: 'The film runs out. A new roll. "Right. Tell me Jim, why the hell we're here and you're here and why does it matter?"' To put it simply: plants don't move, it is only the human emotions which surround the growing of these new varieties which can stand a chance of drawing in viewers, and of holding them against the competition on the other channels.

A few years ago one analysis of viewers' responses suggested that, on average, people learn three or four 'facts' from a 50-minute *Horizon* programme. Television is not at heart an informational medium – when it works, it works below the belt. It is best at communicating atmospheres and attitudes, personalities, motivations, hopes and fears, and the broader political and cultural significance of things. But scientists and social scientists usually claim that fundamentally their work is intellectual, rather than artistic. So when television producers and scientists come together to make or contribute to traditional documentaries, the liaisons formed are bound to be dangerous and not always mutually satisfying.

I shall return to discuss 'documentary', a centrally important kind of programme making, later. But first I want to explore two other ways (via shows with studio audiences and via drama-documentary) in which we producers seek to present science and social science – while keeping actual practitioners at a safer distance.

In the late 1970s I produced the last studio-based run of James Burke's *The Burke Special*. In six programmes we explored developments and issues in psychology and social psychology, along with a studio audience. James can command a studio audience as a ringmaster commands a circus. During a film about the body and body image, he had a woman member of the audience looking at herself in a distorting mirror. 'Okay, now one more test. We're going to make you the incredible fat lady . . . if we can get that up on the mirror.' The audience laughs. 'Okay terrible fat lady, are you ready? When you're normal, say so, coming inwards now. Getting thinner and thinner. Yell "stop" any time you like.' 'Stop!' . . . 'Okay, now the man labouring away behind there is a chap who has been doing the research on this aspect of people's body image, Dr David Clark from Aberdeen University. Can you tell us anything interesting about the way she sees her body?'

David Clark's long journey from Aberdeen was then rewarded with the chance to say four lines about how the woman saw herself. This show was recorded-as-live, so had Dr Clark's mirror apparatus failed, his contribution might have been cut out altogether. To his credit, Dr Clark was very good humoured about what must to him have been an absurd business. In fact, far from being ashamed of it, I am proud to have been associated with this series, even though it was derided by some academics, television critics and fellow more 'serious' members of Science and Features department at the BBC. More than 11 million people were entertained by and exposed to valuable ideas derived from the social sciences (including, for example, an explanation of the clinical value of Kelly Grids and 'personal constructs' in anorexia) and they had their prejudices about their own and other people's bodies challenged.

Of course, David Clark and the other contributors could, in those circumstances, be little more than putty in James Burke's hands. In such cases, social scientists invited to appear must decide if they can trust the producer and presenter (who may come from an arts background) not to misrepresent their work. But the programme makers (professional sceptics, suspicious of their subjects' tendency to claim more significance for their work than it may deserve) will always seek to claim to be more in touch with audiences, and more aware of what viewers will understand, than the expert advisers and scientific contributors can ever be.

The advantage for the scientist of programmes like *The Burke Special* (and with studio-based discussion and interview programmes in general) is that the producer's and presenter's mediation or simplification of the work in question is there for all to see: indeed sometimes the scientist may even get the chance of a direct encounter with a member of the public on screen, while, as Roger Silverstone's book shows so clearly, the mediation involved in traditional documentaries happens in the privacy of the producer's head, and in the cutting room.

The drama-documentary, or 'faction', form is even less open to view and yet another stage removed from the scientific work itself. When Mick Jackson, a former colleague of mine in Science and Features, decided to produce *Life Story*, a drama-documentary about the discovery of the DNA double helix, Dr Jim Watson refused to cooperate. Perhaps, modestly, he didn't want to be turned into a hero or villain, or perhaps, more likely, he thought the movie rights of his book *The Race for the Double Helix* were worth more. But either way, faced with this, the writers concerned simply diligently searched out other sources for the scenes they wrote involving Jim Watson: the way film drama is, writers must in any case invent the actual dialogue and newly create the dramatic ways in which their stories unfold, however many accurate contemporary sources are available. Each television form makes its own insistent demands of its practitioners. But if producers feel guilty when they find themselves doing this kind of alchemy, they can be comforted by the fact that the presence of actors represents a clear 'label' which says: 'what you are seeing is an invention'. They can persuade themselves that their loyalty is to a higher, less literal truth.

How do scientists react to being reconstructed by actors and scriptwriters? In this case, after the event, Jim Watson was reported as telling colleagues that *Life Story* was an excellent film. This is not surprising because, apart from showing that Rosalind Franklin's contribution to the discovery had been seriously undervalued, the film idealized and even romanticized the scientific process, and it did make heroes of both Francis Crick and Jim Watson as the central players. It added a warm musical glow to the idea, deep in our entrepreneurial culture, that vigorous competition gets results. It was the drama equivalent of the classic *Horizon* detective story. *Life Story* went well over budget, but it enthralled millions and won prizes. Scientists I have talked to glow with pleasure about the film: my interpretation is that not only did it glamorize science to the public but it reinforced the scientists' own myths and dreams about what scientific enterprise is all about. 'Of course', you feel as a viewer, 'those scientists deserved every bit of public money they got.'

The *Horizon* editor, Jana Bennett, sought to redress the balance by encouraging producer John Lynch to make *Genes R Us*. For this, the producer's role was to enable a group of researchers to say what they wanted about their working lives. They were given cameras and took videos of themselves over many months. Certainly the film they made was not well shot nor smoothly presented, but at least viewers could see something of the real day-to-day tedium and struggles of scientists at the workbench, unmediated for a change by the usual televisual need to search for detective stories or 'break-throughs'. Some viewers may as a result have questioned the scientists' use of public money, but all will also have realized how very difficult it is for scientists actually to get hold of any of that money.

For me, the high point of my own flirtations with drama-documentary started with the writer Stephen Davis and myself seeking out psychologists who had known the eminent (and sus-pected) father figure of the IQ test and of the 11-plus in Britain, Sir Cyril Burt. The premise of the *Horizon* film we eventually made (entitled *The Intelligence Man*) was that Burt got away with inventing fictional co-workers and fraudulent research findings because of the uncritical way in which the whole scientific community tends to respect and accept 'data', especially when that data reinforces existing prejudices.

I am aware that some psychologists even today question the verdict of the film that Burt was a fraud: but what gave us confi-dence was the fact that Hans Eysenck, Arthur Jensen and Raymond Cattell – hereditarians to a man who had all been inspired by Burt and who knew him personally – told us in our meetings that they had, although reluctantly, accepted the careful evidence set out in Leslie Hearnshaw's biography of Burt. So we felt we had the green light to invent 'composite' visitors to Burt's house on Primrose Hill; a Miss Howard, played by Lynsey Baxter (a beautiful, fictional co-worker dreamed up in the mind of our Burt, played by John Shrapnel); and attacks of Ménière's disease, reputed to have hap-pened to Burt after he had been inventing data. What a tangled web we wove – even interspersing our drama with interviews with the actual witnesses such as Hans Eysenck – but at least we did not call our kind of concoction 'science'.

Writer Stephen Davis has an acute sense of the dangers of institutions and institutional ideas: his work is always iconoclastic. On the other hand, I think of myself, as a producer, as a bit of a courtesan: feeling it is my duty, as it were, across a range of programmes to give pleasure and pain from time to time to differ-ent partners from across the political spectrum. And for me at least the view that a good programme can be 'balanced' within itself is an illusion: love-making is usually best with one partner at a time, and the same is true of film-making.

The BBC's Science and Features department offers a variety of traditional documentary formats. *Antenna* (unlike those documentary strands which have a narrator read the commentary as though he or she is the voice of God) gave a clear signal that it was as it were on the game too. All the stories were 'authored' by their presenter/narrator, who was usually a scientist, or critical expert in the field. Among others, I have made stories for *Antenna* giving Dr Richard Leakey the chance to ponder his difficulties in reconciling wildlife, tourism and popular interests in Kenya, and giving Dr John Seaman of the Save the Children Fund (SCF) the chance to criticize United Nations immunization policies.

I was lucky enough in 1989 to win a Commonwealth Travelling Bursary to explore health care in Uganda. During my travels I had come to the conclusion that the realities of the immunization programmes in the less developed world do not live up to UNICEF propaganda. A prominent academic, who knew what he was talking about, persuaded me that the problems with the immunization programme were real and widespread: he believed that the coverage was not as great as was claimed, that data were often invented to satisfy funders and that the emphasis on immunization as a 'quick fix' was diverting aid from areas which would be more likely to improve health: the provision of jobs, safe water, basic health care services, and so on. The philosophy put forward at the famous Alma Ata conference was being allowed to die, he felt.

Could this academic become the voice for a hard-hitting *Antenna* film? Well, no, this would not be possible: he had just been appointed to a senior role in a British government department and he was soon to be officially muzzled. But he suggested that John Seaman of SCF shared his views, and might be a willing substitute. So Dr Seaman and I negotiated our liaison: I knew it might be dangerous for him because the power of the UNICEF establishment is great. They had tolerated his criticisms expressed during private meetings of development workers, but they might take great exception to his airing them to a wider public. In the end, to his credit, he expressed his point of view on film almost as vigorously as he had when I first met him. And what has happened since the film was transmitted? In the field at least SCF and UNICEF workers are still collaborating in harmony: so this seems to have been one of those cases where insiders were pleased that an outsider could express concerns that they could not voice themselves.

Controversy about 'authored' presentations like *Antenna* can arise in the scientific community from the choices (made by the series editor and the producers) of presenters from amongst those who are out on a limb, or at least idiosyncratic in their approach. But although many of them have a very individual stance they can, when given this kind of 'authorship', demonstrate opinions, experience or research which lets the viewer understand that not all scientists think the same. Of course they must also, if the film is to become 'good television', be vivid and lively performers.

Incidentally, if a producer asks you to look straight into the camera lens, he or she is really saying: 'Now I am making you part of the team, and viewers will know you are colluding with the camera and with the thesis of the film.' So unless you do share those aims, refuse to do it – look at the interviewer off-camera and, through that convention, viewers will tend not to blame you for the way your contribution is edited later. You will also perform much better talking to an interviewer or producer even slightly off-camera: for most people the blank, staring lens is very off-putting.

Renowned neuroscientist Professor Colin Blakemore is an exception. Before I asked him to 'host' our 13-part series *The Mind Machine* for BBC 2 in 1988, he had appeared several times as contributor in television documentaries, and he had written and presented numerous scientific radio programmes. But he had never looked straight into camera. When he did, he was excellent. I had on my hands, through the generosity of American co-producers, documentary material with which to make more than 13 films about the brain and the mind – but now, because I had agreed to give Colin Blakemore the label 'host', I had to negotiate the thesis of a newly constructed version of the series with him.

For example, we had some vivid footage illustrating the apparent personality switches of an American patient with multiple personality disorder (variously calling himself Richard, Dede and Tony, and whose different personas spoke with very different sounding voices). But for Colin, multiple personality disorder is more or less a fiction created in patients by the expectations of the American psychotherapeutic community, working on a patient's need to play to the gallery. He would not allow us to use a single frame of that material.

During the making of that series, I too was wearing my reductionist clothes – luckily, or Colin Blakemore and I could not have worked together. True we dramatized our presentation of science with moving human stories, but underneath I had even more respect for 'real facts', scientific 'breakthroughs' and 'data' than Sir Cyril Burt. I am, indeed, proud also to have helped make that series – and I know one benefit of it to the world of science and medicine has been to inspire many young people to go into the field of research in the brain sciences. But I also feel the protests against it from at least two groups of people were valid, and also deserved presenting (though in other programmes).

The first group, a small minority of anti-vivisectionist viewers, made our lives very difficult and, inspired by Vernon Coleman of the *Sun*, launched a campaign against each new transmission and libellously compared Colin Blakemore to the Nazis. More seriously, in my view, the second group of critics was composed of professionals and others concerned with treating depression and schizophrenia, together with many of their patients. They felt that by concentrating on processes in the brain (in films called *Madness* and *Portrait in Blue*) we were denying the significance of family, social and environmental factors in mental illness and understating the possible value of talk therapies as opposed to psycho-active drugs. Colin Blakemore stuck to his reductionist last, and the series made excellent and coherent television as a result – but a holistic approach to mental disorders would be equally valid for television, (and to his credit, as 'host', he also helped me answer all the letters after transmission, showing concern for patients and respect for different points of view).

My next series (for BBC 2 in 1993) was *The Trouble with Medicine.* For a change, it gave voice to the critics of the scientific reductionism and the 'technological imperative' which together dominate so much of Western-style medicine. But this time there was no one 'host', and the narrator's voice was intended to be not that of God, but of the people – a voice which set out to undermine the assumption that a white coat gives you authority. This time, the protests have come from the professionals – so I know that I have again been working for the people who really pay my salary: the licence payers and viewers.

Finally I return to Roger Silverstone's uncomfortable and revealing analysis of the making of one of my films because I believe that what I have written so far might give the false impression that, as a senior BBC producer, I am free to exercise my whims and prejudices in any direction I choose. Reading *Framing Science* showed me for the first time just how constrained and limited I am as a producer: by the nature of broadcasting institutions and hierarchies, by the personal relationships and subtle deals worked out with contributors during production, by the expectations of audiences and the demands of the medium. It is astonishing how often a very diverse group of people seated in front of an editing machine will all agree that a particular shot, or a segment of an interview, is 'boring'. And no matter how 'important' it seems to any of the parties concerned, or how long it took to set up and shoot, or how many people were inconvenienced in the process, if it is boring it has to go.

One of the biggest constraints comes from the fact that television programmes are extraordinarily difficult to make and complete. Roger Silverstone writes:

> Martin . . . sets out on an adventure, meets his villains, gets his help and returns firstly without recognition and only finally with some success. At no stage was it clear to me (or often even to him) what the outcome would be. He was receiving contra-dictory advice and opinions; his beliefs were leading him one way, his responsibility another. So much was going on that was outside his control. His making of the film was made for folk-lore. Only his ambiguous success lets it down.

By 'ambiguous success' he means, amongst other things, that the film was rejected by my then head of department and could be transmitted only after it had been recut and made much more dramatic. In conclusion Roger Silverstone adds:

> Of course television science is partial and the example of Martin's film should not contribute to a delusion that *Horizon* does not mostly accept the values of the scientific community in its programmes. The first stage of any change is an awareness of how things are and of the constraints on, and the complexity of, present practice. It seems to be therefore that enlightenment, however minimal, is its own justification – though it is a rather old-fashioned view.

I, too, have tried to enlighten readers a little in this chapter about my own particular motivations and sympathies – I must take the consequences if it puts some potential contributors on their guard when I next arrive in their office or laboratory with a film crew. I am old fashioned enough to believe that I have a duty to explain something about how I go about my business to anyone who wants to know more. These days public-service broadcasters are having to fight for their public funds every bit as hard as scientists and social scientists do. But, if we are to hold onto our audiences, we must continue to put the demands of the medium above those of our collaborators and contributors. I make no apology for that.

Chapter 13

From science to journalism

An interview with Oliver Gillie
edited by Cheryl Haslam

When I was young I had always wanted to be a scientist. To become a scientist for me had a kind of magical quality, but I became disillusioned with it. I felt that I was more interested in the subject matter than I was in sitting at a laboratory bench and conducting and analysing experiments (which can be very tedious). I found research very frustrating because of the long-term nature of it and because I was interested in a wide range of things which I was not able to pursue. I had always been interested in writing and I thought I might like to move into that area.

I was unsure what to do when I left Mill Hill but I had had small successes in the form of some scientific pieces published in the *Guardian*. I thought that I would be able to build on that and do freelance work for various newspapers. I wrote to the nationals, but they all had their own science correspondents. I knew nothing about practical journalism, which is essential if you want to get a job on a national newspaper. So I ended up doing some freelance work and got a contract to write a book about cell biology. After a while I obtained a post with a monthly journal called *Science Journal* (since amalgamated with *New Scientist*).

That was my first step in getting a job where I could do what I wanted to do and I was there for a couple of years. Then I was made redundant, because the *Science Journal* folded and was incorporated into *New Scientist*. I could have stayed and worked on *New Scientist* but I opted to try something different. I became editor of the journal *General Practitioner*, a weekly journal for GPs. While I knew a fair amount about medicine, it was a big step going from a monthly science magazine to editing a weekly for doctors. It was very strenuous and I had to cope with directing a team of people.

It all worked out and I remained there for about 18 months, but I knew what I really wanted was to work for a national newspaper.

I managed to do some freelancing for *The Sunday Times*. They were short of a medical correspondent so I tried to build up a relationship and in the end I persuaded Harry Evans to take me on, on a three- or six-month trial. I was there for about 15 years and then finally, excited by the possibility of joining a newspaper at its inception, I left and joined the *Independent*. I was medical editor at the *Independent* for about three years. We pioneered a health page which was so successful that all the other national papers followed us. I was very happy with that but was given the option to move after three years. Having spent some 20 years writing about medicine and health I was glad to diversify. I am interested in numerous areas and I didn't want to spend the whole of my life writing about health and medicine. I feel as if I've taken a degree in medicine because I have studied it so intensively. As a journalist you can end up knowing more about certain aspects of medicine than most GPs or more about some areas of psychology than a lot of psychologists. Of course a journalist is not equipped in any way to practise these subjects but he or she is equipped to be critical of certain aspects of practice. Individuals working in the social and medical sciences have usually specialized in a particular aspect, and as such may know more about that aspect than anyone else. A journalist may become specialized in various parts of the subject and for a short period of time know more than GPs or academics.

On the other hand, many journalists skate on very thin ice and patch together stories knowing much less about an area than they should do and the results can be superficial. The experience Cheryl Haslam had with reports of drug taking in medical school is a good example. A journalist may see articles in the specialist press, and take them at face value, without bothering to phone up the expert for clarification. That happens more often than it should in journalism. There is a saying in journalism 'Don't knock a good story'. That means if you have a good story don't ask too many questions because if you do what appears to be a good story disappears in front of your eyes.

Of course, journalism is a very broad church and one has to make distinctions between both different kinds of newspaper and indeed different types of journalist, with different aims and different standards. The best journalists will take a good deal of trouble to talk to a variety of experts even if they have very little technical knowledge in the first place. By talking to experts who are good communicators they will be able to find out and understand what the important aspects of the story are from the point of view of the public. Journalism is not just a matter of writing, like science, it is a process of enquiry which can be conducted in various different ways. You get good science and bad science, good journalism and bad journalism. The best journalists will conduct a very thorough enquiry.

Many journalists now are graduates though a significant minority are not. Having a degree doesn't necessarily make for better journalism. But the journalistic process is one of enquiring and absorbing knowledge of various kinds and it does help if you have some sort of scientific background when you are writing about psychology or medicine. There are certain stories that I would not have been able to write had I not had some technical knowledge to begin with.

An example is a series of articles on childbirth which I did with my ex-wife, Louise Panton, who is a BBC producer. Without the scientific knowledge and perspective I have and also Louise's expertise (she is also a science graduate) we would have found it much more difficult questioning the induction of childbirth. At the time of writing, it was being done quite indiscriminately and some doctors were saying that women should be induced between nine and five in office hours in the week and that no births should take place at the weekends. This seems a very extreme view now, and indeed the position has totally changed. It would be fair to say that the change came about partly as a result of the questions that we asked.

I am currently a writer/reporter and since giving up my role as medical editor I have written about slavery in modern Britain, specifically about African girls taken in by Lebanese families and brought to Britain. These girls have never been paid and they are forced to work all hours. Two of these girls ran away and I have written about them. I went to the Gulf during the Gulf War and I now write about everything from Scotland to parking problems. I am enjoying the freedom to write about everything, working as a reporter/writer.

COMMON INTERESTS

There are lots of areas that we are interested in as journalists that social scientists are also interested in, and social scientists are among the people that we contact when we are looking at these issues. The work of social scientists comes to the media to be reported on from time to time. The annual general meeting of the various academic societies, for example the British Psychological Society meetings, are now broadly covered by the press.

Newspapers have different departments just like universities: health and social services (which covers the politics and management of these services) is one, medicine (covering treatments and causes of illness) and science are others. We have four people covering health and health politics and they are divided up into those covering the clinical aspects and those who focus on social or political aspects, although they work together and cover for each other. We also have a home affairs desk which covers, for example, prisons, the law, homelessness and various aspects of social policy. We also have education journalists in touch with academics conducting research in that area. They are all taking an interest in social policy, so while social policy as a broad topic is not covered, its components are covered by the various sections. Journalists writing about politics may also occasionally get involved in social policy because of particular issues raised by politicians in the House of Commons.

JOURNALISTIC OBJECTIVES

A journalist has to have multiple objectives and that is what makes the job difficult. It is quite unlike writing a scientific paper, which is rigid and organized in a particular way. A scientific paper has a very definite structure where certain sorts of information are expected in certain parts. A newspaper story also has a definite structure but it is quite different from scientific articles. The most important goal is to grab the reader's interest. The story may be about a mundane matter, such as parking, but because it affects the reader it may still be of great interest to them. Nevertheless, the reader's interest cannot be taken for granted, the reader must always be wooed and won. Alternatively, the article might be about something horrific, like murder. Either way the first sentence is absolutely crucial. The first sentence has to give the reader a reason for reading on.

This is more or less opposite to the way things are written in scientific journals, where you often have to go to the last few sentences to find out why the research is really interesting. In journalistic pieces you begin with the first few sentences grabbing the reader's interest, then having grabbed their interest, you give more detailed information. Readers are able to take in the factual detail once they are interested, once their mind is focused. In the fourth or fifth paragraph you quite often find a quotation because that gives further authority for what is being written and adds interest. A quotation is a way of using a different voice and getting people's attention. Further down, in the middle the story begins to expand and to provide detail about some incident that happened. Then, if it is a nicely turned out story, the final paragraph may have some kind of a punchline which wraps up the story and gives people something to go away with and think about.

As a journalist you aim to fulfil various objectives. The objectives are to tell people something that they do not know about. When it comes to news there are various different definitions of news but my definition would be telling people something that they don't know anything about. It might be results from current social scientific research or some event which happened five or even 10 years ago that has been totally overlooked and is for some reason of interest now. A journalist's first objective is to write about something that is new and relevant, the next objective must be to communicate to people in the most interesting way possible. The first sentence, the technique of writing and the accuracy of the story are absolutely vital.

There is another concept which I have often found helpful: you must be fair to both your reader and your source (who might be a social scientist who supplied you with the information). To be fair to the readers is not to mislead them. For example, you may mislead them if you repeat learned language with a specialist meaning which is different from the meaning that is attached to it by the ordinary person. Language used by specialists is often not used in the same way that we use it every day. So it might be that a journalist using specialist language could suggest a meaning that was sensational when in fact the real meaning is more mundane. If you fail to explain such differences to your readers early on in a story then you are not being fair to them.

In order to be fair to the social scientist you are dealing with you must be accurate. Some experts actually do not explain what they are doing at all well and so in communicating their work you need to tidy up certain points. When I am unsure as to whether I have the right meaning, I get back to them (time permitting) and I may read the story to them and check the details. Academics vary in their ability to work with the press. Some of them are totally paranoid and are very difficult to deal with, they want to change everything that you write. Some know nothing about newspapers, indeed some don't even read newspapers and have no conception of what we are trying to do. So reading back a story can cause difficulties. However, I find that most are very understanding and realize that journalists have their own expertise. When this trust is established an academic can discuss a story with a journalist and each can help the other.

Trust and mutual respect are essential if this is to work, and, of course, this relationship takes time to develop. There has to be mutual respect in that the expert has to respect what the journalist is trying to do just a much as the journalist has to respect what the expert is trying to do. An academic may be guilty of exaggeration or of seeking publicity when he or she has little of great interest to say. In such a case the interests of the expert and the journalist do not coincide.

However, often the interests of the expert and the quality journalist are the same. They both want to communicate something relevant and interesting to the public. But you do have to be careful. Some journalists, like some social scientists, are not straightforward and honest and want to make a story when there is no story there. I would say that there is quite a lot of that in journalism. If social scientists want to get the best publicity they have to control the publicity by channelling the information through journalists they can trust. For an academic working in the fields of psychology, health and so forth this is likely to be the specialist journalists on the quality papers. Whatever the newspaper, there are some journalists who are prepared to take a bit of a flyer. This may come from an academic presenting some fairly dodgy ideas. I believe that there is always a place for the expert who challenges a professional opinion, even when the challenge may look shaky, as there may be and perhaps there should be a place too for the journalist who publicizes that work. However, it often ends with the general public becoming hopelessly confused.

For example, there have been some ideas put forward which have challenged the conventional view of AIDS. This view seems to be saying that HIV is not the primary cause of AIDS. Such contentious statements may have a useful role in the learned literature. Mavericks who have very challenging views force people who are close to this subject (who may not have tested all the arguments and all the loopholes) to go back to the data and look at it afresh. It is not always possible in science to produce final and conclusive proof. Scientists are usually never more than say 90 per cent certain of the facts relating to a particular issue. People like Professor Duesberg, who challenged the conventional view of AIDS, can get the AIDS experts to spend a lot of time going over their data and I think that may actually be a useful function. However, they are sometimes seized on by the media in order to make a story. Then it may be questionable whether the evidence is presented in an even-handed and responsible way. For example, I would say the way in which *The Sunday Times* presented Duesberg's work has not been even-handed and fair to the reader. It has given a wrong impression of the state of research on AIDS and has done a disservice to the reader.

A journalist who has written a story must always have a very large responsibility for that story. The whole atmosphere in a particular newspaper office can contribute to mistakes being made. Mistakes are made in newspapers, just as they are by scientists. There is an editorial process that we go through, just as learned papers are edited and subjected to peer review. Every newspaper article is subjected to peer review within the newspaper office where it is generally read by three or four different people. Peer review can involve seizing on a particular aspect of the story and saying 'Well this is the interesting thing we will project that.' This process of projection can sometimes cause distortions or can magnify errors of interpretation.

RESPONSE OF SOCIAL SCIENTISTS TO HAVING THEIR WORK REPORTED IN THE PRESS

When social scientists present their work at a meeting or publish it in the learned press they get very little response. But when research results are published in an accurate way in the national press they are drawn to the attention of a much wider audience. Social scientists might, for example, find that the local police or someone from Home Office or a head teacher takes an interest. Possibly a specialist in a different field may, as a result of a newspaper story, get into correspondence with them. Sometimes an article will lead to correspondence being printed in the newspaper and this may be important to the social scientist whose work triggered the letters.

The vast majority of social scientists I have dealt with over the years have been very pleased to have their work written up in a quality newspaper. They are usually happy with the reporting of their research and the implications it has for them. In my experience the number of academics who complain about their work being misrepresented is very small. Having said that, I think I have a reputation for being fair and accurate and not all journalists have that reputation. Based on information from my colleagues, I would say that in quality papers complaints are the exception.

There has been a discernible change in the attitudes of academics toward the press. When I started off in this business the universities did not have press officers, but virtually all have them now. The British Psychological Society and the British Medical Association have press officers. I think they have press officers for two reasons: one is in order to be able to influence the way in which the news is written and the other reason is actually to project their discipline and get publicity. The social and medical sciences need publicity for two reasons: one is the immediate contacts that are made through publicity; the other reason is that newspaper stories show that scientists are doing socially relevant work. Politicians may then be more inclined to support their research financially.

There are certain individuals that journalists come across, not just scientists, but in any walk of life, who feel that the press is a lower grade of life. Such people believe that the press is totally exploitative and doesn't care about accuracy and they are afraid to have any dealings with us. In the scientific community that takes the form of people who are obsessive about details and want a certain emphasis to be put on things. If social scientists want publicity for their research they have to emphasize the points that they think are important and interesting, but at the end of the day the journalist has to pick out the things that he or she thinks are important. Sometimes it is better to recognize that journalists and social scientists are coming from different directions. Most of the time I would hope that social scientists and journalists have objectives which are close enough to avoid problems.

The specialist science journalist has a position which is similar to that of the critic in the arts. They need a very broad understanding of the subject and should endeavour to write about it in a way that connects up with the average person. They have to be critical because some social scientists actually make silly and outrageous claims, or may be naïve about another branch of science. I would say that some psychologists are naïve about genetics, for example. The situation is that a psychologist who knows a little bit about genetics can appear to be very clever amongst colleagues who know nothing about genetics and can persuade them of certain ideas which would never cut any ice with geneticists.

The journalist ideally has to talk to experts on both sides of an argument and then has to make up his/her own mind. This is particularly important in the case of controversial areas which are often fraught with difficulties. Social science has the special problem that we don't come to the discipline without pre-conceptions. We have preconceptions because we have all lived lives which connect up with the research material of social science. We derive theories of life based on our individual experience whether we are social scientists or anyone else. We come with preconceptions and with ideas which stem from our families, friends and society in general. So we are not coming to the subject with a *tabula rasa* as we might if we were studying physics, for example. The journalist has mental baggage just as the social scientist has and both will be influenced by that mental baggage.

THE CYRIL BURT AFFAIR

Sometimes journalists have a role in exposing dubious or fraudulent work of social scientists. A notable case in point is that of the educational psychologist Cyril Burt. Sir Cyril Burt, who died in 1971, was widely held as one of the founders of psychology and was an immensely influential figure in education. But five years after his death, allegations were made that he had fraudulently invented his data on the inheritance of intelligence. Media coverage and public interest in this scandal was sparked off by my article in *The Sunday Times* on 24 October 1976 headlined: '**Crucial data was faked by eminent psychologist**'. This article was followed up with further stories and there was enormous correspondence in *The Times*.

My current position on Burt is that the original allegations that I made all stand. He was a fraud, he invented data and he invented research assistants who did not exist or at least did not do the work attributed to them. Burt was a plausible man, much loved by his pupils who I am sure learned a lot from him. The problem was that he never had enough of his own data and he was far more interested in pushing his theory. Inspired by scientists such as Darwin he wanted to provide a sociobiological theory of society, which gave a certain authority to the class system in Britain.

Ten years after the publication of my article in *The Sunday Times* the debate continues and three books have been published. Two found in favour of Burt and one against. In 1991 there was a defence of Burt, the *Guardian* published some misinformed articles about it and there is a pressure group that is trying to re-establish Cyril Burt. In my opinion the charge that he was guilty of fraud still stands and the pro-Burt books and newspaper articles have not considered all the available evidence.

ADVICE TO SOCIAL SCIENTISTS

If you have an article that you think might make a newspaper story, it is well to remember that 99.9 per cent of scientific papers do not make good newspaper stories. But if you have some results which you consider to be 'pretty hot stuff' and you want to get good publicity I would suggest that you send copies of it to any specialist writers in the quality press that you think would be interested. Do not assume that a specialist correspondent in one department is necessarily going to pass it on to another section. It might not occur to them that others would be interested. So if the results cover more than one specialist area, disseminate the findings as widely as possible. It is helpful, if you send something to more than one person on a newspaper, to include a note indicating that you have sent it to others.

If there is a future publication date for your research, specify that the material is embargoed until such a date. Send a covering letter which explains, in ordinary language, why you think it is interesting and what issues it connects with. Do not be afraid to stress why you think it is interesting as this is important. Give your daytime and home telephone numbers and make sure you are ready to answer questions from the press during the day, evening and weekends following despatch of the letters.

At the end of the day you are in the hands of the journalist. He or she is going to decide if the story is interesting and, if so, how to write it. You have to accept that, but you can alert them to any worries you may have and ask them to clarify any details with you. Ask them to check any quotations with you so that there is no question about accuracy, because it is always possible with selective quotations to make mistakes. It is also possible for the journalist to have misunderstood you. Few journalists are going to agree to reading the story back to you to make sure the whole thing is correct. I sometimes do that with people when it is very detailed and complicated or when I know them well but I would be anxious about doing that with a social scientist that I did not know. Some scientists really don't understand what the journalist is trying to do and they raise objections to the story even when it is a perfectly good and fair story and when actually they will be delighted when it comes out. It may not be a good idea to place the social scientist in the position of being some kind of editor or censor of the story in case they get carried away; most journalists will try to avoid that situation.

Social scientists and the media: an overview

Cheryl Haslam and Alan Bryman

The focus of this book has been the media coverage of the social sciences. But before drawing together what we have learned from our contributors we should consider the fate of the physical and biological sciences at the hands of the media. There are two good reasons for this. First, while social scientists are more likely to be contacted by journalists than other scientists (Dunwoody, 1986), the literature dealing with media reporting of the physical and biological sciences vastly outweighs that on the reporting of the social sciences. We hope this book goes some way towards redressing this imbalance. The second reason for turning our attention briefly to the media coverage of the physical and biological sciences is that the issues are germane to the social sciences. Indeed, some studies of science in the media include the social sciences within their purview. The following section is inevitably highly selective, but we hope it will provide an impression of the main issues.

SCIENCE AND THE MEDIA

As might be anticipated, the accuracy of scientific reporting in the media has been a major focus of attention. The results of such research are broadly consistent, though there are difficulties about how to interpret the results of the studies. Tichenor *et al.* (1970) presented newspaper science stories to members of the public who were asked to summarize those stories. Scientists were generally very satisfied with the accuracy of the original stories, though less happy about readers' summaries. Tankard and Ryan (1974) sent to scientists whose work was reported in newspaper articles questionnaires in which they were asked to indicate whether the stories contained any of 42 types of error. The mean error rate per story was 6.22 and only 8.8 per cent reported no errors. The commonest errors (all over 30 per cent) were: omission of information about methods; omission of relevant information about results; investigator misquoted; names of other investigators on the research team omitted; qualifications of statements omitted; and misleading headline. A partial replication of this study was undertaken by Pulford (1976), but a smaller number of types of error (11) was used in the questionnaires. The list was chosen by taking the most frequently cited errors in the Tankard and Ryan research and by combining the less frequently cited ones into more general types. The mean error rate was 2.16, with 29.4 per cent having no errors. As Pulford observes, the error rate is quite similar to the rates found in news accuracy studies in general.

A different methodology was employed by Borman (1978) in science reporting in magazines. Taking three scientific issues that had emerged in the period, 10 evaluators with expertise in each area assessed the accuracy of the articles. Like Pulford, Borman concluded that accuracy was generally good and that problems tended to occur in relation to details that were omitted. Borman also found that longer articles tended to exhibit fewer errors. Singer (1990) carried out an assessment of news accuracy in the reporting of hazards. Her research covered newspaper and magazine articles and television news broadcasts. Each story was independently coded on several dimensions. Only 7.1 per cent of articles were error free. Sometimes 'errors of commission' were discerned. These were of two types: incorrect reference to the published source and 'when one or more of the statements in the news story is substantially different from a statement in the original research report' (p. 106). As with the other studies, the most frequent occurrence was omission of details rather than errors. The typical omissions were similar to those found in the Tankard and Ryan (1974) study. Singer also found that lengthy research reports were particularly prone to omissions or errors. The chief problems were selective presentation of results, omission of some qualifying statements, and a tendency to over-generalize the findings.

The results of these studies point to a degree of inaccuracy in science reporting and clearly certain problems tend to recur. However, the evidence about the accuracy of science reporting is not especially gloomy, though the absence of unambiguous yardsticks against which to gauge levels of accuracy makes the evidence difficult to interpret.

In part, the fact that science reporting comes across as reasonably accurate can be attributed to a slightly surprising tendency,
based on US evidence, that scientists and science journalists share
similar attitudes to science news coverage (Ryan, 1979). Those
problem areas that have been identified can be attributed in large
part to the demands of journalism which have also been a prominent focus for researchers and commentators. For example, from
his interviews with US science journalists, editors and television
producers, Winsten (1985) concluded that competition within
journalism could distort science reporting. He quotes one science
reporter:

> I'm in competition with literally hundreds of stories every day,
> political and economic stories of compelling interest . . . . We
> have to almost overstate, we have to come as close as we can
> within the boundaries of the truth to a dramatic, compelling
> statement. A weak statement will go no place. (p. 9)

A similar point was made by Ruth McKernan, an industrial neuro-
biologist who acted briefly as a science correspondent for the
Independent in the UK, when she wrote:

> The only guaranteed space for science is the weekly feature
> page. On the news pages, a science article must fight for space
> with the latest scandal in the Cabinet, the most recent rift in
> royal relationships, or a juicy case of fraud or bankruptcy. Since
> most advances in science are incremental and big break-
> throughs are rare, a science writer must carefully tread the path
> between playing up aspects of a report and sensationalising it.
> (McKernan, 1992, p. 16)

However, as Winsten also notes, there are strong competitive pressures in science as well, so that exaggerated claims about the impact
or significance of a piece of research can often be attributed to the
ambitious scientist, rather than to the journalist. Journalists are
frequently critical of scientists who are often seen as manipulative
and presenting a distorted picture of their work and its significance (Nelkin, 1987).

Friedman (1986) has provided a useful catalogue of additional
factors associated with the work of journalists that can have an
impact on accuracy. For example, she notes that priority is given to
'hard news', where the conclusion opens the story. Science stories
do not readily fit this format, so that if the hard news genre is

superimposed, some distortion may ensue. The pervasive influence of deadlines may inhibit the science reporter's ability to examine more than one source when writing a story. Miller (1986) notes that the restricted space which journalists have for presenting information means that certain details can easily be squeezed out.

However, the question of accuracy in science reporting is a somewhat restricted issue. Just as interesting from the point of view of achieving an understanding of science reporting has been work on the social construction of science reporting. Nelkin has observed that science reporting is surprisingly homogeneous, reflecting a frame that 'organizes the world for journalists, helping them to process large amounts of information, to select what is news, and to present it in an efficient form' (1987, p. 9). As a result, certain motifs, images and themes continue to surface, such as notions of progress and of dramatic breakthroughs, the depiction of scientists as stars, an emphasis on imagery rather than content, and a sensitivity to the competitive nature of science.

The aim of this section has been to provide an inevitably selective picture of writings on scientific journalism. These considerations have implications for journalistic reporting of the social sciences that are valuable to bear in mind when we draw together the conclusions from the previous chapters. Many of the themes explored in this section recur in the context of the social sciences.

PERENNIAL PROBLEMS FOR THE SOCIAL SCIENTIST

Our contributors have recognized the possible advantages for social scientists of media contact, as have other writers (e.g. Etzkowitz and Mack, 1975; Adler, 1984) but they have also drawn attention to many pitfalls. This section draws together the recurrent problems described by our contributors in the earlier chapters.

Sensationalism

Academics have little control over the media treatment of their work. So the reporting of science (social, physical and biological) will inevitably suffer from the problem of sensationalism. Advances in the physical and biological sciences are portrayed in the media as 'breakthroughs'. Findings in the social sciences are reported with undue finality and closure (Weiss, 1985; Weiss and Singer,

1988). The apparent reason for this is the fierce competition among journalists in obtaining limited newspaper space or air-time. To beat the competition, stories must seem significant and 'newsworthy'. However, as Oliver Gillie notes, there are occasions when scientists themselves are guilty of exaggerating the import-ance of their research findings. So a charge of sensationalism cannot be laid exclusively at the door of the media.

Hans Eysenck is no stranger to being on the receiving end of media sensationalism. He gives an overview of how the media have portrayed him as a 'controversial' figure who is totally at odds with the rest of the scientific community. He explains how the media have systematically associated his name with controversial view-points. They have also attributed certain social scientific advances to him, such as the development of the IQ test, which, as he readily admits in this book, happened before he was born.

As regards the media treatment of research that he has done, Hans Eysenck notes that this has sometimes been misrepresented for the sake of sensationalism. He provides an example which relates to his work on risk factors for illness that received some gross misreporting, implying that he discounted smoking as a health risk. Another example is his work on the effects of vitamin supplementation on intelligence. The findings of this research, he argues, have been both misrepresented and wrongly dismissed in the press. He fears that such misuse of social science by the media is a disservice not only to the social scientist but also to society.

Distortions

Bob Burgess explains how some proposed research on 'Teaching and Learning about Food and Nutrition in Schools' was grossly distorted in press reports. In the press reports, the study was portrayed as a study of children's eating habits. The newspaper stories, which gave Bob Burgess titles such as 'Burger-Master' and 'Dr Din-Dins', stated that he was to be paid £1.4 million to eat school dinners and 'share bags of chips with kids for two years': a severe case of distortion by anyone's standards. An interesting idea though – how many social scientists out there would be prepared to share chips with school children for two years if it meant boost-ing their research income by £1.4 million?

Helen Haste describes how the reporting of her work on the social and psychological aspects of metaphor focused on what was a minor illustration of her argument. This distortion resulted in her portrayal in the media as a world expert on Madonna. This perpetual problem of media distortion stems from the fact that social scientists and journalists often have different goals. Graham Murdock suggests that there is an inevitable clash of interest between social scientists wanting to put their ideas across to the public and journalists aiming to provide entertaining copy. However, as Helen Haste points out, there are different kinds of journalists. A journalist working for the tabloid press has the task of creating a 'story', which will necessitate some sensationalism. In these cases she notes that there is a chasm between the needs of the social scientists and those of the journalist. To bridge this gap the social scientist must give clear, straightforward statements. However carefully social scientists put forward their ideas, at the end of the day they must be prepared to tolerate some distortion from the tabloid press.

But, as Helen Haste points out, other journalists are far removed from the tabloid ethic. These are the professionals who write and broadcast for the 'intelligent lay audience'. These people understand the gulf between what scientists would like to say and the demands of the media. These journalists also seek a 'good story' but one with substance and accuracy. They often have a background in science and are highly skilled in communicating complex ideas to their audience. They bring out the best in social scientists, and indeed may compensate for any inadequacies in the communication skills of some social scientists.

Omission of important details

As mentioned above, omission of detail has been shown to be a problem in media reporting of the physical and biological sciences. So it is not surprising to find this problem cropping up in the realm of the social sciences. A good example of omitting an important detail comes from the press reports of Cheryl Haslam's work on drug use among medical students. The statement that '30 per cent of medical students use cannabis' is quite different from saying that '30 per cent have tried cannabis, but only 7 per cent currently use the drug'. Omitting details such as the distinction between one-off, experimental drug use and regular, current drug use gives a very distorted picture of research findings. Clearly journalists often need to prune some detail to make a story more reader-friendly, but they should try to retain the original meaning of research results. Otherwise they are not only misrepresenting a piece of research, but also misleading the reader.

Divulging sensitive details

Investigative journalism involves uncovering details about the nature of a piece of research. Some journalists seem to delight in ruthlessly uncovering and reporting confidential information. Examples are sensitive details such as the names of the actual organizations or individuals that took part in a piece of research. This can cause much embarrassment to the researcher and those being researched. It can also have serious consequence for the research itself.

A classic example is the study by Morgan (1972) of female factory workers. Journalists uncovered the identity of the two factories involved in the research. Some women respondents felt very betrayed when the names of the factories were printed in newspaper reports, particularly as these reports suggested that these women treat the workplace as an extension of their home environment and that the social rewards associated with work were as important as the financial rewards.

These unplanned 'media events' can have serious consequences for the continuation of a piece of research. As Cheryl Haslam and Alan Bryman discovered, having 'confidential' comments made by university senior managers and their staff liberally plastered over the front page of *The Times Higher Educational Supplement* is not the way to ensure the future cooperation of the research project participants. When reporting preliminary findings of ongoing research projects, journalists should be sensitive to the potential for doing harm to the research itself. Similarly the researchers themselves should be cautious about disseminating preliminary research findings.

Sometimes these 'leaks' can be turned around and given a positive emphasis. When Cary Cooper reported on organizational research without giving the identity of the organization involved, reporters at the conference managed to obtain and print the name of the organization. The press reports were not regarded kindly by the organization initially, but Cary Cooper was able to convince the organization that this incident could be perceived as good for the public relations of the company.

Selective gatekeeping

The question of biased selection of social scientific research to report was raised by Weiss (1985) and discussed in the introductory chapter. The experiences of some of our contributors certainly support the idea that the media show biases in their reporting of social scientific research. This is apparent in both their selection of which types of social science research to report and also, within a given piece of research, the aspects that are focused upon.

As regards the selection of which types of social science research to report, Jane Ussher discusses the role of the media as gatekeepers for dissemination of knowledge. She notes that certain aspects of psychology (such as her work on female sexuality) receive considerable attention while developments in other areas of psychology (e.g. neuro-psychology) are seen as much less newsworthy. There is not only selectivity as to which areas are publicized but also selectivity about which social scientists are quoted. As Jane Ussher points out, this selectivity gives the public a distorted view of what the social sciences are about.

Selective reporting further operates within a particular aspect of social science. As Jane Ussher points out, sex sells newspapers, but not *all* research on sexual matters is deemed newsworthy. Her work on gay and lesbian sexuality, menstruation and women's mental health has received no press coverage. She notes that research showing no performance decrement in the premenstrual phase (Ussher 1992b) does not grab the attention of the media, probably because such evidence pours cold water on the popular notion that women are victims of their raging hormones.

The role of the media as gatekeepers of news is examined by Dennis Howitt who points out that scientific research (social, physical and biological) often impinges on the activities of certain pressure groups. As such, pressure groups may use scientific research selectively as part of their pressure-group rhetoric. He describes the uses made of the Home Office report on pornography, not only by the media but also by certain pressure groups and other academics. While the report received much press attention, the actual content of the report was rarely the focus of the discussion.

Dennis Howitt acknowledges that some journalists wrote fairly accurate summaries of the report. But other journalists used comments made in other contexts prior to the publication of the report almost as if they were part of the report. This tendency to misrepresent the report for political ends was also reflected among certain anti-pornography campaigners. Howitt describes how anti-pornography campaigners, and indeed other social scientists, manipulated the media coverage of the report to support their particular causes. His experience of the way in which the report on pornography was used by various groups certainly concurs with the notion that social scientific research can be used selectively by social institutions, the media and other groups.

The gatekeeping function of the media has a pervasive influence on our society. Not only does it shape the public view of the nature of the social sciences, it also contributes to the public perception of social problems. Indeed, some would argue that the media are capable of perpetuating social problems. This point is demonstrated by Eric Dunning in his analysis of the role of the media in perpetuating football hooliganism. He points out that rather than operating as neutral reporters of 'the facts', the tabloids play a role in the construction of problems such as football hooliganism. Since the mid 1960s the popular press have been sending reporters to football matches to report on crowd behaviour as well as reporting on the game. Eric Dunning argues that violent incidents have always tended to occur at or around football grounds but the fact that they were regularly reported contributed to the impression that they were increasing at a faster rate than was the case. Another factor is that the tabloids tended to sensationalize football-related violence, for example by publishing 'league tables' of fan violence. In this way football grounds began to be portrayed, or 'advertised', as places where fighting regularly takes place. This, Eric Dunning suggests, has had the effect of attracting young, violent men to football matches and deterring other people from attending football grounds.

So the selective gatekeeping role of the media is manifested in the emphasis on certain aspects of a piece of research, in the selective reporting of certain types of research and in the perpetuation of particular social problems. Social scientists would do well to keep these influences in mind in their dealings with the media. Moreover, reporters should be aware of the power they wield in moulding public perception and use this power responsibly.

So what can the social scientist do to use this gatekeeping function to the benefit of the social sciences? Media reporting, as pointed out by Jane Ussher and others, forms the public perception of psychology. Similarly, Walum (1975) notes that what the media cover as sociology becomes equated with the public image of sociology. She argues that sociologists should not put their heads in the sand because they are powerless to control the media. On the contrary, they should consider what aspect of media coverage they can alter to increase the authenticity of the public image of sociology. So the onus is on the social scientist to influence the media reporting to make it more representative of the social sciences.

Love–hate relationships

There seems to exist a love–hate relationship between social scientists and the media. Jane Ussher explains how the media may be initially flattering but ultimately dismissive of the social scientist. She has observed the contempt of certain media representatives towards academics when she worked on the other side of the fence, conducting interviews with fellow psychologists and members of the public for a BBC radio series. Jane Ussher describes how psychologists (and psychiatrists) were used and abused by producers and presenters. They would be kept waiting and after eventually being interviewed much or all of the interview might be ditched. Jane Ussher found herself persuading colleagues to give up their time (unpaid) and go though the nerve-racking experience of talking on the radio to find that their interviews were rejected, without explanation.

She poses the question of why social scientists subject themselves to such potentially humiliating experiences in trying to publicize research. The first reason is that public exposure can ensure that academic research reaches a far wider audience than will ever be reached through publication in academic journals. Another reason is that social scientists may wish to put forward their research findings or state their views in the media to influence public opinion. In terms of personal benefits, she argues that social scientists do not seek publicity for money but rather for the potential ego boost. As she points out, students, friends and parents are really convinced that your work is important when it's reported in the media.

A further question Jane Ussher addresses is why academics are subjected to derision within the media. Certainly there are academics who treat media requests with hostility or arrogance, which clearly does nothing to engender good relations. A further problem is the reliance of the media on experts. This, Jane Ussher suggests, may breed a certain amount of resentment. In the love–hate relationship the social scientists have most to lose, and those in the media have everything to gain. So how can social scientists cope with the love–hate treatment they receive from some quarters of the media? As Jane Ussher suggests, one solution is for social scientists to retreat to the ivory tower, to content themselves with knowledge dissemination through the usual academic channels. The other, more positive, solution is for social scientists to engage actively with the media and to develop effective skills (along the lines of those displayed by politicians) so that they are less vulnerable to the potential abuses. As regards the latter, Richardson (1991) describes her extensive preparations to enhance her image and improve her communication skills prior to a prolonged tour to promote her book on 'the other woman'.

Rubin (1980) outlines the press coverage of his work on couples' relationships or 'love research'. He acknowledges the problems he faced because of adopting a passive role in relation to the media. Based on his own experiences he concludes that non-cooperation or avoidance of the media only results in increasingly less desirable reporting of research. Rubin argues that researchers should adopt an active and discriminating stance including issuing well thought out press releases. They should establish ground rules for interviews and generally prepare themselves for reporters' questions.

Second-class academic/media tart

An inherent risk of publicizing one's research is the possible negative effect it may have on one's standing in the academic community. Canter and Breakwell (1986) note that academics who write for national newspapers often admit that they have to try even harder to maintain their academic credibility after having media exposure.

By working with the media, an academic's credibility may be dented in many ways. Cary Cooper describes the snobbery that pervades some academic circles, the notion that wide publicity somehow 'cheapens' the scientific endeavour. Sometimes publicity can be regarded very negatively, possibly even affording second-rate academic status to the recipient of that publicity. Helen Haste notes that some academics are scornful of those who wish to communicate widely, and use terms like 'trivialization', 'slumming' and even 'prostitution' to describe working with the media. She argues that 'popularization' to some academics is anathema, a term of abuse rather than a desirable skill. As Cary Cooper points out, the end result of this snobbery is that only the more well-established social scientists have the confidence to work on a regular basis with the media. He feels this is unfortunate because many young social scientists are conducting important research and have interesting things to say to the media, but are reluctant to put themselves forward for fear of jeopardizing their academic careers.

Turning to the other side of the coin, the attitudes of those in the media, Jane Ussher explains that academics who regularly consort with the media are regarded by people in the media as 'media tarts'. This seems unfair because, as Dunwoody (1986) points out, journalists need information from scientists while scientists do not necessarily need the publicity that journalists have to offer. Dunwoody calls for the evolution of a 'shared culture' between scientists and journalists as is enjoyed between the media and politicians (Blumler and Gurevitch, 1981) whereby participants know the ground rules and abide by them.

Instant answers, comments and 'expert opinions'

In dealing with the media, social scientists are often torn between their natural modes of explanation of their work (offering suitable qualifications and caveats) and the media's incessant need for instant answers. The media often expect social scientists to offer a quick 'expert' comment on whatever issue is at the top of the media's agenda on a particular day. Cary Cooper is often in this position but, as he explains, it is possible to manage this sort of media contact and not let it get out of hand. Cary Cooper makes the important point that when a social scientist is telephoned by a journalist wanting a comment on a news story, it is not compulsory to respond immediately. It is quite reasonable to ask the journalist to call back, thus allowing time for more careful consideration, a strategy to which we will return in the final section of this chapter.

A related problem is that as well as wanting instant answers or comments, the media are not usually too bothered if the issue is well beyond the remit of the social scientist they are speaking to. Social scientists are bombarded with requests to comment on areas which fall outside their sphere of expertise, indeed outside the sphere of the social sciences. The social scientists who have contributed to this book have been asked to comment on a staggering array of issues. Here are just a few examples: Cary Cooper was asked to comment on the health of George Bush following a collapse of the then President in 1992 at a formal dinner; Jane Ussher was asked to provide a psychological explanation of toe sucking during sex, the wearing of sexy underwear and leg shaving among women. Interestingly, while Cary Cooper agreed to comment on the Bush incident, Jane Ussher has typically refrained from comments on the litany of topics mentioned.

Helen Haste notes that such requests for comments pose a difficult dilemma: does the credibility that social scientists have established through their research entitle them to give comments based on little more than common sense? She argues that the press will often need some expert comments and it is probably better that these come from social scientists than dubious pseudo-experts or individuals with extremist views.

Individual social scientists will clearly vary in terms of how comfortable they feel in making general comments. Helen Haste states that some social scientists have made the transition to become 'media persons', willing and able to talk about any civilized topic. Such individuals have an important role in the promotion of the social sciences. As she points out, some psychologists have 'carved a place for psychologists amongst the intelligentsia, rather than merely among the ranks of newsworthy boffins'. Other social scientists, with little experience of dealing with the media, may feel distinctly uncomfortable about commenting on issues well beyond the remit of their research-based knowledge. Journalists should not push such social scientists for these types of comments.

Social scientists who publicize their work through the media are required to proffer short, easily understandable snippets. The coverage of the developments in the social sciences often comprises quick, simple and unequivocal statements. Jane Ussher argues that such treatment of research findings makes the social sciences appear banal and common sense. It is not surprising then that the social sciences (as distinct from the physical and biological sciences) are more open to derision and labelled 'garbage science' by the media and the public.

In discussing the relationship between economists and the media, Weinstein (1992) states that, among his colleagues at *The New York Times* the term 'academic' means irrelevant. Conversely, among his former colleagues in academic circles to describe a piece of work as 'journalistic' is to characterize it as shallow. Weinstein suggests that in recent years economists have come a long way in bridging the gap between 'thoughtful irrelevance and engrossing superficiality'. He fears that this process may have gone too far in that nowadays journalists have ready access to smart and fast-talking economic analysts on nearly every issue. Weinstein concludes that the relationship between economists and the media has been turned on its head. There is certainly no problem in getting economists to come down from the ivory tower. In fact he argues that:

> the profession has grown media savvy, the distribution of academics has been radically reshaped. The tail with engaged, glib pundits has grown tall and fat. But the tail of thoughtful, irrelevant scholarly discourse has shrivelled. And dangerously so. (p. 77)

As this remark and the comments from our contributors reveal, there are difficult balances to be struck in contacts with the media.

POTENTIAL SOLUTIONS AND PRACTICAL ADVICE

To be effective in disseminating research to a wider audience, and to project a good public image of the social sciences, social scientists must surely take the initiative. As Canter and Breakwell (1986) suggest, we must 'abandon the passive respondent model of interaction with the media'. McCall and Stocking (1982) argue that psychologists should take a more knowledgeable and active role in interacting with the media. Rather than waiting to be asked for their opinions, social scientists should adopt a more active position. They should solicit publicity and work on a more equal basis with those in the media. Bob Burgess agrees with this view and states that social scientists cannot simply rely on journalists ringing up to ask about their research. They should get to know journalists with whom they can discuss their research, and develop the ability to identify newsworthy research and to communicate it successfully to the press.

The British Psychological Society (BPS) and British Sociological

Association (BSA) have embraced this 'active' model of attracting publicity. The BPS has a Director of Information and Standing Press Committee with an impressive record in media relations. They actively promote psychology, by informing the government, other agencies and the public at large of recent developments in the discipline. The BPS responds to specific requests from psychologists for advice on dealing with the media. They also run training sessions for social scientists to develop their skills in relation to all aspects of media contact. The BPS Standing Press Committee has produced a *Media Handbook* (British Psychological Society, 1989) containing valuable advice on: writing press releases, being interviewed for newspapers articles, radio and television broadcasts, obtaining a fee for interviews, effectively using press offices at conferences and complaining about unsatisfactory media reports. The BSA also has a Publicity Committee that offers advice on disseminating research through the media (Fox, 1992). Most universities now have active external relations/public relations departments through which social scientists can bring their work to the public's attention.

In the remaining sections in this chapter, we offer some practical advice for social scientists in their dealings with the media. The suggestions are derived from the advice given by our contributors in the earlier chapters of this book combined with the guidelines of the BPS Standing Press Committee (British Psychological Society, 1989) and BSA Press Committee (Fox, 1992).

The press release

Taking an active role may well involve the social scientist initiating the media contact. The first stage in this process might be to draft a press release. The *Media Handbook* written by BPS Standing Press Committee (British Psychological Society, 1989) offers detailed instructions on how to write a press release and gives examples of good and bad press releases.

Press releases must be short, certainly no more than 250 words, and in simple language tell the reader about a piece of research. Bob Burgess points out that press releases need to be carefully designed because they are often used in their entirety by journalists in preparing an article. He also notes that issues of interest to social scientists are not necessarily of interest to journalists and the public. So when writing a press release, the aim should be to emphasize those aspects that will attract the attention of journalists and the public. In his chapter he shows how social scientists could learn a trick or two from estate agents, when it comes to writing press releases.

Press releases should be written in a journalistic style to grab the reader's attention. This is not the usual style of writing for the social scientist. As Oliver Gillie explains, the journalistic style of writing is opposite to the way in which things are written in scientific journals. In adopting the journalistic approach to writing press releases, the conclusion and main points of interest should come at the beginning, further expansion and detail should come in later paragraphs. Oliver Gillie suggests that if there is a future publication date for your research, specify that the material is embargoed until such a date. Include a telephone number and make sure you are ready to answer questions from the press.

So if you have a piece of research or theory that you think deserves publicity you should issue a press release to the local and national media. University publicity/external relations departments will handle this process on your behalf. You may wish to target specialist writers in the quality press or specialist presenters in radio or television. An important point to bear in mind, mentioned by Oliver Gillie, is that you should not assume that a specialist correspondent in one department of a national newspaper will pass information on to another section. It might not occur to them that others would be interested. So if the piece of work covers more than one specialist area, disseminate the findings as widely as possible. Obviously, if you send something to more than one person on a newspaper you should include a note indicating that you have done so. However, as Dennis Howitt found, there can still be problems that stem from the way in which a press release is interpreted by the media.

Initial media contact

Canter and Breakwell (1986) argue that it is just as important for a social scientist to establish the capabilities of the media representative as it is for the media person to assess the social scientist. So we suggest that when you are approached by a reporter (from the written or electronic media) you should ask about the reporter's organization, position in the organization (if such information is not offered) and what aspect of the topic is to be emphasized in the coverage. Paul Wilkinson suggests that if you are not familiar with the publication/organization you should find out what you can about its reputation for quality and accuracy. If you have serious doubts about the publication/organization you should carefully consider whether you wish to talk to them.

It is also important for the social scientist to find out if the reporter has pre-judged the issue and has some definite conclusions. There may be a tendency for some journalists to 'put words in your mouth'. As Cary Cooper points out, occasionally journalists telephone for a comment when they really want you to agree or disagree with *their* comment. They call up knowing the kind of comment they want and they lead you down a particular path. In these instances the journalist has a hidden agenda.

Eric Dunning provides a classic example of the hidden agenda strategy. When he was contacted by a reporter from the *Sun* purportedly writing a piece on multi-sports clubs and wanting a sociological statement on the functions of sport. During the interview the journalist slipped in a comment about her belief that her husband's rugby playing is a childish activity. Eric Dunning remarked that sports can provide adults with a socially sanctioned opportunity to regress to childhood levels. The article that appeared in the *Sun*, which reported him as saying that 'taking part in sport is childish', was all about adults doing childish things and had nothing to do with multi-sports clubs whatsoever. Another example of the 'hidden agenda' phenomenon comes from Bob Burgess when, as President of the British Sociological Association, he was interviewed by a journalist from *The Sunday Times* who wanted to do a story on the discipline of sociology to mark the fortieth birthday of the British Sociological Association. When the article appeared it was entitled 'The 'ology we all love to hate' and was filled with comments from people who were antagonistic to sociology. When journalists use these hidden agendas, they do nothing to foster mutual trust between social scientists and the media.

In agreeing to be interviewed for television or radio, it is a good idea to send the interviewer, in advance, a brief written statement that reflects the main points or topics you would like to discuss. However, as Cary Cooper points out, in any interview, whether for newspapers, television or radio, you should be prepared for unexpected questions. Before the interview you should establish how long the interview is likely to last, and if it will be live or pre-recorded, if pre-recorded, whether it will be edited. If it is to be a long interview, or one which necessitates some background work on your part, you should negotiate a suitable fee (the BPS *Media Handbook* contains suggestions for dealing with the issue of payment for interviews). You also need to know how you are to be introduced. As Paul Wilkinson points out, it is important to ensure that your name, position, institution and discipline are correctly stated. You should also ascertain if you are to be interviewed alone or with other guests. Had the fictitious Dr X discussed by Peter Evans asked such questions she could have saved herself from a very unpleasant experience.

Interviews for newspaper articles

Information for newspaper articles is most commonly obtained through telephone interviews. When a journalist calls up, remember you should not feel obliged to give an interview there and then. If it is a topic you feel comfortable talking about you may be happy to give an immediate response. If this is not the case, ask the journalist to call back later that day, thus allowing time for more careful consideration of your responses. Another possibility is to arrange a face-to-face interview. Either way, this will give you some time for preparation. During this time you may wish to write down the main points that you would like to put across in the interview. It is also a good idea if you have time to write down any quotations you wish to make. Spoken comments often look rather different when they are in print so it is useful to write them down first to check that they are succinct and that they convey the meaning that you intend. Cary Cooper notes that the competition between newspapers means that there is a greater danger of the press, more so than radio and television, using the more 'risky' comments that you may have made.

When being interviewed over the telephone it is a good idea to keep in mind the rule of thumb mentioned by Jane Ussher. This is the guideline she was given by Stephen White, Director of Information of the BPS, to pretend that your professional colleagues are seated in your room and avoid saying anything to the journalist that you would not feel comfortable saying in front of these colleagues. Paul Wilkinson stresses that it is important, in any interview, to avoid making 'off the record' comments.

After giving the interview ask the journalist to check the story with you. They will usually refuse to send a draft of the article because of their deadlines but also because this gives the social scientist a role of editor or censor. But, as Oliver Gillie notes, you can alert the journalist to any worries you may have and ask them to clarify details with you. Ask them to check any quotations with you because it is always possible with selective quotations to make mistakes. It is also possible that the journalist may have misunderstood you. So ask the journalist to check quotations, or, better still, ask them to check the whole story with you over the telephone. That way the end product should meet with your approval and that of the journalist. You will then feel inclined to talk to the journalist on future occasions.

Radio interviews

As Peter Evans points out, it is inappropriate to treat radio as an undifferentiated medium. The experience of being interviewed about your research for, say, a BBC specialist science programme will be quite different from the experience of participating in a local radio chat show. In the latter case you will represent one of many, possibly opposing, viewpoints on the topic of discussion. So the first thing to establish is what form the radio interview will take, how you will be introduced to the audience, whether the interview will be live or pre-recorded, if pre-recorded whether it will be broadcast untouched or re-edited prior to broadcasting. As Paul Wilkinson notes, it is important to be well briefed on the format of any broadcast programme to which you intend to contribute.

Taking the one-to-one interview for a specialist radio broadcast first, as with the telephone interview above, it is a good strategy to work out in advance the main points that you wish to convey in the interview. You may choose to take some notes along as an *aide mémoire*. Ideally you should not rely too heavily on notes as this would detract from the spontaneity of the interview.

An important part of the interviewer's responsibility must be to create an appropriate setting in which the interviewee is encouraged to relax and talk about their work. Obviously, different interviewers, whether from radio, television or the press, will vary in terms of their ability to get the best out of their interviewees. If you are lucky enough to be interviewed by a highly skilled and experienced radio presenter like Peter Evans, you will soon be put at your ease and talking about your subject quite naturally.

In the radio interview you should try to use clear, simple, every-day language. As Peter Evans stresses 'radio needs pictures' and by using everyday examples, metaphors or analogies you may be able to invoke an image in the minds of the listeners which will bring the subject to life. Another very important point made by Peter Evans is that in a radio interview you should be sensitive to the audience. The tone or turn of phrase which you might use when presenting material to your academic peers or when lecturing to a group of students may be quite inappropriate for sustaining the interest of the listeners. If it is a pre-recorded interview you might ask to repeat a section if you feel you did not do justice to the subject, yourself or the audience.

At the other end of the spectrum of radio broadcasts are the live radio debates or the audience participation 'phone-ins'. In these situations you may be asked to comment on anything and you may have to respond to people holding fiercely different positions on the topic of discussion. You may have to answer questions from callers on a wide range of topics. As Paul Wilkinson points out, when you are asked to comment on a matter outside your specialism it is worth stating that the issue is beyond your own expertise, though this should not necessarily preclude you from offering an answer. In radio 'phone-ins', the BPS Standing Press Committee recommends writing the caller's name down and making brief notes while the caller is speaking. Always respond in a courteous manner even with rude callers. It may be a useful strategy to compliment callers on their question regardless of the angle you take in responding to them – rather similar to the ploy used by politicians.

Television

Television interviews may take place in your office, at a television studio or some other relevant location. Wherever the interviews take place it is wise to make some preparations. Unlike the radio interview situation, you will be unable to take notes with you during the interview. But before the interview you should find out the nature of the interview and whether others will be taking part. When Eric Dunning appeared on *TV AM* to discuss football hooli-ganism he was confronted with another guest of a right-wing persuasion who was very much of the flog 'em and hang 'em school of thought. This guest was also of the opinion that the decline in standards of behaviour in our society was due to the advent of 'the permissive society' and he saw the rise of sociology as part of this process. Clearly it is important to establish if there are to be other guests and, if so, whether they are likely to be antagonistic to your area of research or your discipline.

You need to know if the television interview will be a live broadcast or pre-recorded interview. It is vital to establish the exact purpose of the interview and the sorts of question you will be asked. If you can be provided with a list of likely questions this will give you the opportunity to prepare your answers. The BPS Standing Press Committee advises that during the interview you should try to look alert and yet relaxed. You should look at the interviewer and avoid looking directly into camera. The exception to this is the unusual circumstance of the remote studio interview where your interviewer is in a different studio and you receive questions through earphones. In these instances you have to deliver your answers directly to camera. Eric Dunning describes the unfortunate consequences of not looking into camera.

During a television interview aim to keep your answers simple and succinct and don't be afraid to inject some of your natural enthusiasm for your subject into your responses. Be prepared to (calmly) challenge the interviewer if you disagree with something. Always avoid responding with long, monotonic, jargon-based ramblings. As Martin Freeth points out, low-key, diffident expositions do not make for good interviews. Even in the case of information-focused programmes like *Horizon*, viewers will take away only three or four facts. Rather more compelling to the viewers are the motivations, hopes, fears, and concerns of scientists working in a particular field.

If you are being interviewed for a documentary be prepared for the fact that only a small proportion of the film shot may actually be used in the broadcast. As Graham Murdock points out, much depends on how your contribution fits with the production team's ideas about how the programme should be organized. Eric Dunning describes being interviewed about the problem of football hooliganism and how to deal with it. In the interview he talked of the need for positive as well as punitive measures. Yet, everything he said on the former was discarded, leaving a very brief appearance giving one side of the argument.

It is striking that a number of our contributors refer to their displeasure about the selective use of interviews in television programmes. David Canter's remarks in a letter to the *Independent* regarding the treatment of his contribution to the Central Television documentary *Murder in Mind* on serial killers exemplify this annoyance:

> My own contribution to police investigations are based on extensive research, published in scientific journals. Yet, although Central filmed detailed examples of this work, it was kept out of the documentary in favour of the interviews with violent, remorseless criminals. (*Independent*, 29 January, 1993, p. 18)

So be prepared for the fact that your interview may be used selectively and that possibly only a tiny proportion of the interview may be used. However, the likelihood of the residual material being put together and marketed as a separate video (as happened to Cary Cooper) is, mercifully, low. BBC producer Martin Freeth explains how he is constrained by the nature of broadcasting institutions and hierarchies, by the deals worked out with contributors during a production, by the expectations of audiences and by the demands of the medium. He points out that diverse groups of people sit in front of the editing machine. So no matter how 'important' a particular piece may seem to you, or how long it took to set up and shoot, or how many people were inconvenienced in the process, if it is deemed 'boring' it has to go.

Studio based one-to-one interviews and group discussion programmes (especially live ones) can be stressful. The social scientist is literally in the spotlight. So it is important to look as relaxed as possible. Pay attention to your posture, try to find a happy medium between looking both alert and yet relaxed. As Helen Haste notes, the aim is give fairly short, pithy answers. If it is a pre-recorded television interview ask to re-do any sections that you feel unhappy with. In a live television broadcast be sure to avoid any sort of fidgeting, as even small movements can be magnified by the camera. In a group discussion programme you may be on camera when you least expect it, as Helen Haste recalls in her description of participating in *After Dark*, the open-ended discussion programme broadcast during the early hours of the morning. Here, the ambience of the programme is that of an after-dinner discussion, so, as Helen Haste points out, you could easily say something indiscreet or be filmed fidgeting or looking bored.

The audience participation programme is potentially the most risky public forum for the social scientist. Graham Murdock states that such shows are based firmly on the premise that expertise grounded in knowledge of relevant research is no more valid than opinion based on personal experience. In the audience participation programme, the social scientist is faced with members of the public who object to the very notion of an expert. Ideas based on empirical research which counter their beliefs (based on their own experiences) are dismissed out of hand and treated with the utmost derision. As Jane Ussher explains, the function of the expert in audience participation programmes is to provide a contrast to the 'real' views of the audience.

Livingstone and Lunt (in press) provide an in-depth analysis of the audience discussion programme based on content analyses of shows such as *Kilroy!*. They conducted interviews with experts and studio audiences who participated in such programmes along with the viewing audience. These authors explain how the audience participation programme radically alters the relationship between the lay participating audience and the experts. Traditionally experts are valued and are seen as objective and rational. Statements from experts are assumed to be grounded in data. The public collectively provide these data points but their unique, individual experience is considered subjective. The audience participation programme is set up so as to challenge these traditional notions. Statements from the participating audience are perceived as relevant and authentic while experts come across as alienated and their comments appear fragmented, irrelevant and superficial. Livingstone and Lunt note that the programme format itself undermines the very idea of an expert. The invited experts are part of the participating studio audience. Lay members of the participating studio audience can insult and interrupt experts but not vice versa. The nature of the discourse is conversation not dissemination; narrative not factual; informal not formal.

In these programmes, the host sides with the public and the experts are marginalized. The underlying rationale seems to be that there are no facts, it is what the ordinary person thinks that counts. When social scientists come across badly in the programmes, viewers blame the scientists themselves. But Livingstone and Lunt argue that the media manipulate this situation such that the social scientist or any other invited expert is bound to fail. For the social scientist who is relatively new to working with the media this forum is definitely not recommended. This is clearly the forum most social scientists would need to build up to, in large part because it is the one over which they have least control in terms of what they are able to say and how their remarks are presented. Indeed, it is highly questionable whether social scientists should participate in these programmes.

FINAL REMARKS

The rewards associated with media contact (a wider audience, greater recognition of one's work) may, as we have seen, be accompanied with costs such as over-simplification and even distortion. One factor that can cause some of the distortion that our contributors have pointed out is the tendency for media representatives to pander to popular images (which often they themselves have helped to foster in the first place) of academics in general and of social scientists in particular. It is this posture which helps to explain Bob Burgess's experience of finding an apparently anodyne interview on sociology being given the headline 'The 'ology we all love to hate' or his research being construed as a waste of taxpayers' money by conveying the impression of his having received £1.4 million to eat chips with school children. The academic social scientist is paraded by implication as an unworldly pseudo-expert who, with the aid of taxpayers' money, trades in common sense dressed up with jargon and whose musings are frequently less valid than common sense.

Undoubtedly, we sometimes earn this image, but the persistent use of the assumptions that underpin it frequently leads to some of the distortions that appear in the earlier chapters and to a great many of the adverse experiences of media contact that are reported. The reference in Dennis Howitt's chapter to his ivory tower and to the use of public funds to cast doubt on his questioning of something that 'everyone knows' is true is symptomatic of this tendency. Equally, the sending up of Eric Dunning and Norbert Elias for their use of jargon or the derision faced by Jane Ussher for her views on working mothers in a talk show provide illustrations of incidents in which social scientists are set up by the media in order to indulge popular prejudices. It is no wonder that many social scientists become wary. However, the image with which some media representatives operate can lead them into absurdities; Graham Murdock's experience of *New Society* wanting to translate 'social structure' into 'social shape' is an illustration. It is hard to believe that *New Society*'s readers would have understood any better what Murdock was seeking to convey by this translation, but the conviction that as a social scientist he necessarily traded in jargon nearly lay behind a new concept entering everyday discourse.

Of course not everyone in the media distorts findings and perpetuates the popular perception of the social sciences. As in any discipline there are good and bad practitioners and the media are no exception. James (1983) states that distortions in each of the vital areas – communicator, receiver and medium – will always occur but can be reduced by planned communication procedures properly carried out. He argues that the onus must surely be on the communicator (the social scientist) to get the message across in a clear and concise form. The receiver and medium cannot be blamed for distorting a message that was unclear in the first place. Given that the dissemination of social scientific research has implications for people (personal and political), careful communication of research findings is crucial if social scientific research is not to be abused. James concludes that psychologists should be offered training in effective presentation so that their ideas and research findings remain intact and are received and understood by the public. The editors of this book would agree that some form of training should be available to social scientists to improve their skills for working with the media and publicizing research. We feel this is a priority for the social sciences. Courses on research methods for social scientists in universities (especially at post-graduate level) and in other research establishments should address the dissemination component of the research process. This might entail role-playing exercises to improve the oral presentation skills and practice at preparing press releases to develop written presentation skills.

We should like to leave the reader with a quotation from Lerner (1968), who, in summarizing a conference on behavioural sciences and the mass media, to which prominent academics and journalists were invited, stated:

> Journalists and social scientists are jointly engaged in the process of demystifying the human mind in some sense – reducing ignorance and prejudice, increasing rationality and enlightenment. (p. 258)

In this book we, and our contributors, have outlined the benefits of publicizing social scientific research along with the problems and pitfalls. The discussion of these issues has been based on real examples and we have addressed these issues from both sides of the fence – the media and the social sciences. We have suggested ways to alleviate, or at least to minimize, some dangers inherent in publicizing social scientific research. We firmly believe that social scientists and the media should be equal partners in the process of reporting research. By bringing together representatives from the social sciences and the media, we hope to have contributed in some way to the forging of links between the two disciplines. If the two groups can work effectively together in the name of disseminating knowledge, this is surely to the benefit of social scientists, the media and society.

Bibliography

Adler, P. (1984) 'The sociologist as celebrity: the role of the media in field research', *Qualitative Sociology*, 7: 310–328.

Barlow, G. and Hill, A. (1985) *Video Violence and Children*, London: Hodder and Stoughton.

Baruch, G. and Kaufman, D. R. (1987) 'Interpreting the data: women, developmental research and the media', *Journal of Thought* 22: 53–57.

Baxter, M. (1990) 'Flesh and blood', *New Scientist*, 5 May: 37–41.

Berelson, B. and Steiner, G. A. (1967) *Human Behaviour: An Inventory of Scientific Findings*, New York: Harcourt, Brace Jovanovitch.

Blumler, J. G. and Gurevitch, M. (1981) 'Politicians and the press: an essay on role relationships', in D. D. Nimmo and K. R. Sanders (eds) *Handbook of Political Communication*, Beverly Hills: Sage Publications.

Borman, S. C. (1978) 'Communication accuracy in magazine science reporting', *Journalism Quarterly* 55: 345–346.

British Psychological Society (no date) 'Subliminal messages in recorded auditory tapes and other "unconscious learning" phenomena', prepared by a working party of the Scientific Affairs Board of the BPS.

British Psychological Society (1989) *Standing Press Committee Media Handbook*.

Burgess, R. G. (1983) *Experiencing Comprehensive Education: A Study of Bishop McGregor School*, London: Methuen.

Burgess, R. G. (1990) 'Sociologists, training and research', *Sociology* 24: 579–595.

Burgess, R. G. and Wallis, M. (1991) 'Sociology – the 'ology we all love to hate?', *Newscheck* 2: 6–7.

Burgess, R. G., Candappa, M., Galloway, S. and Sanday, A. (1989) *Energy Education and the Curriculum*, University of Warwick, CEDAR Report.

Canter, D. and Breakwell, G. (1986) 'Psychologists and the media', *Bulletin of the British Psychological Society* 39: 281–286.

Carol, A. (1991) Letter. *Index on Censorship*, 1: 33.

Check, J. V. P. (1991) *Review of 'Pornography: Impacts and Influences'*, unpublished ms. Department of Psychology, York University, Canada.

Cherns, A. (1986) 'Policy research under scrutiny', in F. Heller (ed.) *The Use and Abuse of Social Science*, London: Sage.

Cline, V. B. (1974) *Where Do You Draw the Line?* Provo, Utah: Brigham Young University Press.

Cohen, S. and Young, J. (eds) (1973) *The Manufacture of News*, London: Constable.

Commission on Obscenity and Pornography (1970) *The Report of the Commission on Obscenity and Pornography*, New York: Bantam.

Cooper, C. L., Cooper, R. D. and Eaker, L. (1988) *Living with Stress*, London: Penguin Books.

Cumberbatch, G. (1984). 'Sorting out little white lies from nasty pieces of work', *Guardian*, 25 April.

Cumberbatch, G. (1989) 'Violence and the mass media: the research evidence' in G. Cumberbatch, and D. Howitt, *A Measure of Uncertainty: The Effects of the Mass Media*, London: John Libbey.

Cumberbatch, G. and Howitt, D. (1989) *A Measure of Uncertainty: The Effects of the Mass Media*, London: John Libbey.

Cumberbatch, G., Hardy, G., Lea, M. and Jones, I. (1987) *The Portrayal of Violence on British Television*, London: British Broadcasting Corporation.

Davis, F. (1959) 'The cab driver and his fare: facets of a fleeting relationship', *American Journal of Sociology* 65: 158–165.

Dunning, E. and Rojek, C. (eds) (1992) *Sport and Leisure in the Civilizing Process: Critique and Counter-Critique*, London: Macmillan.

Dunning, E. and Sheard, K. (1979) *Barbarians, Gentlemen and Players*, Oxford: Martin Robertson.

Dunning, E., Murphy, P. and Williams, J. (1988) *The Roots of Football Hooliganism*, London: Routledge.

Dunwoody, S. (1980) 'The science writing innerclub: a communication link between science and the lay public', *Science, Technology & Human Values* 5: 14–22.

Dunwoody, S. (1982) 'A question of accuracy', *IEEE Transactions on Professional Communication*, PC-25: 196–199.

Dunwoody, S. (1983) 'Mass media coverage of the social sciences: some new answers to old questions', paper presented at the meeting of the Association for Education in Journalism and Mass Communication, Corvallis, OR.

Dunwoody, S. (1986) 'The scientist as source', in S. M. Friedman, S. Dunwoody and C. L. Rogers (eds) *Scientists and Journalists: Reporting Science as News*, New York: Free Press.

Dunwoody, S. and Ryan, M. (1985) 'Scientific barriers to the popularization of science in the mass media', *Journal of Communication* 35: 26–42.

Einsiedel, E. F. (1988) 'The British, Canadian and U.S. Pornography Commissions and their use of social scientific research', *Journal of Communication* 38: 108–121.

Elias, N. and Dunning, E. (1986) *Quest for Excitement*, Oxford: Blackwell.

Etzkowitz, H. and Mack, R. (1975) 'Media, social researchers and the public: linkages of legitimation and deligitimation', *American Sociologist*, 10: 109–112.

Everywoman (1988) *Pornography and Sexual Violence: Evidence of the Links*, London: Everywoman.

Eysenck, H. J. (1985) 'The theory of intelligence and the psychophysiology of cognition', in R. J. Sternberg (ed.) *Advances in the Psychology of Human Intelligence*, Vol. 3. Hillsdale, N.J.: Lawrence Erlbaum.

Eysenck, H. J. (1990) *Rebel with a Cause.* London: W. H. Allen.

Eysenck, H. J. (1991a) 'Science and racism', in R. Pearson (ed.) *Race, Intelligence and Bias in Academe,* Washington, D.C.: Scott-Townsend Publishers.

Eysenck, H. J. (1991b) 'Science, racism and sexism', *Journal of Social, Political and Economic Studies* 16, 217–250.

Eysenck, H. J. (1991c) *Smoking, Personality and Stress: Psychosocial Factors in the Prevention of Cancer and Coronary Heart Disease,* New York: Springer Verlag.

Eysenck, H. J. and Barrett, P. (1985) 'Psychophysiology and the measurement of intelligence', in C. R. Reynolds and V. Willson (eds) *Intellectual and Statistical Advances in the Study of Individual Differences,* New York: Plenum Press.

Eysenck, H. J. and Eysenck, S. B. G. (1991) (eds) 'Improvement of IQ and behaviour as a function of dietary supplementation', *Personality and Individual Differences* 12, Whole No. 4.

Eysenck, H. J. and Nias, D. K. (1978) *Sex, Violence and the Media,* London: Maurice Temple Smith.

Fox, N. (1992) 'Sociology among the headlines', *Network: Newsletter of the British Sociological Association* No. 54, October.

Friedman, S. M. (1986) 'The journalist's world', in S. M. Friedman, S. Dunwoody, and C. L. Rogers (eds) *Scientists and Journalists: Reporting Science as News,* New York: Free Press.

Fritz, S. (1988) 'Dinosaur love tail', *OMNI,* February: 64–68.

Golding, P. and Elliott, P. (1979) *Making the News,* London: Longman.

Goslin, D. A. (1974) 'Social science communication in the United States', *International Social Science Journal* 26: 509–516.

Gouldner, A. W. (1978) 'News and social science as ideology', *Quarterly Journal of Ideology* 2: 4–7.

Greek, C. E. and Thompson, W. (1991) 'Antipornography crusades and religious fundamentalism: A comparison of the United States and the United Kingdom During the 1980s', Paper presented at the American Society of Criminology 50th Anniversary Meeting, San Francisco, California, 20–23 November.

Grossarth-Maticek, R., Eysenck, H.J. and Vetter, H. (1989) 'The causes and cures of prejudice: an empirical study of the frustration-aggression hypothesis', *Personality and Individual Differences* 10: 547–558.

Grotheer, M. H. (1973) 'The use of marijuana by medical students', *Journal of the Kansas Medical Society* 74: 142–144.

Harding, S. G. (1986) *The science question in feminism,* Ithaca: Cornell University Press.

Harris, R. (1991) *Good and Faithful Servant,* London: Faber and Faber.

Haslam, C., Bryman, A. and Webb, A. (1991) 'An evaluation of university staff appraisal', BPS Occupational Psychology Conference, Cardiff, January.

Haste, H. (1990) 'Beyond the barriers: taking psychology to the wider world', *The Psychologist* 3(5): 212–14.

Haste, H. (1991) Media Watch: 'Psychology at the British Association for the Advancement of Science', *The Psychologist* 4(11): 497.

Haste, H. (1992) 'Splitting images: sex and science', *New Scientist* 133 (1808): 32–34.

Hayward, M. (1991) Letter. *Index on Censorship* 1: 32–33.

Howitt, D. (1972) *Trash: Some Audience Reactions*, Centre for Mass Communications Research, University of Leicester.

Howitt, D. (1982) *Mass Media and Social Problems*, Oxford: Pergamon.

Howitt, D. and Cumberbatch, G. (1975a) 'Does television teach our children violence?', *Psychology Today*, 16–23 September.

Howitt, D. and Cumberbatch, G. (1975b) *Mass Media Violence and Society*, London: Elek Science.

Howitt, D. and Cumberbatch, G. (1990) *Pornography: Impacts and Influences*, London: Home Office Research and Planning Unit.

James, R. (1983) 'Communication is too important to be left in the hands of the media', *Bulletin of the British Psychological Society* 36: 81–82.

Kay, J., Howard, T. and Welch, G. (1980) 'Health habits of medical students: some perils of the profession', *Journal of the American College Health Association* 28: 238–239.

Kitzinger, C. (1990) 'The rhetoric of pseudo-science', in I. Parker and J. Shotter (eds) *Deconstructing Social Psychology*, London: Routledge.

Koop, C. E. (1987) 'Report of the Surgeon General's workshop on pornography and public health', *American Psychologist* 42: 944–945.

Krieghbaum, H. (1968) 'A new challenge for mass media: reporting the social sciences', *Science Forum* 1: 21–22.

Lerner, D. (1968) 'Summary and conclusions' in F. T. C. Yu (ed.) *Behavioural Sciences and the Mass Media*, New York: Russell Sage Foundation.

Lewis, C. D. (1986) 'Doctors and drugs' (editorial), *New England Journal of Medicine* 315: 826–828.

Livingstone, S. and Lunt, P. (in press) *Talk on Television: Audience Participation and Public Debate*, London: Routledge.

Longford Committee Investigating Pornography (1972) *Pornography: The Longford Report*, London: Coronet.

McAuliffe, W. E. (1983a) 'Recreational opiate addiction in a dentist and a nurse', Proceedings of the 44th Annual Scientific Meeting of the Committee on Problems of Drug Dependence, Inc., Rockville, MD: National Institute of Drug Abuse.

McAuliffe, W. E. (1983b) 'Non therapeutic opiate addiction in health professionals: a new form of impairment', *American Journal of Drug and Alcohol Abuse* 10: 1–22.

McAuliffe, W. E., Rohman, M., Fishman, P., Friedman, R., Wechsler, H., Soboroff, S. H. and Toth, D. (1984) 'Psychoactive drug use by young and future physicians', *Journal of Health and Social Behavior* 25: 34–54.

McAuliffe, W. E., Rohman, M., Santangelo, S., Feldman, B., Magnuson, E., Sobol, A. and Weissman, J. (1986) 'Psychoactive drug use among practising physicians and medical students', *New England Journal of Medicine* 315: 805–809.

McCall, R. B. (1988) 'Science and the press – like oil and water?', *American Psychologist* 43: 87–94.

McCall, R. B. and Stocking, S. H. (1982) 'Between scientists and public. Communicating psychological research through the mass media', *American Psychologist* 39: 985–995.

McCall, R. B., Gregory, T. G. and Murray, J. P. (1984) 'Communicating developmental research results to the general public through television', *Developmental Psychology* 20: 45–54.

McKernan, R. (1992) 'Goodbye lab, hello news desk', *Independent*, 9 November: 16.

Maddux, J. F., Hoppe, S. K. and Costello, R. M. (1986) 'Psychoactive substance use among medical students', *American Journal of Psychiatry* 143: 187–191.

Mennell, S. and Elias, N. (1990) *Civilization and the Human Self-Image*, Oxford: Blackwell.

Meyer, P. (1973) *Precision Journalism: A Reporter's Guide to Social Science Methods*, Bloomingtan: Indiana University Press.

Miller, J. A. (1986) 'Neuroscience as news', *Trends in Neuroscience* 9: 409–410.

Morgan, D. H. J. (1972) 'The British Association scandal: the effect of publicity on a sociological investigation', *Sociological Review*, 20: 185–206.

Murdock, G. (1984) 'Figuring out the arguments', in M. Barker (ed.) *Video Nasties: Freedom and Censorship in the Media*, London: Pluto Press.

Murdock, G. (1992) 'Citizens, consumers and public culture', in M. Skovmand and K. C. Schroder (eds) *Media Cultures: Reappraising Trans-national Media*, London: Routledge.

Murdock, G. and McCron, R. (1978) 'Television and teenage violence', *New Society*, 14 December: 632–633.

Murdock, G. and McCron, R. (1979) 'The television and delinquency debate', *Screen Education* No. 30, Spring: 51–67.

Murdock, G. and Phelps, G. (1973) *Mass Media and the Secondary School*, London: Macmillan Education.

Murphy, P., Williams, J. and Dunning, E. (1990) *Football on Trial*, London: Routledge.

Nelkin, D. (1987) *Selling Science: How the Press Covers Science and Technology*, New York: W. H. Freeman.

Nicolson, P. (1992) 'Menstrual cycle research and the construction of female psychology', in J. T. E. Richardson (ed.) *Cognition and the Menstrual Cycle*, New York: Springer.

Nobile, P. and Nadler, E. (1986) *How the Meese Commission Lied about Pornography*, New York: Minotaur Press.

Pulford, D. L. (1976) 'Follow-up study of news accuracy', *Journalism Quarterly* 53: 119–121.

Rawnsley, K. (1984) 'Alcoholic doctors', *Alcohol and Alcoholism* 19: 257–259.

Richardson, L. (1991) 'Sharing feminist research with popular audi-ences', in M. M. Fonow and J. A. Cook (eds) *Beyond Methodology: Feminist Scholarship as Lived Research*, Bloomington: Indiana University Press.

Rubin, Z. (1980) 'My love–hate relationship with the media', *Psychology Today*, 13: 7–13.

Russell, D. E. H. (1980) 'Pornography and violence: what does the new research say?', in L. Lederer (ed.) *Take Back the Night: Women on Pornography*, New York: William Morrow.

Russell, D. E. H. (1988) 'Pornography and rape: a causal model', *Journal of Political Psychology* 9: 41–73.

Ryan, M. (1979) 'Attitudes of scientists and journalists toward media coverage of science news', *Journalism Quarterly* 56: 18–26.

Schlesinger, P. (1978) *Putting Reality Together: BBC News*, London: Constable.

Short, C. (1991) *Dear Clare . . .* , London: Hutchinson.

Silberman, C. E. (1964) *Crisis in Black and White*, New York: Random House (Vintage Books).

Silverstone, R. (1985) *Framing Science: the Making of a BBC Documentary*, London: British Film Institute.

Simpson, A. W. B. (1983) *Pornography and Politics*, London: Waterlow.

Singer, E. (1990) 'A question of accuracy: how scientists and journalists report research on hazards', *Journal of Communication* 40: 102–116.

Slaby, A. E., Lieb, J. and Schartz, A. H. (1972) 'Comparative study of the psychosocial correlates of drug use among medical and law students', *Journal of Medical Education* 47: 717–723.

Smith, A. (1974) *British Broadcasting*, Newton Abott: David and Charles.

Snyderman, M. and Rothman, S. (1988) *The IQ Controversy: The Media and Public Policy*, Oxford: Transaction Books.

Tankard, J. and Ryan, M. (1974) 'News source perceptions of accuracy of science coverage', *Journalism Quarterly* 51: 219–225.

Tate, T. (1990) *Child Pornography*, London: Methuen.

Taylor, Lord Justice (1990) *Hillsborough Stadium Disaster: 15th April 1989, Final Report*, London: HMSO.

Tichenor, P., Olien, C., Harrison, H. and Donohue, G. A. (1970) 'Mass communication systems and communication accuracy in science news reporting', *Journalism Quarterly* 47: 673–683.

Tizard, B. (1990) 'Research and policy: Is there a link?', *The Psychologist* 3: 435–440.

Tracey, M., and Morrison, D. (1977) *Whitehouse*, London: Macmillan.

Ussher, J. M. (1989a) *The Psychology of the Female Body*, London: Routledge.

Ussher, J. M. (1989b) 'Sex and marital therapy with gay couples', paper presented at the BPS annual conference, St Andrews, April.

Ussher, J. M. (1992a) 'Madonna or whore? Female sexuality and the regulation of women', paper presented at the Women and Psychology conference, Lancaster University, July.

Ussher, J. M. (1992b) 'The demise of dissent and the rise of cognition in menstrual cycle research', in J. T. E. Richardson (ed.) *Cognition and the menstrual cycle*, New York: Springer.

Ussher, J. M. (1992c) 'Science sexing psychology', in J. M. Ussher and P. Nicolson (ed.) *Gender Issues in Clinical Psychology*, London: Routledge.

Van Den Haag, E. (1971) 'Quia ineptum', in J. Chandos (ed.) *To Deprave and Corrupt*, New York: Association Press.

Vine, I. (1990) 'How not to understand pornography', University of Bradford, Unpublished manuscript.

Walum, L. R. (1975) 'Sociology and the mass media: some major problems and modest proposals', *American Sociologist* 10: 28–32.

Weaver, D. H. and McCombs, M. E. (1980) 'Journalism and social science: a new relationship?', *Public Opinion Quarterly* 44: 477–494.

Weinstein, M. (1992) 'Economists and the media', *Journal of Economic Perspectives* 6:73–77.

Weiss, C. H. (1974) 'What America's leaders read', *The Public Opinion Quarterly* 38: 1–21.

Weiss, C. H. (1985) 'Media report card for social science', *Society* 22: 39–47.

Weiss, C. H. and Singer, E. (1988) *Reporting of Social Science in the National Media*, New York: Russell Sage Foundation.

White, D. M. (1950) 'The "gatekeepers": a case study in the selection of news', *Journalism Quarterly* 27, 383–390.

Wilcox, B. L. (1987) 'Pornography, social science and politics: when research and ideology collide', *American Psychologist* 42: 941–943.

Williams, B. (1979) *Report of the Committee on Obscenity and Film Censorship*, London: HMSO, cmd 7772.

Williams, N. (1992) 'Dinosaurs "more like birds than reptiles"', *Guardian*, 28 August: 6.

Wingens, M. and Weymann, A, (1988) 'Utilization of social sciences in public discourse: labelling problems', *Knowledge in Society: The International Journal of Knowledge Transfer* 1: 80–97.

Winsten, J. A. (1985) 'Science and the media: the boundaries of truth', *Health Affairs* 4, 5–23.

Zeta (1990) 'Dear Readers', *Whitehouse Quarterly* 59: 3.

Index

fragmentation 7
Franklin, Rosalind 168
Freeth, Martin 14, 165, 206, 207
Friedman, S.M. 188–9
Fritz, Sandy 89–90, 92

'garbage' science, social sciences
  as 10–12, 198
gatekeeping, selective 127–9,
  193–5
gay/lesbian sexuality 127–8
gender metaphors 90–1, 190–1
General Practitioner 175–6
Genes R Us 168–9
Gibson, Ken 27
Gillie, Oliver 14, 175, 201, 204
Golding, P. 148
Goslin, D.A. 1–2, 4, 5
Gould, Stephen Jay 67
Gouldner, A.W. 1
Greek, C.E. 94, 95, 96, 101
Greenway, Harry 57
Gregory, Richard 88
grenade case incident 61, 64
Grossarth-Maticek, R. 67
Grotheer, M.H. 76
group discussion programmes 207
Guardian 29, 37, 101, 127, 138, 184
Gulf War (1991) 94
Gurevitch, M. 197

Halstead, Beverly 89
Hames, Michael 101
Hampshire LEA 23–5
Harding S.G. 128
Harris, R. 94
Haslam, Cheryl 1, 13, 14, 186;
  medical students and drug use
  13, 75, 76–7, 78, 79, 191;
  university staff appraisal 13,
  80–1, 82, 192
Haste, Helen 13, 84, 92, 190–1,
  197, 198, 207
Hayward, M. 95
Hearnshaw, Leslie 169
hidden agenda 42, 202

Highfield, Roger 85–6
hijack simulation 141–2

Hill, A. 95
Hillsborough football tragedy 53
Home Office report on
  pornography 97–107, 193–4
Hooligan (documentary) 59
Horizon 166, 169, 173
Hospital Doctor 76, 78
How to Survive the 9 to 5 45–7
Howitt, Dennis 13, 93, 94, 95, 96,
  97, 193
Hungerford massacre 119
Hurd, Douglas 118–19
imagery 114–22, 162, 205
immunization programmes 170
inaccuracies in reportage 6–8,
  139; science 186–7
inadequate scrutiny 7
independence, academic 144
Independent 60, 69–70, 71, 176, 207
independent radio 152, 163–4
induction of childbirth 177
information, types of 4
initial contact with media 201–3
instant answers 5–6, 197
'intellectuals' 113, 114–15
'Intelligence Man, The' (Horizon)
  169
intelligence testing 65–7, 73, 190
'Inter City' Firm 59
interim findings 83, 192
International Herald Tribune 146–7
interviews 39–40, 202–3; for
  newspaper articles 203–4; radio
  39–40, 204–5; television 205–7
intrusion 37–8
invention of data 183–4
ITV 58
Itzin, Catherine 101, 103, 104,
  105, 106

Jackson, Mick 168
Jackson, Robert 22
Jagger, Mick 108–9
James, R. 210
jargon 110, 210
Jarman, Derek 119
Jensen, Arthur 169
Johnson, Paul 120
journalists 175–85; approach